Origins of the Novel

ORIGINS
OF THE NOVEL

MARTHE ROBERT

INDIANA UNIVERSITY PRESS

Bloomington

Copyright © this translation, The Harvester Press Limited, 1980

Translated by
SACHA RABINOVITCH

First published in France as
Roman des Origines et Origines du Roman
Editions Bernard Grasset, Paris 1972

Library of Congress Cataloging in Publication Data

Robert, Marthe.
  Origins of the novel.

  Translation of Roman des origines et origines du
roman.
  Includes bibliographical references.
  1. Fiction—History and criticism   2. Psychoan–
lysis and literature.   I.   Title.
PN3353.R613   1980   809.3   80-7970
ISBN 0-253-18824-5   1 2 3 4 5 84 83 82 81 80

To the memory of Arthur Adamov

Contents

I
AN UNDEFINED GENRE

I Why the Novel?

A novel is a life in the form
of a book. Every life has an
epigraph, a title, a publisher,
a foreword, a preface, a text,
foot-notes, etc . . . It has them
or may have them.

Novalis

The modern novel, whether it was born with Don Quixote's
memorable escapade or on Robinson Crusoe's desert Isle,[1] and
notwithstanding the distinguished and historically acknowledged ancestry it claims, is a newcomer to the literary scene, a
commoner made good who will always stand out as something of an upstart, even a bit of a swindler, among the
established genres it is gradually supplanting. From as early as
the sixteenth century the genre has doubtless included a great
many famous names (especially if Rabelais is seen as a novelist), and Cervantes finally confirmed its status at the start of
the seventeenth century when, creating the Book of books,
the prophetic Bible which put an end to the Golden Age of
Belles Lettres, he inaugurated the uneasy era of Modernity.
Nonetheless in 1719 — a date usually accepted as its official
birthday — it was still held in such disrepute that Daniel
Defoe, its presumed begetter, took great pains to ensure that
his masterpiece would not be assimilated to this much despised
byproduct of literature. According to him *Robinson Crusoe* is a
true story[2] whereas the novel is a lie, insipid and sentimental
by nature and created to corrupt men's hearts and their tastes.
Moreover such an unfavourable assessment was no exception.
Indeed, during the previous century people had to read the
books they most enjoyed — which were precisely those they
publicly condemned — in secret. And such was still the
attitude of Diderot, another shamefaced novelist, if we are to
judge from his dismissal in *Jacques le Fataliste* of the arbitrariness and conventionality of fictional narrative's customary

3

methods. In fact he was so prejudiced against the novel that, when writing his *Eloge à Richardson*, divided as he was between his admiration for this novelist and his scorn for the genre, he claimed that Richardson's works should be classed in some other category than that of the novel, which was wholly unworthy of them. True, the scorn of the intelligentsia did not hinder the novel's progress: by the middle of the century neither readers nor writers of novels had any further cause to blush at their predilection. And a century later Balzac could assert without fear of ridicule that he was 'history's secretary' and claim that *la Comédie humaine* was no less important than Napoleon's heroic exploits.

In fact the novel achieved its devastating success as an upstart. All things considered, its victories were mainly due to its encroachments on the neighbouring territories it surreptitiously infiltrated, gradually colonising almost all of literature. Graduating from a discredited sub-category to an almost unprecedented Power, it now reigns more or less supreme over the world of literature which it influences aesthetically and which has become economically dependent on its welfare. With the freedom of a conqueror who knows no law other than that of his unlimited expansion, the novel has abolished every literary caste and traditional form and appropriates all modes of expression, exploiting unchallenged whichever method it chooses. And while it squanders an age-old literary heritage it is simultaneously intent on monopolising ever wider provinces of human experience, of which it frequently claims an intimate knowledge and either presents them to the reader straight, or else interprets them ethically, historically, theologically or even philosophically and scientifically. Similar in many respects to the imperialistic society from which it sprang (its adventurousness inevitably recalls Robinson Crusoe, whose colonisation of a desert island was surely not fortuitous), it is irresistibly drawn towards the universal and the absolute, towards generalisations of events and ideas. Thus it inevitably standardises and levels down literature while simultaneously providing it with unfailing outlets, since it can write about everything under the sun. Revolutionary and middle-class, democratic by choice but with a marked tendency for totalitarian over-rulings of obstacles and frontiers, the novel is free, free to the point of arbitrariness or total anarchy. Yet paradoxically its uncontested freedom is strangely parasitic; for the novel is naturally compelled to subsist both on the written word and on the material world whose reality it purports to 'reproduce'. However its twofold parasitism, far from restricting its activity, seems only to increase its energy and extend its frontiers.

Obviously the novel owes its historical success to the enormous privileges literature and the material world have granted with equal generosity. The novel can do what it wants with literature; it can exploit to its own ends description, narrative, drama, the essay, commentary, monologue and conversation; it can be, either in turn or at once, fable, history, parable, romance, chronicle, story and epic. There are no proscriptions or restrictions to limit its choice of subject matter, setting, time or space. The only prohibition it generally observes, because it defines its 'prosaic' nature, is not even compulsory for it can include poetry at will or simply be 'poetical'. As to the material world to which it is more intimately related than any other form of art, the novel is free to represent it faithfully, to distort it, to preserve or modify its proportions and colours, to judge it and even to speak in its name and claim to transform existence by recreating it in a fictitious world. If it so wishes it can feel responsible for its assessments and descriptions, but this too is entirely optional: neither literature nor the world will ever take it to task for the way it exploits their property.

Unlike traditional forms whose excessive regularity is not only subjected to prescriptions and proscriptions but is actually created by them, the novel knows neither rule nor restraint. Open to every possibility, its boundaries fluctuate in all directions. This is doubtless the main cause for its increasing popularity as well as for its appeal to modern societies whose inventiveness, restlessness and vitality it mirrors. Yet theoretically such quasi-unlimited potentialities entail a fatal indeterminacy. Indeed, if the genre is undefined and virtually undefinable, can it constitute a form recognisable as such? Should we not rather consider each work as an isolated case to be appreciated on its own terms according to the descriptive criteria it suggests? In other words, can a theory of the novel, based on a few indispensable, adequate and relatively stable principles, be formulated which would make it possible first to classify such works rationally, and then to analyse them from a standpoint that would be as free as possible from pre-conceptions? Such a question, though mainly ignored by our own literary historians,[3] is given considerable prominence by their German and Anglo-Saxon colleagues in what they rather emphatically and optimistically call the 'science of literature'. However, its implications are practical rather than speculative, for until it has been answered the various schools of thought cannot be reconciled, and misunderstandings will continue to proliferate between the novelist and part of the reading public, and especially between the novelist and the critic. Indeed critics seem to take the novel form for granted. At least such are the implications when they assert that a certain book is a novel and that another is not and should be classed in a different category. Such an assessment is only acceptable if it is based on a general principle which takes simultaneously into account the infinite peculiarities of works of this kind, that is to say the freedom they enjoy and the definite requirements dictated by their common form. Otherwise the novelist has every right to challenge it with Maupassant's irrefutable argument to a reviewer who praised *Pierre et Jean* while denying it the status of novel:

After *Manon Lescaut, Don Quixote, les Liaisons dangereuses, Werther, les Affinités électives, Clarissa, Emile, Candide, Cinq-Mars, René, les Trois Mousquetaires, Mauprat, le Père Goriot, la Cousine Bette, Colomba, le Rouge et le Noir, Mademoiselle de Maupin, Notre-Dame de Paris, Salammbô, Madame Bovary, Adolphe, Monsieur de Camors, l'Assommoir, Sapho*, etc., a critic who can still write 'This is or is not a novel' seems to me to be more incompetent than discerning. . . . If *Don Quixote* is a novel is *le Rouge et le Noir* also a novel? If *Monte Cristo* is a novel what about *l'Assommoir*? Is it possible to compare Goethe's *les Affinités électives*, Dumas' *les Trois Mousquetaires* and Zola's *Germinal*? Which of these works is a novel? On what imaginary criteria can the distinction be based? Where do they come from? Who established them? On what principles, what authority and what arguments? . . .

The novelist's argument is well founded and we could add to his list a number of titles — multinational and very dissimilar — which would further confirm it. For we might ask the reviewer what *The Trial* has in common with *Gone with the Wind, Lolita* with *Anna Karenina, No Orchids for Miss Blandish* with *Du Côté de chez Swann* or Robbe-Grillet's *la Jalousie*, while stressing the fact that such comparisons, drawn at random from the latest catalogue of our vast universal library, are not by a long stretch among the most ludicrous. And, strictly speaking, the reviewer ought to admit that, until rules have been laid down which, where ignored, preclude a work from being included in the category 'novel'; and so long as he does not know what makes the use of the term legitimate or, on the contrary, proscribes it from being applied to past, present, or future works, he must defer his judgement.

For the novelist then the novel's power resides precisely in its total freedom. For the critic, on the other hand, such freedom is highly suspect. He feels that some kind of boundaries should be established. But in the absence of any known rules he can only trust his own personal taste and particular state of mind to decide where they should stand — and thus as a rule 'his taste is law' as Remy de Gourmont suggests. This naturally creates a state of permanent conflict, which might perhaps have been avoided if at least the grammarian's definition of the term could provide some sort of basis for an agreement. But what indeed have dictionaries and encyclopedias to say about the novel? For *Littré* it is 'a fictitious story written in prose where the author depicts emotions, actions or strange adventures in order to capture his reader's interest'. True this only applies to the modern novel; when written in medieval French it is described as 'a true or fictitious tale'. Whence it can be deduced that the distinction between fiction and truth is not decisive, or that it is only so in the case of the modern novel which (but why?) is denied the right to 'truth' enjoyed by its predecessor. If the modern novel is necessarily 'fictitious',[4] the many novels based on historical events or on news items (*War and Peace, le Rouge et le Noir*) cannot be considered as novels, nor indeed as literature, since they have no place elsewhere. Moreover what does 'fiction' and 'truth' signify in a sphere where even empirical data are not experienced but written and therefore interpreted? Is 'novelistic truth' identical, similar or simply analogous to 'real truth'? What vouchsafes the proper transition from one to the other? The nineteenth-century *Larousse* is no more concerned than *Littré* with such crucial problems, which it settles with a similar opposition of classical ('a true or fictitious story') and contemporary novels ('a prose narrative of imaginary adventures invented and contrived to engross the reader'). Once again the grammarian appears to take for granted the fact that contemporary novels are the product of imagination, while their traditional counterparts are naturally more akin to history. However such a position is only tenable when the story is considered exclusively from the point of view of its plot, without taking into account all the factors an author can and must exploit to realise his purpose. But the subject matter, where it can be labelled, will only give a precise idea of the novel's value when it corresponds entirely to the author's overt intention: that is if he makes it clear from the start that he set out to write a historical, erotic, popular or detective novel. Otherwise we would have to classify *The Trial* and *Crime and Punishment* as detective stories, *Moby Dick* as a sailor's yarn and *Robinson Crusoe* as an adventure story — a logical classification if you will, but quite ridiculous in view of all the factors it ignores which constitute the particular significance of each of these works. Whether the subject is based on reality or is purely fictional is not what makes a novel. Still less can it be expected to clarify the relation between 'true' and 'fictional' which is infinitely more complex than the dictionaries' peremptory opposition would lead us to believe. Indeed strictly speaking anything is 'fiction' in a world created for the sole purpose of writing about it: however it is treated and in whatever way it is conveyed the novel's reality is fictive or, more precisely, it is always the reality of fiction, where fictional characters are fictionally born, fictionally die and have fictional adventures. In this respect *Guilliver's Travels* is neither more or less real than *Madame Bovary*; *The Castle* than *David Copperfield*; or *Don Quixote* than a novel by the Goncourts or by Zola. Kafka's Prague is not less real than Dickens' London or Dostoevsky's St Petersburg; the three cities only possess the empirical reality of the books that created them, the reality of objects that are not substitutes for something else but are actually there among the rest of our world's real objects. The degree of reality of a novel is not something quantifiable; it depends on the amount of illusion the writer chooses to activate.

Fantastic or realistic, utopian or naturalistic, 'fictitious' or true, whatever relation it may claim to have with reality, a novel's subject matter can thus never provide a reliable criterion for defining the genre, since it is never more than a strictly literary structure having no other connection with empirical reality than that of pure convention. Neither can it serve for purposes of classification, since to subdivide novels according to their subject matter — geographical or historical environment, social standing or profession of the main characters — doubtless gives some indication of the illusion the writer maintains with his readers' complicity, but reveals nothing as to what gives each individual category the right to claim it is a novel. Furthermore the different dictionary definitions can never be exhaustive, for the novel's peculiarity consists in its freedom to choose its characters with their environments and social circumstances, and to manipulate them at will (it can even be totally 'unfocused' if it wants, for there are as yet no rules to which it must adhere); thus theoretically there is no reason why the novel's subdivisions should not correspond to every conceivable human environment, trade, profession — not to mention all the books whose subject matter is too singular or insignificant to warrant any kind of classification. Thus the twenty odd subdivisions the dictionaries provide could be supplemented by whatever ideas or events the inventive novelist may contrive to exploit. But even when such a list has been completed, unclassifiable 'fantasies' will continue to crop up that will require new subdivisions if they are not to be misfiled. This is the main drawback of the system since classifications according to subject matter[5] can never in the nature of things be exhaustive, and though they are extendable they tend to fragment rather than to unify. Moreover it does not serve the purpose of criticism since it destroys the notion of genre — which is the only valid notion in the circumstances — before it has been established.

Thus although grammarians are satisfied, most definitions fail to solve the problem of reality which continues to divide succeeding generations of novelists and critics. True, there is a tendency to take it rather more seriously nowadays, though inferences are rarely drawn (except in the *Encyclopedia Britannica* where the *Oxford English Dictionary* entry is discussed in great detail). The 1964 *Robert* for instance defines the novel as 'an imaginary work in prose of considerable length, which presents as real certain characters living in a given environment and describes their attitudes, fate and adventures'. This is obviously an improvement, especially since 'presents as real'

introduces the preliminary supposition, the 'as if' on which
fiction survives exclusively — though it tries very hard to
make us forget it. However the formula is too vague — or too
precise, for here paradoxically vague and precise are one, as in
the case of most definitions — for it implies that the intention
to deceive is common to all novelists, almost a warranty of
their trade. Whereas, in fact, the desire to mislead, to 'ring
true', is by no means general in a field where everything is
permissible, even intentional improbability, incredibility or
unreality. Though illusions of reality may be the novelist's
favourite device, there are many novelists — not the least
among them — who, far from attempting to pass off their
characters as real, overtly stress the fictive nature of their
creations. Such were Swift, Hoffmann and Kafka, to name
only three of the greatest among those who established their
reality on the negation of common experience and in favour of
the fantastic and utopian, without for that deserving any less
than Balzac, Dickens, Zola or other 'illusionists' of reality, the
title of novelist. It is the novel's great privilege to be under no
definite obligation other than that which it assumes or ought
to assume in its own right. Moreover the desire for verisimilitude is not more legitimate in the circumstances than the
opposite desire, though it may seem more natural or more
consistent with our preconceptions. Whether the novel
chooses to 'ring true' or to flout reality, it cannot be classified
according to its intentions: every intention is permissible
though none can claim to have the backing of a law.

The inadequacy of definitions should thus discourage criticism. If it is true, as the *Encyclopedia Britannica* openly suggests,
that the term 'novel' is simply a time-honoured convention
and therefore reveals nothing about its object; if it is also true
'that critics have questioned the existence of a fictional genre or
described the novel as too vast, varied and amorphous to be
considered as a genre or a literary form', then we must resign
ourselves to the fact that it can only be apprehended empirically and always anew; quite unsystematically, in fact, since no
generalisation is possible on the subject. However, judging by
the number of specialised books, this is far from being the case:
as the genre gets older and looser, even more intricate, elusive
and anarchic, so the need to constrain it within the boundaries
of law and order increases — the need, that is, to restrict, if not

deny its freedom. Since all criticism requires a general law, and in the circumstances the licit and the illicit are theoretically indistinguishable, the novelist is judged instead according to standards of right and wrong in the same way as his public or private actions might be assessed. Of course the novel is not the only genre to suffer from the tyrannical Thou Shalt of philosophers and moralists; similar laws and restrictions borrowed piecemeal from empirical reality are imposed on all advanced literature and incessantly call art to order. But the novel, because of its inherent anarchy, its natural lack of organisation and of respect both for tradition and society, is more vulnerable than most traditional forms to the restrictions moral censorship would impose on imagination's freedom and lawlessness. Since the novel is so ill-defined and disorganised, and consequently at the mercy of overbearing imaginary desires, its theoreticians must be of necessity primarily fault-finders and its critics moral assessors.

That the novelist has contributed in no small measure to the misunderstandings from which he is the first to suffer, is another fact that transpires from the dictionary entries already mentioned, whose inconclusiveness is amply compensated for by salutary warnings — sententious remarks, commonplaces and rules of conduct suggesting what the novel ought to be rather than what it actually is. By and large such cautions obviously stress the anarchy of the genre, but they represent no more than a cross-section of opinions or, at best, a certain amount of optimism. Individually, however, each one expresses a supposedly self-evident principle which, as such, can be neither refuted nor proved, whence its apparent weightiness. For example, Voltaire asserts that 'History relates what has been, a good novel what should be'; for Huet 'a fable represents what has not and could not have occurred, a novel represents what might have but has not occurred'; the same writer further declares that 'antiquity had no novels because at the time women were slaves'. A professor (Villemain) announces from his rostrum: 'Gentlemen, this much must be said: the eloquent, passionate, moral and virtuous novel is the epic of a modern nation.' Naturally none of these opinions is seriously motivated and each writer puts forward his own as if it were self-evident. But what entitles the novel to improve on history? What peculiarities enable it to represent history for female readers exclusively? How can it contrive to be both passionate and exemplary? The improvised theoretician has no time for such questions (indeed, they will not be asked till the Russian structuralists appear on the scene and the notion of a theory is considered seriously for the first time). He states a fact which he takes for granted (the novel is . . . , the novel represents . . .) and which therefore has to be imperative ('the novel is' should be read as 'the novel must'). Thus the genre as a whole comes under a supreme jurisdiction so unequivocally competent that it cannot be questioned, not even by those mainly concerned. History (true or idealised, past or present), Ethics (from the most elevated to the utterly trivial or the mere observation of conventions), Truth (religious, philosophical or metaphysical) — all such extra-literary categories are erected as so many 'courts of justice' before which the novel is summoned. To date the novel has never *officially* enjoyed the freedom to which it is and should be entitled. For the movements which succeed each other in their endeavour to 'set it free' simply replace a court of justice deemed outmoded by a new one (thus we have the rule of experimental science, of realism, socialist or otherwise, of social engagement, etc.) no less tyrannical and no more competent than the last. True, the novel continues to thrive, undisciplined and licentious as ever, but so torn between innumerable external compulsions and swayed by the inextricable combination of ethics and aesthetics which is seen as a peculiarity of this art, that its creation, inevitably accompanied by guilt, occurs in a state of inner conflict whereby it usually evades one form of tyranny only to succumb to another.

The worst enemies of the novel's freedom are those who demand it most urgently. This much is clear from all the requests writers have made — starting in the eighteenth century and continuing right through the nineteenth — that fictional liberty be both restricted and appreciated, that it should be controlled while nonetheless they condone its wildest extravagance. After Defoe — who declined the title of novelist to avoid any association with a false and futile genre — the novel was unstintingly granted all the natural characteristics most incompatible with those tradition had formerly favoured. Not only was it no longer (as it remains for *Littré*) a 'fictitious love story skilfully written in prose for the delectation of readers', but it had become a public asset endowed with specific qualities which enabled it to further the cause of righteousness and truth. The author of *Manon Lescaut* did not hesitate to assert that 'this work is, from start to finish, a Moral Treatise in the guise of a pleasant pastime'.[6] And we should not be misled by the statement's artlessness— or artfulness: in the following century such assertions became, if more considered, sophisticated or apparently cynical, no less current among even the foremost writers — apart from the odd exception such as Flaubert in France and James in America. As a matter of fact, though morality has undergone many a change since the days when it could be pleasantly disguised as a love story (at the expense of pleasure which has become increasingly suspect), moral principles are more and more indispensable to the novelist, especially when his style or subject matter might suggest a certain moral laxity.

'Fiction', says Madame de Staël, 'should reveal the mystery of our fate through our virtues and our passions'. 'Perhaps', suggests George Sand, 'the story-teller's art consists in making the guilty and the unhappy, whom he would save and comfort, take an interest in their own fate'. The same writer credits romantic fiction with the power to 'alienate the reader from sin, immunise him with a shot of realism'. And Victor Hugo: 'So long as the three problems of the present century — man's degradation through poverty, woman's degradation through starvation and the stunting of children through darkness . . . so long as ignorance and need are on earth, books like this (*les Misérables*) will not have been written in vain. . . .' Thus the novel is not the frivolous, deceitful genre tradition mistrusted but, indeed, a medium for progress, an immensely efficient instrument which, in the hands of a conscientious novelist can become a real public asset. It brings the sinner back to the fold, comforts the needy and highlights the horrors of individual and social injustice. In other words it has a mission which it accomplishes either by transmitting its message through the plot or, more subtly, by creating stimulating examples; or again by revealing life's seamier side, for it can describe evil without foregoing its purity. This last method which consists, in fact, in curing evil by evil, is usually invoked when a writer is in danger of being attacked on moral, religious or political grounds. Thus Barbey d'Aurevilly exclaims: 'Yes passion is revolutionary and that is why it is essential to expose its strange and abominable glamour. It is for the sake of Order that the history of Revolution is worth writing.' And Sainte Beauve, more guardedly, in his preface to *Volupté*: 'Can the difficult cure of such a vice be attempted otherwise than in secret? . . . That is a question I considered at great length. Then . . . I gradually realised that the publication of an honest work could hardly add to the sum of evil, and that it might even do some good to some people.' Other writers have been far less cautious on this henceforth vital subject of fictional truth. Following his famous statement about 'competing with the registry office', Balzac declared that he was unquestionably superior to the various scholars whose specialities *la Comédie humaine* exploits: 'I have excelled the historian, I am freer.' In such cases freedom and truth mutually reinforce one another. A novel is true insofar as it is free to understand and to express everything; it is true because it is in direct contact with existence whose mysteries it instinctively solves. Such was Zola's contention concerning the 'experimental novel' inspired by the methods of experimental science but free from the restrictions that constrict its scope. Zola too excels Claude Bernard whose methods served as a model for his own, since Zola does not confine his work to collecting and classifying data in order to deduce general laws; he has the means and the right — and thus the obligation — to assess them: 'We novelists are the examining magistrates of men and of their passions.' The story-tellers of old could not have dreamt of such a reversal! Where once they were pleasure-seekers trading on the notorious collusion of idle pastime and deceit, henceforth they are cast in such weighty roles as scientist, priest, doctor, psychologist, sociologist, judge and historian (without even having to assume their responsibilities, since they are only answerable to the tribunal of their calling — the tribunal of aesthetics). Moreover, as substitutes for every expert in human thought and activity, they have the advantage over each of these of being free, farseeing, profound and gifted with an unmediated knowledge of reality and all its intricacies. Far from merely telling stories to fool themselves and their readers they are credited with sufficient innate truthfulness, rightness of judgement and discrimination to make each novel a message and the wildest anecdote instructive.

Since such requirements cannot be theoretically defined, the novelist simply asserts them brutally in a manner that leaves no room for discussion and is not a little disturbing. Maybe if the novel were more assured of its own truthfulness it would not have to make such a great show of sincerity. Indeed why should it be so keen on assuming all the onus of reality besides imitating it, if it did not want to make amends for its actual inadequacies and shelve its responsibility? This plea for sincerity which serves to avert inquiry reflects less a desire for clarity than an uneasy desire to justify itself. It is a symptom of guilt, of the bad conscience from which it has always suffered and which, instead of abating is, on the contrary, aggravated by the progress of modernism. The modern novel, at least insofar as it aims at truth, will achieve nothing unless it overtly abandons the flights of fancy on which its frivolous reputation has rested for so long. However such a break is the one thing it cannot make, except in theory. Moreover in trying to make us believe otherwise, the novel can only sink further into its congenital vice, which consists precisely in pretending that it is not lying while simultaneously consolidating the delusions it creates by wilfully exploiting its resemblance to reality (delusions are never more successful than when they disown their true nature). Virginia Woolf, with the common-sense of a profound intellect, suggests that the novel is the only form of art which tries to make us believe that it gives a complete and truthful account of a real person's life. Which sums up the whole problem; for the genre's originality and paradox consist in thus 'trying to make us believe'; in the wilful delusion always created in the name of truth but for the sole purpose of deceiving (unlike all other literary genres, or even all other forms of art, where the thing represented is shown together with the method of representation). Such an insight makes the question of truth and untruth a little clearer; the novel is neither true nor untrue but merely creates the illusion of being one or the other. In other words it can only choose between two ways of deceiving, between two kinds of deceit which exploit the reader's gullibility in unequal proportions. For either a story does not pretend to anything else and reveals even its texture, the conventions to which it has decided to submit; or it masquerades as reality, in which case it must naturally beware of betraying its intention to delude. Since the most innocent lies are the most obvious, a novel can only be convincingly truthful when it is utterly deceitful, with all the skill and earnestness required to ensure the success of its deception. This is one of the reasons for its megalomania — it can do anything since it can make us believe anything without revealing that it is doing so — and for its vague but nonetheless profound sense of guilt which it partially alleviates by indulging in crime fiction.

The novel's truth is never more than its greater ability to delude. But from what does such an ability derive and, more important, what reason is there for the irresistible urge to exert it? Though such questions may not trouble theoreticians, popular opinion knows the answer, or so it would seem, judging by certain expressions which sum up its views. Thus in current parlance story-telling and lies are so intimately related that they share the same discredit. However such synonymy is more ambiguous than it might appear, for it presupposes a reciprocity between the two terms, a natural relation, which is not wholly detrimental to art (art is less degraded by its association with falsehood than falsehood is upgraded). Thus we say of some incredible piece of gossip: 'It's pure fiction'; while 'It was better than fiction!' implies that it was too extraordinary or moving to be classed among normal events. In the first case fiction stands simply for untruth; in the other it represents an experience or event unheard of in everyday life and far more thrilling and beautiful. The same *double entendre* can be found in the French expression 'faire un roman' which, according to *Littré*, has two distinct meanings: either 'to capture the heart of a person of higher social standing, as in popular love stories', or 'to report events otherwise than they occurred'; that is, either to *behave* like the hero of a romance, or to *lie* like a novelist or writer of romances. The way deceit switches here from action to words, forces us to admit that fiction does not lie in vain, but possesses a power which it wields without scruple or sincerity. Thus popular opinion ignores the theoretical alternative — a novel is either true and beneficent or untrue and noxious — by which critics stubbornly abide (if only to their greater discomfort). According to the popular view deceit and fictional action are not only easily compatible, but there is a definite relation of dependence, almost of causality between fiction's deceitfulness and its success. The novel is not successful despite the 'stories' it tells but because of them; precisely because of its tendentiousness and the delusions it chooses to serve. Since the novel's purpose is to deceive, lying is the law by which it abides and to which there is little point in being unfaithful since its reality derives from it.

Doubtless according to popular opinion the novel is no better nor worse than reality. But neither is it a pointless imitation of reality. For if reality is permanently beyond its reach, nevertheless it has access to it at one crucial point and that is in its endeavour to transform it. 'Faire un roman' is to express a desire for change which can be satisfied in one of two ways: either by altering *what is*, or by altering *who one is* through an alliance with someone above one's standing. However, both solutions are a rejection of empirical reality for a personal dream presumed to be attainable by dint of deceit and charm. The conquest of a world thus deceived and charmed can only be achieved once its hierarchies have been rejected. Thus the man who decides to use women as a means to social success is primarily a rebel, one who refuses to accept the circumstances into which he was born and undertakes to revise his personal biography. Unlike the tragic or epic hero who endures the fate he stands for, the 'faiseur de roman' is by intent a disturber of the peace who scorns degree and rank even while he attempts to attain the highest. He is a social climber whose hopes are based on intrigue and mythomania. But he is furthermore someone whose mind is set on freedom, who refuses to accept the irreversibility of existence; who is in revolt against preconceived ideas and pre-established situations; who is subversive in spite of his fundamental conventionality. With his complex aspirations — responsible both for his insignificance and for the sort of heroism to which his initial impulse testifies all the same — the 'faiseur de roman' is well equipped to establish that contact between dream and reality to which he apparently owes his rather dubious reputation. For although he is unquestionably a dreamer, his dreams refer to reality, since his aim is to alter it. And although he deliberately refashions his life, his dynamic faith in change and in the powers of imagination constitutes, nevertheless, a highly instructive example. For if it is true, as popular opinion suggests, that he epitomises the essence of romanticism, then his subversive rejection of things as they are may help us to understand the real novelist's vocation.

Is the novelist a 'faiseur de roman' who writes instead of acting out his dreams in order that his fictions may provide a stimulating model for those who share his thirst for success? The difference between acting and writing is not so great as to preclude such a possibility. But before seeking a more solid basis for the parallel it may be noted that, insofar as the aims and means of the 'faiseur' are straightforward in the extreme, he provides a more rewarding specimen for observation than his over-complex and ambiguous counterpart. At first sight his scheme — to wed above his condition — might seem too limited to sum up the practically boundless possibilities the novel is able to present. But on further inspection it becomes clear that it could stand for the exemplary romantic act and hence become proverbial. For it combines love and ambition, falsehood and truth, reality and imagination in such a way that it suffices to vary the pattern's disposition to obtain an endless number of unprecedented situations — more or less complex, restricted or idealised, but all involving a basic desire for change (a desire that might well account for the pursuit of progress the novel's history reveals together with a tendency for ideological and formal innovations). Without even having to invoke Rastignac or Julien Sorel, whose aims are overtly those of the 'faiseur' (nor, for that matter, Balzac who admitted that, for him, to have achieved an aristocratic marriage was more important than the success of *la Comédie humaine*), there is no doubt that the novel differs from every other literary and artistic form in that it is able — not, as is usually believed, to reproduce reality — but to stimulate life in order to provide it with ever new situations and different ways of combining its ingredients. The general notion that the novel has a dual emotional and social mission is not unfounded, though the interdependence of the two is not usually obvious. For love is essential to it as a powerful motive for the great upheavals it takes such pleasure in inscribing in its spurious registry office; while it is intimately concerned with society, since that is where all the human categories and situations it intends to *displace* are evolved. Thanks to its compulsive recasting — which might well be the secret of its popularity as of its elusive unity — it exploits at will the resources of utopia, of satire (in spite of its

ambiguity and its ultimate need for orthodoxy, a critical
tendency is inseparable from such a vocation), even of meta-
physics or philosophy, when it is able to take its hero's
inevitable onslaughts on reality seriously. Its parasitic, protean
nature doubtless reflects the rebellious, go-ahead, upstart who
apes it in the lower ranges of ambition; but so, unquestionably, does its monumental inconsistency and the opacity that
makes it so exasperating a literary specimen. Indeed, by virtue
of its initial plan of conquest, it can only be simultaneously
democratic and conservative[7] (even when it claims to be
totally committed); dare-devil and thrusting (even when its
aims are most respectable);[8] liberated and despotic, typically
middle-class, order-loving and restless. Little wonder in the
circumstances that it should either remain undefined or be
forced into a mould. For it knows no law but the utopian
desire to which it is rooted — a meaningless desire within
established literary conventions, a desire whose existence is
restricted to the frontier between literature and psychology,
where the novel does not, perhaps, reveal what it is so much as
what it wants, that towards which it is striving by means of its
apparently arbitrary structural and ideological growth. So that
is where we must now venture. Not indeed to fetter it with a
new set of abstract regulations, but to try and discover the
basic nucleus which alone can account for its culture and its
primitivism, its social influence and its individualism, and for
its profound unity despite its generic vagueness. In other
words, to take the plunge and reconstruct its private history —
or simply the primal novel.

Notes

1   *Don Quixote* is certainly the first 'modern' novel, if modernity is
     understood as the self-searching, self-questioning literary movement
     which uses as subject matter its own doubt and belief in the value of its
     message. *Robinson Crusoe* can claim another sort of priority: it is
     'modern' insofar as it expresses very clearly the tendencies of the
     mercantile middle class which emerged from the English Revolution.
     Thus it has been possible to assert that the novel is a middle-class genre
     and that, before it became international and universal it was specifi-
     cally English. Further analysis will reveal the similarities and the
     differences between 'Crusoism' and 'Quixotery'.
2   Of course Defoe does not tell us what it is that makes pure fiction true.
     Can fictitious illusions that are false by definition be truer in some

cases than in others? And how? But then, are we entitlèd to condemn an eighteenth-century author for not having solved problems that we are not much nearer to solving today?

3   Albert Thibaudet, an expert on the novel, has restricted his efforts to dividing the different kinds of novel with which we are familiar into a given number of categories: family novels, adventure stories, highbrow novels, amusing novels, painful novels, etc. This is a more subtle version of the usual classification according to subject matter, which can also be done according to the strata of society in which it is enacted or to its characters' class and profession (thus the nineteenth-century edition of *Larousse* refers to the religious novel and even to the hunting novel). Classifications by nation (English, Russian, German novels, etc.) correspond to the same need to reduce the chaos to some kind of order. But however much we multiply the novel's subdivisions, the resulting variety cannot explain the genre, which is invariable.

4   Incidentally such a definition clashes with the English notion of the 'novel', which was originally seen as the relation of real events or, in other words, as a chronicle. *Littré's* definition would apply more exactly to the 'romance', which is purely imaginary. But, as *The Oxford English Dictionary* observes, 'novel' and 'romance' are not strongly contrasting categories, and English novelists have frequently combined them.

5   The same could be said of 'national' classifications which, however useful they may be for a study of national literatures, throw no light on the concept of the novel.

6   Preface to *Manon Lescaut* in *Anthologie des Préfaces de romans français du XIXe siècle*, Juillard 1964, p.43.

7   A novel's conservatism may be expressed in its political bias or its ideology, but its democracy resides in the very movement that enables it to exist. This much is confirmed by ethnologists who report that fiction is unknown among caste societies or primitive populations whose social structure is firmly fixed by tradition. 'No novels spells theocracy' writes Etiemble; 'theocracy spells no novels!' (*C'est le Bouquet*, p.227).

8   The novelist's social ambitions — source and caricature of his highest spiritual aspirations — are one of the obscure yet significant themes underlying Kafka's *The Castle*. K., the Land Surveyor whom Kafka saddles with a vocation for honest, realistic and total art, is no better, in the eyes of the Castle authorities, than a common social climber who uses women as a means to his ends.

II Telling Stories

Abandoning the field of theory — none too reliable in this case — for the world of romantic desire we must now explore, let us consider another kind of imagination, the non-literary imagination which, in the purely psychic sphere it normally inhabits, has all the ingredients of an unformulated novel, of an incipient fiction. Since Freud — whose discovery of it was based on his patients' day-dreams, or on what might be called their personal folklore — we are aware of a certain type of elementary story-telling, half-way between literature and psychology, conscious in childhood, unconscious in adult life, but compulsive in many forms of neurosis, whose quasi-universal significance cannot be ignored in view of its remarkable prevalence and the consistency of its content. Elementary yet compulsive, and lending itself both structurally and thematically to the expression of all sorts of conflicting intentions that only an adequate analysis can unravel, this 'pattern' of a story may vary greatly from case to case and pass through different stages of development, while its setting, characters and subject matter remain constant. Its affective complexion and the obscure desires which force it into hiding have a permanence which suggests that such monotony may correspond to some basic need or even to the essence of imagination as such.

Freud, drawing on his unique clinical experience, describes

it as a sort of day-dream which, at some time or other, sank into the depths of the psyche to become a forgotten fragment of our archeology, part of that residue which we can safely ignore without ever realising how much we owe to it. Thus it is something which primarily concerns psychology; yet simultaneously it is a chunk of unvoiced literature, an unwritten text, soundless and entirely unwitnessed, but possessing all the intensity and significance of a genuine creation. The dual psychological and literary character of this rediscovered myth, the originality of its structure, the peculiarity of its content and the pathological nature of its revival could not have been more aptly epitomised than in Freud's now classicial definition: 'the family romance of the neurotic'.[1]

From Freud we learn that in early childhood we all consciously fabricate this fabulous, wholly mendacious and fantastic tale, but that we forget or 'repress' it as soon as the requirements of our development make it impossible for us to take it seriously. Small wonder then that we had to wait for the psychoanalyst to extract it from oblivion; unknown by normal adults, and thus without significance or status in everyday life, only the peculiar circumstances of analytical treatment will enable it to surface with any consistency, as a set of more or less well preserved remnants which, when completed and assembled by means of adequate analysis, finally falls into place as a coherent whole. Though conscious and normal at its incipience in early childhood, it is unconscious and pathological during the remainder of our lives; and although it may indeed subsist as no more than a symptomatic archaism in the adult psyche, it is more than merely the manifestation of an outgrown stage of our development or its pathological survival; for it may be said to possess a kind of undying universality, since each child re-invents it in the privacy of his dreams as if it were always new.

The child does not invent his Family Romance simply as a game for the sake of inventing — though game and invention are certainly not foreign to his motives — but, as Freud says, to overcome the first disappointment whereby his parental idyll is in danger of foundering. The young child continues to see his parents as tutelary deities for a long time; they dispense their loving care and he, in exchange, invests them not only with absolute power, but with an inexhaustible store of love and an infallibility that sets them apart from and above the rest of humanity. For the puny creature threatened by danger on all sides, such idealisation is not without considerable advantages; indeed, it provides precisely what he senses that, in his precarious state, he most lacks: first a token of security (all-powerful protectors are obviously more effective than the unarmed); then, a respectable excuse for his own weakness (no cause for shame in feeling small before perfection itself!); and furthermore, a means of reversing the whole situation, since the offspring of divine parents can only be an infant god. Thus the apologist is the first beneficiary of his idols' presumed virtues: the love he bestows is reciprocated, he basks in the reflected light of his parents' glory and the magnifying mirror of his admiration reflects his own image suitably enlarged. Since infantile narcissism, basic to such parental glorification, amplifies and immortalises all that with which the young child can identify, his hyperbolic world naturally tends towards permanence. Life, however, decrees otherwise; as the child grows up and ceases to be the object of unremitting attention, he imagines that his parents love him less; and thus — especially when he has to share their affection with a newcomer or two — he cannot help feeling deprived, swindled or even betrayed. Not only has he ceased to be the one beloved infant monarch or god entitled to unmitigated, undivided attention; he further begins to suspect that his mother and father are not the only parents in the world: a foretaste of social experience has shown him that there are others, a great many others, some of whom may be superior to his own, wittier, kindlier, wealthier or more distinguished. The blind veneration that once epitomised all his assessments is a thing of the past; spurred on by his disappointment and humiliation, he now observes, compares, evaluates or, in other words, substitutes scrutiny for faith and temporal reality for eternity. Obviously such an inevitable transition is not without jolts as the child is torn between the dictates of awakening intelligence and his attachment to the outgrown beliefs to which he desperately clings in dread of what the consequences of their relinquishment might be. Obliged to go forward or forego the benefits of development, yet unable to give up the paradise in whose eternity he still trusts against all odds, he can avoid disaster only by taking refuge in a more amenable imaginary world. That is why he starts to tell himself stories; or rather *a* story which, in fact, is a tendentious version of his life, a biographical fantasy expressly conceived to account for the unaccountable disgrace of being un-aristocratic, unlucky and unloved; and in which, further-more, he can indulge in self pity, self comfort and revenge through a single act of his imagination where veneration and rejection vie for primacy.

To make up the plot of his Family Romance, the child does not have to resort to over-complex inventions; he only needs to find an external cause for the inner transformation whose motives elude him: his parents, unrecognisable since he has discovered that they are human, are so different he cannot accept them as his own and thence assumes that they are not his true parents but literally strangers, people with whom he has nothing in common except that they have given him a home and brought him up. Once the estrangement he now feels for his idols has been accounted for in this way, he can henceforth think of himself as a Foundling, an adopted child to whom his true parents — Royal, needless to say, or at least noble and influential — will eventually reveal themselves and restore him to his rightful status. Formerly he had felt neglected, wronged, unfairly treated by fate and afflicted with unworthy parents; and he was right, since he has indeed been abandoned and his unknown parents are unable to bestow their love and their wealth upon him. The fantasy makes it clear at one go: it makes every form of retaliation permissible and explains his rejection of former idols (the imaginary sins of his imaginary noble parents are visited on his real parents whose redoubled lowliness accounts for their unworthiness). Meanwhile the subtle displacement that results simultaneously in accusations and false excuses — the parents are guilty of seeming to be what they are not, but it is not they, in fact, who are impli-cated, since their failings have been ascribed to strangers[2] — enables the child to resolve, at least in his imagination the otherwise insoluble problem of growing up while still remain-ing a child. For although he rejects his parents to signify his desire to become independent, and thus dispense with the irrational faith of his past, on the other hand he closes the gap which separated him from them, since his imaginary parents are exact replicas of his old idols; so that while taking a first tentative step towards independence and self reliance, he nonetheless succeeds in prolonging, however briefly, the parental idyll he knows will eventually come to an end.

The first stage of the Family Romance ends in this purely narcissistic conflict which the child, conditioned by the psychic experiences proper to his age, neither wishes nor is able to resolve.[3] Alone between the apparently antithetical couples towards whom he feels the same veneration and the same resentment, he is immune to love and to its inherent conflicts; indeed, he would be at peace were it not for the concessions he has to make to his pride, and if he suffers it is as it were, regally and without prejudice to his vanity. Within a space restricted to himself and therefore limitless — 'mine' and 'yours' are barely distinguishable; others and the self constantly exchange possessions; accuser and accused are one; so that vengeance inevitably strikes the avenger, rebellion and dissent fall back on the rebel. And here the tale inevitably reaches the last stages of its evolution: for want of individualised characters sufficiently distinct and distanced from each other to agree or disagree, it deals only with a vague desire for freedom, with attempted evasions that are no more than differed regressions.

In fact the Romance will not reach a more lively stage until sexuality appears on the scene, together with notions of *otherness* which alone make agreement, conflict, union or separation properly intelligible. So long as the child considers his mother and father as undifferentiated beings, there is no reason why he should not love or hate them both, without any thought for the fundamental distinction which presides over their union and has always unwittingly dictated his preferences; but as soon as he becomes acquainted with the facts of life (and, since he is still entirely self-centred, he is only really interested in finding out how he himself was born), he cannot fail to imagine the major and most disturbing consequence of this discovery: that his two parents have two distinct functions in the story of his birth. Moreover their official respective titles do not correspond to the truth in an equal degree of certitude, the one being invariably undisputed and the other dubious and practically unverifiable. Now if it is true that genealogical insecurity always depends on paternity, the dual rejection which enabled the child to invent his own genealogy is henceforth inadequate; the story can no longer be based on it without becoming anachronistic and thus less credible — and, contrary to its purpose, regressive. The answer consists in accepting the mother, while excluding her from the fantasy, and promoting the father to the required rank. Once the child has decided to keep his real mother with all her familiar features and humdrum circumstances, he will concentrate his efforts on his father whose uncertain status has been revealed to him (uncertainty promptly changing to another certainty). Thus, with an ordinary mother and an imaginary, noble father ever more distant as he rises in rank, the child assumes an illegitimacy that opens, for his pseudo-biography, new vistas with untold consequences. In this way the parental couple's indissoluble union is firmly refuted; each parent is available to other partners and utterly independent; the mother, excluded from the fantasy, re-integrates reality while the father emerges from it, so that the two figures no longer inhabit the same universe; they pertain to two distinct categories, one feminine, familiar and insignificant; the other masculine, remote and noble; but each divided in two by a constant conflict of emotions and ideas. The Romance as such begins with this opposition which involves — insofar as it is based on sexual differentiation and all the antitheses and distinctions it sym- bolises — infinite possibilities for adventure, intrigue and conflict; in other words for all manner of activity which will enable it to achieve its ends without in any way departing from its ambiguity.

The Romance's new, sexual preoccupations are apparent even in its efforts to disguise them. Indeed, by placing him in the position he obviously aspires to, the child's asserted illegi- timacy reveals his true motives and the orientation of his sexual desires. For he thus keeps his mother beside him, and such a proximity encourages a relationship which, being henceforth the only concrete one in the story, grows increas- ingly intimate; and furthermore — though the two operations are so intricately linked that is hard to dissociate them — he relegates his father to an imaginary kingdom beyond and above the family circle — a form of tribute, maybe, but in fact an exile, since this royal, unknown father who is forever absent might just as well not exist for all the part he plays in everyday life: he is a phantom, a corpse, who may be the object of a cult, but whose vacant place cries out nonetheless to be filled. If we consider that the unconscious stage-manager

directing the play sees every relationship as a sexual relationship, every absence as a murder (the unconscious ignores death
and can only conceive it as an extended absence), we must
realise that the parents' *social* disparity is more than a symbol
for the assessment of values which seems to motivate it — in
fact it stands for a shocking emotional predicament, for that
indeed is the Romance's purpose to relate without revealing,
and simultaneously to resolve. What is here represented in the
form of unequal circumstances obviously refers to the most
painful childhood ordeal, to that inner conflict Freud associated with the legendary figure of Oedipus[4] in order to stress
the inevitability for all men wherever they are born of the dual
disaster which befell the Theban king. To kill his father and
possess the mother he covets in the face of formidable interdictions may not be the clearly stated intention of the youthful
Oedipus of our Romance; but his evasiveness amounts to a
confession, and though he expresses himself by euphemism
and allusion, his roundabout path unfailingly leads to the
truth. Thus he does not kill his father, he only excludes him
from the family circle; but by treating himself to a remote,
kingly parent whose virtues moreover cast a flattering glow
on himself, his mother becomes conveniently unattached and
he is entitled to interfere with her love life, supervise her
feelings, change her children's civil status. Such unadulterated
intimacy constitutes a substitute for the possession he craves,
and has the further advantage of evading the dreaded punishment such possession entails (castration, according to Freud,
or its attenuated symbol, blindness). Within the family triangle whose emotional space he has organised, he alludes to
what he has to renounce, reveals the goals he must avoid,
skirts the danger towards which his forbidden passion unerringly draws him, in fact, manipulates Oedipus' tragic fate
with such dexterity that he is able to savour transgression
without ever actually succumbing to it.[5] Such a remarkable
sleight of hand alone would suffice to account for the Family
Romance's success and the fact that it should be publicly
acknowledged even when its epithet has been forgotten: for it
provides, if not a solution, at least the simplest, most ingenious and most inspired palliative for that typical childhood
conflict, that crisis which is, above all determinating factors,
the distinctive sign of humanity.

It would seem that the Oepidus theme might create a schism
between love and hate; that they would cease to merge as they
had done in the earlier stages of the fantasy when the story-
teller's ignorance impelled them to do so. The Foundling only
perceived his parents in a general projection or identification
which abolished their separateness; hence the ambiguity of his
emotions and the incapacitating lack of conflict. The illegitimate child, on the other hand, is better off in that he knows
whom he loves and whom he hates, together with the reasons
for his preferences; moreover while torn asunder in this critical
situation, he nonetheless shows unequivocally how he would
like to settle the conflict. But in fact the situation is far from
simple for him; he cannot really by-pass ambiguities — indeed, he becomes entangled in them through the intervention
of a further distinction, this time between love and admiration, or between sexual desires and moral aspirations; or again,
and to sum up the antithesis in an accepted formula, between
what the heart desires and the mind dictates. The parents'
unequal circumstances, invented to satisfy Oedipal requirements, is thus a piece of irrefutable evidence, since it exposes
almost indecently the schism between love and ideal which
increases the child's torment; though, admittedly, it assists
him in his difficult apprenticeship. For his mother's lowly
status is the price he has to pay for her intimacy — his love
demeans her, while the loathed father inhabits the ideal regions
befitting his rank. Debarred from her former royalty, she now
occupies a humble social position; moreover, in addition to
her mediocrity and servility she is branded with immorality,
since the fantasy of his illegitimacy necessarily presupposes her
adultery. Morally condemned for the very incident that caused
her social downfall, the mother will now be guilty of as many
love affairs as she has children, or as the story-teller is able to
invent; thus, deprived simultaneously of her throne and her
virtue, she is reduced to the status of servant, fallen woman or
even prostitute (psychoanalysis has no difficulty in demonstrating how such hierarchically conflicting images are intimately related in the unconscious and can further prove the
point by referring to the large section of romantic literature
entirely based on such confusions). The child is now cruelly
torn: having associated sexuality with 'the Fall' — like every
theologian — he is forced to despise his beloved, precisely for

what makes her attractive (indeed, the mother *falls* as soon as she becomes desirable) while he admires, emulates, equals or if possible surpasses the object of his hatred whom he aspires to kill. Such an ambiguous situation is obviously fraught with insoluble complications. But although, when not properly resolved, the consequences may be very serious, the Romance does nothing to overcome it, but tends rather to magnify it, boasting and advertising it in every possible way, perhaps because it knows that it constitutes the only realistic vindication of the revised biography it has to establish (while believing in it in order to be consistent with its new realism). For if the mother were blameless the chance of amending reality, which is the Romance's whole purpose, would collapse; on the other hand if she is guilty and debased the child can eliminate all the humiliating, undesirable factors from his biography — an unimpressive father, a hopelessly restricted existence and brothers and sisters whose presence is a continual reminder of the intolerable fact that love must be shared. Thus his mother's fall is the *sine qua non* of his ascent, and he does not hesitate to turn it to account by claiming illegitimacy as an exclusive privilege that raises him above his siblings and gives him a certain glamour; or else by making his brothers and sisters illegitimate, which provides him with another form of distinction while simultaneously ridding him of his more importunate rivals. But whichever way the providential adultery is interpreted, the blemish in his civil status is the focal point of his Romance, the one on which he relies to create an imaginary realm which will satisfy his ambition and where he can reign with a certain amount of justification as lord and master of his own fate.

Thus the illegitimate hero 'makes' a novel in the social climber's sense of the term: he 'makes it' through women, or more precisely through the one woman who epitomises the charm of all, together too with their characteristic weakness and untrustworthiness ('the eternal feminine' and misogny here re-assert their old alliance). However such purely social success cannot satisfy his appetite for power, though it continues to be his main preoccupation. Through status he aims at total creativity; and this he achieves by the simplest of imaginary feats, the appropriation of what, to him, is the sum of all creative powers, his father's virility. The Foundling's *miracu-*

lous birth could never serve such a purpose; but from the moment it has been transformed into the *shameful* yet *glamorous* birth of an illegitimate child — shame and glamour are here synonymous, one corroborates the other[6] — he intervenes personally in the intimate process of conception; and it is he who displaces blood-relationships, creates kinships, 'competes with the registry office', in short, takes an active part in the mysterious furtherance of life itself — like his father, he peoples the world, or rather, like God, since he ignores material limitations.[7] Having robbed the father-spouse of the doubly desirable women — she is desirable as sexual partner and as a means to worldly success — he proceeds to rob the father-god of his phallic power — the supreme creativity which alone will enable him to surpass his idol.[8] Degraded, dispossessed, castrated, negated by every means imaginable, the father is then imitated in his most representative and most envied role. But imitation is always an act of devotion, proof of an unshakeable, indestructible piety; so the model is inevitably reborn and reinstated as rival. The imitator, bewitched by the spell of his childish cult, can never free himself — the Romance that was to have been final is never more than an impossible leave-taking he can only hope to prolong.[9]

The Bastard has never done with killing his father in order to take his place, imitate him or surpass him by 'going his own way'. Guilty by nature, not by accident, he has no choice but to draw the Romance, condemned by the source of its inspiration, into a cycle of transgressions where, humiliated by the limitations of his being, guilty, ashamed and obsessed with expiation and punishment, he heaps coals on his bad conscience and rebellion.[10] Murder, revolt and usurpation, invariably justified in the plot, are what motivate the Romance even when it is ostentatiously moralistic.[11] Thus the Oedipus complex that encourages dissimulation, intrigue and scheming, will find the means to pass such transgressions off as amusing and trivial, tone down crime and reduce impiety to small-town gossip, disaster to a conjugal mishap or minor scandal. But however protean its subject-matter and methods, the devil himself is responsible for its murkiness and the peculiar talent for bringing situations to a head — from the sombre machinations of melodrama and the equivocations of comedy to spiritual or historical tragedies apparently unrelated to its infantile origins. For it is a fact — and one the critic rightly stresses — that the novel can do whatever it pleases, because the pattern on which it is modelled lends it credibility, while leaving it a free choice of key, modality and compass; it can be sombre or gay, insipid or spicy, cynical, profound, innocent or superficial; when it raises transgression to the height of tragedy it will be heroic; sublime when it concentrates on the quest for the absolute implicit in its concern for origins; realistic when it produces a convincing image of the world — cities, countries, epochs — its characters inhabit; fantastic when it restricts itself to its original narcissistic excesses; learned, philosphical, rational — it may be all these in turn or together, and it is equally entitled to maintain the narrative at the lowest level of adultery, rape, illegitimacy and criminal or political plots; to be naïve and to exalt the noble princes, avenging Bastards or dishonoured damsels who make it 'popular'; or even to reduce Oedipus' two terrible crimes to vulgar Oedipal tittle-tattle. During the whole of its history the novel has derived the violence of its desires and its irrepressible freedom from the Family Romance; in this respect it can be said that this primal romance reveals, beneath the historical and individual accidents from which each particular work derives, more than simply the psychological origins of the genre; it is the genre, with all its inexhaustible possibilities and congenital childishness, the false, frivolous, grandiose, mean, subversive and gossipy genre of which each of us is indeed the issue (to his shame, say the philosophers; to his delight, says the novelist, speaking for himself and for his readers) and which, moreover, recreates for each of us a remnant of our primal love and primal reality.

★

Since the Oedipus complex is a universal human phenomenon, all fiction, invention and image making expresses it more or less explicity.[12] In this respect the novel is only one 'Oedipal' form among many others, its one distinction — and for literature such a distinction is highly significant — being that instead of reproducing a crude fancy according to rules established by a specific artistic code, it is modelled on *a pre-romanticised fancy*, the outline of a plot which is not only the

inexhaustible source of subsequent plots, but the one convention to which it is willing to submit. Whereas tragedy, drama,
comedy, opera or farce set the eternal triangle that dominates
all their themes in an arbitrarily determined time and space,
revealing what they are playing at — or the *rules* of the game
they have undertaken to observe — the novel receives from
literature as such no hard and fast directions or interdictions; be
it popular or highbrow, old or new, classical or modern, its
only rules are derived from the family setting whose unconscious desires it perpetuates; so that while its psychic content
and motivations are completely pre-determined, it is totally
free to choose one or more of the various structures and styles
at its disposal; whereas in every other case, genre determines
the aesthetic modalities of transposition, here it yields its
prerogatives to pure fiction, which has, as it were, a *compulsory
content* and an *optional form*, admitting of as many variations as
the imagination can invent. The genre's ambiguity consists
entirely in this peculiar characteristic that radically distinguishes it from all codified forms of art; its only obligation is to
the imagination whose programme it carries out and it has,
literally, no further limitations than those of the absolute
monarchy wherein it parades its delusions.

Thus the childhood Family Romance determines the novel's
lack of generic features — its notorious inconsistency — and
more specifically, the endeavour to be realistic which, oddly
enough, it considers a proof of its reality. Unlike all other
representational genres the novel is never content to *represent*
but aims rather at giving a 'complete and genuine' account of
everything, as if, owing to some special dispensation or magic
power, it had an unmediated contact with reality. Thus its
characters are presented as real people, its words as actual time
and its images as the very essence of events; which is not only
inconsistent with a healthy conception of art — where *representation* makes itself conspicuous within an agreed time and space
(sets and props for the theatre, verse for poetry, frames for
paintings, etc.) — but even with that incitement to dream and
evasion which, on the other hand, the novel claims as its
prerogative. On the surface such naïve inconsistency — or bad
faith, as it has sometimes been called[13] — is totally inexplicable; it only becomes comprehensible in relation to the
original story's paradox, which has sufficient communicative

power to be convincing.[14] The novel wants to be believed just like the story the child used to invent to compensate for life's disappointments. And there, in fact, is the paradox: for the child only invents because his first contact with reality was a disappointment; without disillusion there would be no cause for dreams; but neither would there by any cause for disappointment and evasion if reality had not begun to obtrude. Unless he decides to regress by telling himself stories he himself finds hard to believe, he will never be sufficiently engrossed in his dreams to ignore the effects of his ever-increasing experience upon the dreams themselves; and however much he may wish to cut himself off from a disappointing universe, he cannot help simultaneously trying to understand and dominate it, especially since that is the only way in which he can hope to regain at least a certain degree of a control he believes he is being denied. For his reality has, in fact, two aspects: one frustrating and in need of suppression; the other full of potential triumphs that must, at all cost, be taken into consideration. Thus the child can only succeed in his private task of sentimental and social education if, fully aware of this duality, he is able to establish a skilful compromise between these antagonistic tendencies. He will have to instal experience at the heart of his dreams, since there is no point in ignoring it if he wants to change reality; indeed, it behoves him to adapt his inventions to circumstances, utopia to temporality, and dream to experience, or, in Freudian terms, subject the 'pleasure principle' to the 'reality principle' — which doubtless will not make the story come true, but will increase its claims to veracity and even make it that much more credible. This dialectic of 'invention' and 'reality', such as it is apprehended by the youthful dreamer torn between conflicting temptations, is what the novel inherits long before it is transcribed; whence the peculiar philosophy on behalf of which the whole genre claims to combine by magic the visible and the invisible, dream and reality, evasion and re-integration, myth and science, time lost and time regained. A philosophy of this kind has obviously no validity as such, since there is no possible link between interior and exterior events, but only between the reality of 'inventions' and the illusion of 'reality'; that is, between explicit invention and unacknowledged invention (deception being commensurate with the art it deploys to remain undetected). However, inconsistency is the least of the novel's concerns;[15] treading the ambiguous paths where its inventor leads it, it always manages to carry out both sections of its impossible task, even when it seems to be taking short cuts and settling the option in favour of some temperamental or stylistic requirement. Indeed, whether it be realistic or utopian, the ingenious Don Quixote who will one day epitomise both its significance and its fate, is already its true master-thinker: he never deals with anything but the windmills of his dream, but neither does he ever abandon reality; his dream has no other object than reality and the forces of reality he hopes to overcome.

Whatever the novel may be, whatever its ideologies or aesthetic preconceptions, it is always a primarily Quixotic undertaking which, possessing only the reality of its dreams, strives nonetheless to depict and encourage experience. Offshoot of an unwritten genre intimately related to the various stages of human development — birth, marriage, death, every transition seen as a social or historical event — its assumed 'worldliness' is based on its indispensable props: time and space — circumscribed, relative, laboured time and thickly populated, shifting space teeming with figures and prospects. The old definitions were perhaps not so misguided in stressing its innate relation to history, or in distinguishing it according to criteria of duration (though obviously in this case duration cannot be calculated in pages). Indeed historical time is intrinsic to its original motivation; time is what it mainly imitates, pursues, annihilates or anticipates; and it is history as such — personal or otherwise — which is forever being retold in its pseudo-chronologies. Thus it might always bear the title one of its most famous exponents found for it: *A la Recherche du temps perdu*; for it is an art that deals with the past yet is intent on a present it would overcome;[16] time is the element in which it bathes, its essence, or at least what it claims to borrow and to repay in order that its images may come alive.

Although what makes the novel a quest for lost time, a sentimental education, a formative period of apprenticeship, or in other words, an *exploitation* of time and space, is its more or less primitive desire to recast life under ideal circumstances (which does not imply that the lives it represents·are necessarily better or happier than ours, only that the writer has to feel that he is correcting his own life as he writes) it is by no means constricted in its manipulation of empirical data, or more precisely, of the illusions on which its effects are based. Broadly speaking — and leaving aside its less permanent manifestations — fictional illusion can be achieved in two ways: either the author acts *as if* there were no such thing, and the book is then said to be realistic, naturalistic or simply true to life; or else he can stress the *as if*, which is always his main ulterior motive, in which case it is called a work of fantasy, imagination or subjectivity, or perhaps classified under the general heading of symbolism. Thus there are two kinds of novel: one purporting to draw material from life so as to produce a 'slice of life' or the famous 'mirror carried around the country-side'; the other acknowledging quite openly that it is only a set of figures and forms, and thus disclaiming all responsibility for what does not proceed directly from its scheme. Of the two, the first is of course the more deceptive, since it is wholly intent on concealing its tricks; moreover it stresses the other's deceit; for if writing and living are not simply analogous, but represent various stages through which every author can hope to evolve, then the novel of pure imagination must, of necessity, be seen as insincere, or at any rate as trying to be no more than a pleasant diversion (which is what the Priest and the Barber in *Don Quixote* held against romances of chivalry). This viewpoint has not always been acknowledged; but the genre's ever-increasing popularity has tended to strengthen it, and it has now prevailed to the extent that it is not even questioned and, indeed, contributes the one solid basis for criticism. Thus, we repeat (since this is the source of most misunderstandings), it is taken for granted that *L'Histoire naturelle d'une famille sous le Second Empire* is truer than *Alice in Wonderland*; that Hoffmann's Berlin is more unreal than Musil's Vienna; that Moby Dick only exists in a symbolic world, while Madame Bovary 'suffers and weeps in, twenty French villages at this very minute';[17] that Don Quixote is an improbable figure and Raskolnikov taken, as it were, from life — which amounts to classifying novels according to their varying degrees of realism — if such degrees can ever be measured. Once again, it is precisely to this that more advanced modern theories take exception:[18] for these, fiction cannot be more or less true to life; Don Quixote is no less alive than Anna Karenina, notwithstanding the improbability of his adventures; Emma Bovary is no more privileged in this respect than Kafka's Land Surveyor, even though she possesses certain features which 'place' a fictional character and make it come alive, while he does not; in short, though the more extremely realistic writers may have thought otherwise, nothing warrants the classification of fictional works according to their realism, apart from an unquestioned tendency to approximate. But then how is it that the criterion of truthfulness to life or credibility should be so generally accepted that it is applied automatically? How is it that Flaubert, otherwise so concerned with theoretical coherence, should reply in detail to Sainte Beuve's criticism of certain minor inaccuracies in *Salammbô* as if he considered they were justified? If the relation between the novel and reality only exists on paper, how is it that Goethe's *Werther* is supposed to have provoked an epidemic of suicides among contemporary adolescents, and that the first instalment of *Crime and Punishment* prompted a Russian youth to actually commit Raskolnikov's fictional crimes? And how is it that the most enlightened among us see the novel as a mysterious emanation of life, to the extent of believing that it has a moral influence or, more oddly still, an impact on political and social events?[19] Strictly speaking this apparently unshakeable belief is doubtless akin to superstition; but although it may be invalidated theoretically, psychology at least can find excellent motivations for it that account substantially for its permanence. Though the superstitions surrounding the novel may be false as such, they contain that portion of truth to which all forgotten psychic phenomena are entitled; for they bear witness to the unquestioning faith we all had once in our own stories, and to the survival of the now unconscious Family Romance, forever seeking an outlet, and whose spell is everlasting. That is why we have little cause to marvel at the persistent obduracy of readers in general and of a large number of novelists, to the theoreticians' censures: notwithstanding cultural distinctions and generation gaps, reader and writer will always be united by something like a complicity of faith or the sharing of a secret vice.

Thus there is a logic to our irrational faith in fiction. The reader may be misguided in giving more credit to a novel by Balzac than to tales of improbable adventures wilfully projected onto a utopian nowhere; but he has every reason to experience Balzac's 'world' quite otherwise than Swift's Lilliput; for they represent two fictional methods it is essential to distinguish because, from the personal standpoint they are compelled to express, they have not attained the same level of maturity. Apart from aesthetic considerations[20] and the intentional significance each writer puts into his imaginary world, the author who imitates human conflicts with their psychological nuances and chronology, events with their consequences and inextricable confusion, people with their characteristics and inconsistencies, *has not the same psychological age* as the novelist whose imagination spontaneously produces wonders and who does nothing at all to make them seem natural. Not that he is more clear-sighted, more able to provide a perfect reproduction, or necessarily a greater genius; but he shows greater maturity, in that he realises that the world is something outside himself, a complex of positive data that no end of invention will ever enable him to penetrate. Insofar as such a writer undertakes to maintain his inventions within the bounds of probability and verisimilitude — which does not imply that he constructs a new fraction of reality, but only that, notwithstanding his suppressed destructiveness, he pays homage to things as they are — he submits to the subtle motivations of realism that intervene at the more advanced stages of the Family Romance's development, emulating in fact the Oedipal Bastard; whereas the visionary, bewitched by his visions and transformations, creating in isolation and against reality a dream world unrelated to experience, is unquestionably at the developmental stage of the Foundling, imprisoned in the pre-Oedipal universe whose only law is still the omnipotence of thought. 'When fighting the world, back the world', Kafka said, presumably thinking of the destructive radicalism of his own Quixotic behaviour, which he was forever trying to assert and to overcome.[21] There, indeed, lies the frontier between the two major directions the novel can follow and which it has, in fact, followed throughout its history — for strictly speaking there are but two ways of writing a novel: the way of the realistic Bastard who backs the world while fighting it head on; and the way of the Foundling who, lacking both the experience and the means to fight, avoids confrontation by flight or rejection.

Such differences of outlook have absolutely nothing to do with literary merit. The Foundling has probably as many masterpieces to his credit as has the maturer Bastard; moreover, though the distinction may help to put some kind of order in the confusion of literary works, it does not provide us with the classifying principle we would so much like to discover. Indeed the Bastard has still a great many features in common with the Foundling from whom he evolved; and while endeavouring to adapt his ideas to the demands of experience, nonetheless, he can never completely free himself from the old spell. The adult novel is also heir to this relic from an archaic age; but on the other hand, it can never be as totally ignorant of the facts of life, nor as completely cut off from reality as the first childhood myth unavoidably is; thus it is never entirely free of Oedipal elements, except perhaps when, by exceeding the genre's limits, it can no longer claim to be a novel. Thus the two attitudes possible to fiction cannot be clearly pigeonholed; it is more a matter of degree; while providing definite *points of view*, they may well alternate in the works of one author, complement each other, disagree, blend together in the same story or even merge completely to produce one of those hybrid works that seem to be made exclusively in order to refute every theory. Since the two stages of the Romance are not antagonistic but, on the contrary, strictly interdependent, Balzac may well be 'realistic' in *la Comédie humaine*, and then cross over to 'the other side'[22] when writing *Louis Lambert* or *Seraphitus Seraphita*; Swift who is typically pre-Oedipal in the fantastic excesses of his *Travels*, can exploit this same tendency to exaggerate for the purposes of political or social satire; Flaubert is capable of realising his theories of art with the utmost precision in *Madame Bovary* and *l'Education sentimentale* while reverting at will to the narcissistic, solitary Saint Anthony whose temptations haunted him all his life; and Cervantes, who wrote the *Exemplary Novels* as a true man of his time, could evoke Don Quixote's madness in such ambiguous terms that even today we do not know what to make of his ideas. Sometimes a realist will instil into a 'slice of life' a dose of the unreal, or some stylistic ingredient that betrays the true visionary (those minute details, endless enumerations and all that grammar of excess by which Zola occasionally runs the risk of turning naturalism into delirium);

at times, on the contrary, the acknowledged visionary uses visions as a means of saying something essential about reality; but the inconsistency is never wholly resolved unless it serves as direct inspiration for art;[23] the Western novel thrives on it — which accounts both for some of its conflicting 'messages' and for the similarity and diversity of its geniuses.

This said — and notwithstanding the fact that the two stages of the novel correspond neither to historical dates nor to categories established by the various schools of thought — generally speaking each novelist is compelled nonetheless to be either for reality (when the Oedipal Bastard predominates); or (when the Foundling has the upper hand) to deliberately create another world — which amounts to being against reality. In the first case he is Balzac, Victor Hugo, Sue, Tolstoy, Dostoevsky, Proust, Faulkner, Dickens and all those who call themselves psychological, true to life, naturalistic or 'engaged' novelists and, claiming to be initiated into life's mysteries by some god or demiurge, enliven their own story by simulating the rhythms and intricacies of existence itself. In the second case he is Cervantes as well as the author of romances of chivalry; he writes *Tristan and Isolde* or Cyrano de Bergerac's *l'Autre monde*; he is Hoffmann, Jean-Paul, Novalis, Kafka or Melville, and he always flies in the face of reality, ignoring or jostling history and geography. At times he is compulsively meticulous, checking every detail he translates into images which correspond to what he believes to be the truth; he learns the art of the craftsman, the tradesman, the banker, the soldier, the philosopher and the scientist. At others, on the contrary, he will acknowledge no exterior boundaries to his vision; his freedom, commensurate with the constriction of his intimate desires, produces the extravagant creatures he calls fairies, giants, dwarfs, Houyhnhnms or performing dogs; and the tendentious orientation of his fantasies alone makes sense of his metamorphoses. In the first instance he respects reality and temporality, so that even his most violent rebellion reveals his piety, and the frivolity of his Oedipal gossip is still tinged with earnestness. In the second, aware of his total or, at best considerable lack of understanding, and thus of his inadequacy for the task of revealing the ins and outs of existence, he simply cancels out all of creation and sets up in its place imaginary worlds where the only limit to adventure is that of his imagination, desert islands where he reigns as an ingenious despotic Robinson Crusoe, and endless spaces where all the clocks have been miraculously or maliciously tampered with. On the one hand he imitates god, taking himself so seriously that he even tries to make his imitation believable; on the other he is god; a god so confident in his powers that he can afford to include the more subtle weapons of satire and irony in his magic arsenal; though, in fact, there is nothing to stop him from changing sides or even doing away with the dividing line altogether — which is what he does in his more exalted moments. But narcissistic Oedipus or Oedipal Narcissus, he nevertheless will always belong to one or other of the two major lines of descent, depending on the attitude he has originally adopted and which, sooner or later, will reveal his true nature.

★

It remains now to discover how the material corresponding to each age-group becomes organised; how each disposes its shadows and its stresses; and by what conventional method or unknown process the infantile desires that set the whole work in motion gradually emerge, are divulged, distorted, isolated or brought under the aegis of some ideal. For although — wholly determined by the Family Romance of which it is the sequel — the novel is never free to select its stage of development nor, in consequence, the level of human relationships it is able to depict — it can choose, nevertheless, between a vast range of methods for mingling invention and reality; and it is precisely in this art of choosing — which is art itself — that the extent of its freedom resides.

Notes

1   'Der Familienroman der Neurotiker' ("Family Romance") was first published in Otto Rank's *The Myth of the Birth of the Hero*, Leipzig and Vienna, 1909, (in *The Standard Edition of the Complete Psychological Works, Collected Papers*, Vol. V, London, 1953ff.). Freud had as it were 'bequeathed' this short essay to his young disciple who was specialising in the analysis of mythology. However, the discovery of the Family Romance predated 1909. Freud had been aware of its existence

since much earlier, having mentioned it in 1897 in a letter to Wilhelm Fliess; and in 1899 he had already given it the name by which it is still referred to in psychoanalytical literature. Actually, the theory of the Family Romance developed empirically and thus reflects the hazardousness of Freudian thought at the time of its arduous beginnings. Freud was impressed by the part this strange fabrication played in the thoughts of most seriously disturbed patients; but, seeing it at first as a pathological symptom particular to paranoia, he called it *Entfremdungsroman* which expresses the notion of a psychotic refusal of reality. Later he was led by experience to alter his views and to realise that the Family Romance was in fact a general, totally non-specific phenomenon. Though the essay's original title is still influenced by his earlier view, in the text proper Freud clearly posits the phenomenon as a normal, general childhood phenomenon. It only becomes pathological in adults who continue to believe in it and to elaborate it. Thus the Family Romance can be defined as an expedient to which the imagination resorts in order to resolve the typical crisis in human development which the Oedipus Complex provokes.

2   'But it is not my father who talks like that!' says Oscar M., the hero of Kafka's unfinished story which is perhaps an early draft of 'The Judgement'. 'My real father would have kissed me all the same, he would have called mother. . .'. André Breton, shocked by the religious undertones he detected in the words 'my real father cannot fail to come. . .' dismissed the fragment as apocryphal. But such an interpretation is far-fetched: Kafka was simply taking a significant fantasy of the Family Romance literally, as he did later in the simultaneously grandiose and grotesque epic exaggerations from which his 'judges' and 'gentlemen' originate. We should not overlook the fact that Oscar's invention of an imaginary father occurs during a row with his real father, whose attitude is unusually harsh and disappointing. Neither should we forget that the over-obvious reference to the Family Romance has been eliminated from the final version of 'The Judgement'; understandably enough, since the fantasy would have become unconscious for this mature hero and thus could only be expressed by means of complex transpositions which would make it unrecognisable.

3   Since Freud did not publish the theory of Narcissism till 1914, 'Family Romance' (1909) does not refer to it explicitly. However its presence is implicit, and the manner in which Freud analyses infantile over-evaluation of the parental image, as well as the general megalomaniac tendency which gives rise to most manifestations of such fantasies, shows how much importance he gave to a notion which was shortly to become central to his enquiry. Thus the typical situation common to all such pseudo-biographies may be considered from the narcissistic point of view, especially since in the Foundling myth it can have no other interpretation.

4   The legend of Oedipus strikingly combines the pre-sexual and, in this respect at least, innocent Foundling theme with that of the incestuous parricide where Freud found a confirmation of his theory of uncon-

scious psychic activity. Oedipus, a King's son, was brought up by shepherds and his birth was Miraculous. In the *Myth of the Birth of the Hero*, where Freud's essay on the Family Romance first appeared, Otto Rank illustrates in a number of examples the extent to which accidents of birth determine the mythical or legendary hero's mission. It is not possible to imagine such a hero, legendary conqueror or religious prophet whose birth was not unusual in some way, whether mysterious, miraculous, fantastic or divine. Nor do such characters ever spend their childhood between their two parents, basking in the warmth of their common affection. They invariably come into the world on the wrong footing, as it were, and that is precisely what determines their vocation. Rank discovers many such unconscious rejection themes, some of which serve to compensate for the inferiority inherent in the premature birth and prolonged dependence characteristic of mankind; others are a call to arms in the age-old conflict between generations; but all provide an excuse for the two major crimes, parricide and incest. Here infantile megalomania plays an important part. Bella Grumberger (Cf. *le Narcissisme*, Paris 1971) — who ascribes the psychology of heroism to narcissism, for which he contributes important new material — defines the hero as *one who does not want to owe his life to anybody*. His birth, unrelated to the laws of nature, is not a consequence of parental intercourse: he is his own begetter, the son of God (the divine child constitutes a narcissistic triad with his parents), or at a more human level, a self-made man. Thus as a rule the hero is not re-united with his real parents (except in the Family Romance and, as we shall see, in its folklore extension, the fairy tale): he has to be parentless, that is he must reject his parents so that his mission may be confirmed by this self-generation and consequent independence. In this respect Oedipus is exceptional in that he encounters Laius and Jocasta and perpetrates on them the dual crime the Family Romance seeks to avoid. But then he is a tragic hero and not a fictional one.

5   The real novelist sometimes goes much further — Dostoevsky consciously desired his father's death at an age when such desires, if they survive the resolution of the Oedipus Complex, have long since become unconscious. When his father was murdered by his serfs — and castrated into the bargain — he was overcome with remorse from which he tried apparently to rid himself by writing books about overt parricide. It should be noted, however, that the complementary theme of incest does not play any obvious part in his novels. Indeed, most novels seem to respect the taboo of the maternal incest theme as such, only dealing with it indirectly through the substitution of fraternal incest, for instance (Thomas Mann, Musil).

6   Dostoevsky, who like all novelists but perhaps more consciously than most, draws his fiction from the inexhaustible sources of the Family Romance, depicts the Bastard with a penetration and depth of analysis which prematurely vindicates Freud's most audacious theories. Thus the character who plays the title role in his novel *The Adolescent*, a youth upon whom chance has bestowed a princely name, but who is

the illegitimate son of a provincial lord and the legtimate son of a former serf, boasts about his illegitimacy so shamelessly that his interlocutor exclaims: 'Such feelings obviously do you honour . . . *You might almost have been at the party!*' (my italics). With these last words Dostoevsky plumbs the depths of the Bastard's boastfulness, which, more than humiliation and a natural reaction to offended pride, expresses a barely veiled desire to participate in his parents' most intimate relations, or as the psychoanalysts say, in the 'primal scene'. Moreover autobiography might well play a part in all this, if we consider Dostoevsky's own version of the circumstances surrounding his first epileptic fit: it took place outside the door of his parents' bedroom. Smerdiakov, another of Dostoevsky's Bastards, is notable for a similar boastfulness in his relation to others. This is what inspires such aversion in Ivan Karamazov, the legitimate would-be parricide who sees him as his double, the ignoble ape of his own diabolism. Here the Bastard commits the murder of which the two legitimate sons only dream, Ivan because of his inordinate narcissism, Dmitry because of his sexual jealousy (to which the author — again in perfect agreement with psychoanalytical theory — adds the motive of gain).

7   Dostoevsky again writes in his Diary: 'To be God', and 'To be the first in everything'. Cf. Dominique Arban, *les Années d'apprentissage de Fiodor Dostoievski*, Paris 1968.

8   The dual role the Family Romance implicitly assigns to women is clearly defined in the situation on which Kafka's *Castle* is based; a situation whose significance is generally overlooked by critics, perhaps because it is too explicit. K. the Land Surveyor is seduced by Frieda at the very moment when he learns that she is the mistress of Klamm — an obvious father-figure, observed with adult irony but with a child's characteristic exaggeration. He wants to marry her, but after a while begins to feel a kind of aversion for her and wonders if it was not perhaps Klamm's 'reflected light' which had made her so 'fantastically beautiful' in the first place and if any of Klamm's mistresses might not have appealed to him as much. Frieda herself accuses him of seeing her as a 'pawn' in his attempts to succeed in reaching Klamm — in other words, simply to succeed — an accusation the Castle authorities do not hesitate to take up.

9   Kafka writes in his famous letter to his father: 'Thus (through literature) I had succeeded in getting quite a distance away from you . . . I was somehow out of reach. . . . Of course it was only an illusion, I was not yet free. My books were about you, I was always complaining in them about the things I could not complain about in your arms. . . . It was a leave taking, an intentionally prolonged leave taking. . . .'

10   It has often been said that every novel might be called *Crime and Punishment*. Indeed the Family Romance shows why and to what extent this is true. But considered from the point of view of the genre's two basic tendencies, every novel might equally be called *The Trial*, 'The Judgement' *l'Education sentimentale*, *The Insulted and Injured*, *La*

Recherche de l'absolu and, or perhaps especially *Vanity Fair*.

11   The fact that the novel is immoral independently from its content and the moralistic, messianic tendencies in which it naturally indulges — precisely because of its origins, — has been acknowledged by all novelists who draw their inspiration from the inner sources that make it worth while, and not from the superficial sphere wherein they find their self-justification. After attempting to turn the novel into a means of doing 'good' Tolstoy came to see it as an agent of the Devil and finally condemned it. For identical reasons Gogol burnt *Dead Souls* and Kafka, who also burnt most of his manuscripts, refers to the joys of creativity as 'the devil's wages'.

12   According to Freudian theory there is no essential difference between the imagination's various languages, whether literary, musical, pictorial or even scientific and philosophical. Freud made the point when he published, as his first analysis of a work of art, not the analysis of a literary text, but of Leonardo's St Anne, where he discovered a birth-fantasy representing a very primitive stage of the Family Romance (the invisible vulture traced within the visible figures of the painting being associated with the legendary phallic mother who engenders her own child).

13   This is Sartre's definition of the offence he imputes to Proust, in particular, whom he accuses of confusing the issue by wilfully sharing out biographical data between himself and his fictional characters. Now Proust (who waited till after his parents' death to write his great novel, because he presumably feared it might kill them and thus realise the secret desire of his Family Romance) wrote mainly to refurbish his biography, with the irrepressible tendency to fantasticate and the preoccupation with detail typical of the genre in its earlier stages. His bad faith stemmed from the same source as his social ambition, his snobbishness and his pronounced partiality for Oedipal gossip. So there is no point in taking him to task for it, unless we consider that his book is not sufficiently distanced from its infantile model, and thus fails to disguise its motives completely. Though in that case bad faith must be imputed, not to the author's dishonesty, but to an aesthetic failure.

14   The peculiar quality of the faith we all put in our Family Romance is the only adequate explanation for the fictional illusion that makes, not only the artless but even the best informed reader, believe that Raskolnikov, Rastignac or Julien Sorel live just round the corner. When Oscar Wilde said that the greatest disaster *of his life* was the death of Lucien Rubempré in *Splendeur et misère des courtisanes*, nobody was shocked at the absurdity of a remark at which everyone would have scoffed if it had refered to Phèdre or Oedipus instead of Lucien. This is because the classical hero is answerable to quite other laws; his reality is not one with his veracity; his time is not clock-time; he is not created to give the impression of having a complete, detailed existence but to stress the unbridgeable gap separating representation from life. Whereas we unanimously allow the novel hero to come and go between life and the printed page.

15   Except when it steps back, as it were, sufficiently to perceive its own delusions and decides to use them as subject matter. I have tried to show elsewhere (Marthe Robert, *The Old and the New: from Don Quixote to Kafka,* Berkeley, 1977) that such active and fictionalised self-scrutiny — or Quixotism, since Cervantes provides the first and most impressive example — is the only means at its disposal to overcome the ambiguity of 'invention' and 'reality', which otherwise inevitably degenerates into bad faith or ártlessness.

16   Incidentally, science fiction, despite the dating of its adventures, does not deal with the future. Like all true descendents of the Family Romance, its inventions are more or less explicit critiques, or even satires, of the present. Neither indeed is it really based on the present, but on an unconscious nostalgia for the past (whence the remarkable prehistorical symbolism of such works).

17   According to Flaubert himself in a letter, where the author attributes his success, not only to the fact that his heroine is life-like but also to the fact that she resembles the majority of ordinary women.

18   They cannot possibly all be named here. A substantial list can be found in Wellek & Warren: *The Theory of Literature,* New York 1963.

19   Here Kafka's case is once again a good example of such singular incoherence: formerly rejected by Marxist critics (Lukács) on account of their abstractness and social pessimism, his books are now expressly associated with the Prague Spring Uprising, either as sources of inspiration for the revolutionary youth, or as an instrument in the hands of the reactionaries.

20   It is self-evident that everything we have said so far takes no account of the novelist's talent nor of the vast aesthetic differences between works. Before we could find out if the Family Romance would assist us in elucidating that point as well, we had to try to discover the basic features common to all artistic productions at their inception, independently from their value.

21   Elsewhere he writes: 'You don't have to go out of the house. Stay at your desk and listen. Don't even listen, just wait. Don't even wait, be absolutely still and alone. The world will come and offer itself to you so as to be unmasked, it can't do otherwise, it will writhe before you in ecstasy'. The Foundling's utter faith in the magical power of self-absorbtion cannot be better expressed. But Kafka was never content with such an ideology. Throughout all his writings we see it conflicting with his aim for the maturity and action which typifies the Bastard's attitude. K. the Land Surveyor is the main exponent of such a conflict.

22   *Die andere Seite* (The other side) is the title of a novel of fantasy by Alfred Kubin, where the author proves himself to be a true spokesman for the Foundling.

23   A novel's greater or lesser success in achieving the balance between Foundling introversion and the Bastard's relative extrovertedness might serve as a criterion when assessing its value. Thus the most accomplished work would be that where *a purely literary combination of elements* achieves the near-impossible feat of making it simultaneously

for and against reality, completely on 'the other side' and entirely here (Cervantes, Flaubert, Kafka).

II
THE OTHER SIDE

I Castles in the Air

In those days when people still
believed that wishes came true . . .
Grimm

As true as if Mr. Gulliver had
said it . . .
Swift

Since we now know what the Family Romance's hidden aims really are we will not be surprised to find such aims realised to the letter in the traditional children's story we call the Fairy Tale.[1] For such tales derive directly from the original daydream, and although their motives necessarily undergo a certain amount of editing before they can appear in public, they are still close enough to the first magic Romance to serve as a more or less unadulterated model. In this respect Romantic literature was not far wrong when it gave them a significance it longed to possess itself: *once upon a time* is indeed the best way to begin a story, as E. T. A. Hoffmann asserted.[2] It is even the only possibly way, the one at which every novel hints while doing all it can to re-invent it.

Apart from its many different and wonderful ways of making wishes come true, the fairy tale can be reduced to a stereotyped pattern, where everything is contrived in view of an inevitable happy ending. Since the happy ending is obviously its main preoccupation — indeed it could not omit it without automatically foregoing its character, for no fairy tale ever ends unhappily — everything has to lead up to its hero's success, though in the more typical instances this may be delayed by numberless unforeseen obstacles. Thus the tale's ending is literally the end: it has nothing to tell apart from the deliberately delayed success which is its meaning and what it has set out to prove.

No matter what happens in the imaginary space where the

story purports to be lost, its object consists in proving, through the example of a suffering, pathetically youthful hero — usually a child or adolescent, but occasionally a grown man[3] — that even the cripple, the infirm, the humble, the unloved or those who are cruelly treated by wicked relations, can still attain the highest degree (Kingship, symbolising perfect happiness 'for ever after') through love's magic, or by winning the hand of a prince or a princess (thus, furthermore, confirming the incredible fact that the child will one day be grown-up and acquire what, to him, seems quite inaccessible). To account for the underprivileged hero's remarkable luck in getting his own back on life the tale — exploiting the same means (presumably for the same reasons) as the Foundling or 'faiseur de romans' — lays great stress on an accident of birth which may be a natural phenomenon, an ill omen or some magic spell cast by a malevolent power. The hero's handicap may consist in his having lost his mother (the basic theme of the orphan and the cruel stepmother); in being poor (Tom Thumb); in a distinctive sign fraught with danger (the child born with a cawl); in a sinister prophecy (the son who will murder his father and usurp the throne); in a change of background (the child abandoned because of such a prophecy, found and brought up by foster parents); or again in an oversight (the omission of some gesture, time-honoured ritual or even of a conventional formula). When the handicap does not occur at birth it invariably manifests itself at puberty and is the result of an imprudent wish (*The Seven Ravens*); a vow made by thoughtless parents to the Devil (*The Young Girl Without Hands*); or, at its worst, of an unnatural father's incestuous desires (the French *Peau d'Ane* and the German *Skin-of-a-Thousand-Beasts* where the threat of incest follows the young mother's death in child-birth). Since such mishaps are the consequence of events that precede or immediately follow the child's birth, he can hardly be held responsible for them. Indeed, it is the parents to whom must be imputed the unfortunate circumstances surrounding procreation and child-bearing. Thus the tale always depicts the child as victim; and though it may try to clear the parents by incriminating magic, they remain, either together or singly, no less the involuntary accomplices or even perpetrators of his misfortune. Not that they are invariably weak or cruel; but even when they happen to be good, poverty tends to make them selfish and hard (the child seen as an extra mouth to feed and 'lost' in the woods); or, when the father is loving then he is unfortunately widowed and falls into the clutches of a second wife who makes him sacrifice the children of his first marriage more or less unconsciously (the main theme of *Cinderella* and similar tales). Or if instead of being a poor man he is a king, then he condemns his infant son to death so as to eliminate an eventual rival, or pursues with his unnatural attentions his only daughter, the living image of his beloved, dead wife; or again, if the mother is a beautiful, virtuous young queen, she then dies in childbirth and can be no more to her orphaned child than an ideal image incapable of protecting him. The handicap always derives from this unequal distribution of power within the family circle: the good parent — either poor and humiliated, weak and dominated by a cruel partner, or dead — is never in a position to oppose the bad parent's actions. The bad parent, having the advantage of absolute dominance and of being very much alive, can indulge his wicked impulses to his heart's content. Thus, loved at best by a weak or a dead parent, persecuted by a tyrant whose wishes are orders, at the mercy of a cruel stepmother who may be half-witch or half-ogress, terrified, starved, in danger of being maimed or made into mince-meat and devoured, the child-martyr can only hope to survive by contriving to run away — as all 'persecuted' children dream of doing and frequently do. Of course this flight for dear life never puts an immediate end to his troubles; in every corner of the earth lurk his parent's agents in the form of ogres, dragons, witches and evil spirits who delight in carrying out their wicked plans. But though he only jumps out of the frying pan into the fire, so to speak, at least he has escaped from under the parental roof; and this suffices to make him worthy of the crown his trials and tribulations ultimately earn him.

Through the accusations which transpire despite its exemplary claims, the fairy tale is unquestionably related to that ancient store of myths and legends wherein our forefathers expressed their horror at having been born. A superstitious horror, perhaps, but not entirely unfounded in a time when birth was still a perilous adventure whose complete success depended on luck or on a miracle. Indeed the fairy tale child encounters the tragedy of birth in a relatively attenuated form: his entry into the world does not give rise to a battle of Titans and has no cosmic repercussions (though the sun, moon and stars are frequently linked to his fate, either as magic auxiliaries or as symbols of the 'Other World' where the child seeks refuge).[4] He is merely born in unfortunate circumstances that somehow single him out and set him apart from his family, or in the middle of some domestic tragedy, as when he causes the death of his life-giving mother. Handicapped from birth, suffering from some absurd deformity, undersized or, more generally, orphaned and thus unwillingly responsible for a death that leaves him defenceless, he is a living example of the savage indifference with which, according to universal mythology, nature treats the truly gifted. Nonetheless he survives. And this alone, in an age when birth always involves a considerable risk, is an undisputable sign of predestination. Taking his stand against a relentless fate that ill-treats, disinherits and abandons him to the mercy of a no less cruel stepmother, the fairy-tale child represents the conqueror of mysterious or super-human (which in this case is identical) powers apparently combined for his undoing. This is precisely what makes him a hero: having honourably endured the hardest trials, he will overcome all the others unharmed, and his spirit of survival will invariably triumph over whatever further tribulations fate may have in store for him. In other words the fact that he has succeeded in being born has made him invulnerable and capable of defying death to the extent of being practically immortal.

This memory of the precarious living conditions of our remote past is linked in the fairy tale to no less primitive and equally mythological reminiscences of destructive family despotism and its unfortunate effects on the new-born child. For if parents favour the cruel designs of nature by thoughtlessly procreating — as may be deduced from their oversights, omissions and imprudent wishes in the most inappropriate circumstances — they further constrict the new-comer in a system of regulations purporting to protect and unite the family group, but which automatically tend to ignore the needs of its most defenceless member. In the name of rites and customs serving the sole purpose of adults (as well as expressing the evil intentions of parents), the child is either *abandoned* (then found and adopted as in the Family Romance), subjected to cruel taboos, left in a dark wood to undergo frightful dangers, or even sacrificed when paternal power sees fit to do away with him (the tale usually substitutes for the sacrifice a metamorphosis where the child, turned into a bird or a stone, is restored to human shape in the end). Born into a world that was created without him and against him, where he has to fight every inch of the way, he passes from torture to torture and from terror to terror until, saved by the love through which he achieves manhood, he is promoted to his rightful place in the generation sequence as Father-King (and simultaneously evicted from the fairy tale, which only deals with unaccomplished beings).

The fairy tale's unambiguous association of a disastrous birth with a brilliant future corresponds to one of the more significant aspects of myth and legend. Indeed according to this tradition those who are destined to be great — whether prophets or founders of empires or religions — are beings who should never have been born and who, having come into the world against all odds, can survive only at the cost of an unremitting struggle with malicious powers (usually represented by the father or a despot who symbolises him). This is a feature shared by all folklore heroes, however diverse they may otherwise be: exceptionally gifted human beings or those born for superhuman achievements are inevitably misfits, children who are abandoned, sacrificed or ill-treated by the very people in charge of their welfare. Not that the hero is distinguished merely for his resistence to early misfortunes; the main reason for his ascendency is that, evicted from his home and forced to break all family ties, he is free from the mental and physical constraints which dominate the lives of ordinary men. Such is the lesson which, under cover of metamorphoses and marvels, the myth has to impart. For although it tells us that no one is a prophet in his own land, it also sets out to prove that only he who has neither family nor constraints can be a prophet, he who is nobody's son, who is literally self-made, an exile without hope of return and who, for this very reason, is cut out for greatness.

Thus Moses, abandoned by his real parents and adopted by an Egyptian princess, has two families just like the fairy-tale Foundling, with this difference, however, that his parents were innocent since they did not abandon him so as to be rid of him but to save him from the slaughter of male Hebrew babies enforced by Pharoah. In fact Moses should not have been born: his father, determined not to conceive a son condemned in advance, had lived apart from his wife for three years and only rejoins her on the instigation of his daughter Myriam, to whom God has revealed in a dream that the child who will be born to them is to be the saviour of the Children of Israel. So Moses wrests his life from a threatening non-existence. Like most Foundlings he is born to an ageing couple and thanks to a prophecy that predetermines his vocation. Thus he is a Man of God and of Fate prior even to existing: he is born *to save* — or more precisely he is a saviour because he was 'saved from the waters' (he saves the Hebrews from the waters of the Red Sea and thus helps them to be reborn).

The Oedipus legend expresses a similar theme in a context that convincingly re-asserts the myth's basic tendency. Laius, warned by the Delphic Oracle that he will be murdered by his own son, ceases to have relations with Jocasta his wife, until one day under the influence of drink, he infringes his self-imposed rule and conceives Oedipus. The child is abandoned in the mountains three days after his birth. According to Sophacles, the shepherd who has been entrusted with the task gives the baby to one of the shepherds of the Corinthian king Polybus. According to other sources the child is cast out to sea in a basket and saved from the waves by Polybus' wife Mreboe. When Oedipus later learns that he is a foundling, he consults the Oracle to find out who are his real parents and, after communicating the Oracle's now famous answer to his foster-parents, he flees from Corinth to Thebes where he inevitably accomplishes the predicted actions. But before reaching Thebes he had interpreted the Sphinx's riddle and thus delivered the city from the plague which was ravaging it. Once again — though the tragedy of parricide and incest overshadows the beneficial aspect of Oedipus' role — the hero's soteriological vocation is linked to the three indispensable features of all mythic undertakings: a fatal prediction, sombre machinations at birth and the timely rescue of the new-born child from sacrificial death. What distinguishes Oedipus from all other saviour-figures is that his rescue at birth as well as his assistance to a foreign city, both relate him to the mystery of birth, since it is as the solver of riddles, the initiate who has fathomed this mystery, that he saves Thebes. True, his superior knowledge does not help him to recognise his parents nor save him from the Oedipal predicament. Indeed it is responsible for bringing about his ruin (in this respect Oedipus represents a transitional stage between the Foundling and the Bastard of the Family Romance: his awareness of sexuality sharpens his wits on the one hand, while on the other it casts him into the abyss of his own psyche where he wanders blindly).

Christian versions of the legend are notable in that, while the crimes attendant on the mythic birth are more dreadful, they are absolved through the agency of a saviour-hero to whom, in the eyes of the community, such sins confer the distinction of spiritual guide. For instance, Saint Gregory the Stylite, the son of an incestuous union, is cast into the sea by his parents in a basket. Found and brought up by fishermen he is destined for holy orders, but leaves the monastery to become a knight. One day, after yet another of his many successful battles, he is granted in reward the hand of an unknown woman who turns out to be his mother. When he discovers the incest which mirrors that of his parents, Gregory retires to a rock in the middle of the sea to do penance for eighteen years. But despite his crime, or because of it, God raises him to the status of Pope.

Oddly enough, the prophecy omitted from the legend of St Gregory, plays a prominent part in that of Judas, that most ominous of figures who, as the direct opposite of Christ, serves as foil to the Redemption. Judas' mother is forewarned in a dream that she will give birth to a depraved son who will be the undoing of his people. She and her husband therefore decide to get rid of the new-born babe according to the well-tried method[5] of putting him out to sea in a basket. Washed up on the island of Scariot, Judas is adopted by its queen who happens to be childless. However the royal couple later have a child of their own, whom Judas murders out of jealousy. Forced then to escape, he takes refuge at the court of Pontius Pilate whose counsellor he becomes. He marries the widow of a neighbour he has killed in a dispute without knowing his identity. When he evetually discovers that this neighbour was in fact his father, he confesses his sin to Christ who allows him to join his disciples. But Judas, instead of redeeming himself, betrays the very man who trusted him as brother and disciple, thus putting the finishing touch to the picture of the born traitor. Fratricide, parricide and incestuous into the bargain, Judas the Foundling is in all respects a negative of the Child Jesus whose miraculous birth is pre-eminently holy. He comes to destroy humanity where Christ comes to save it. Yet he ultimately contributes in equal measure to its salvation, since his betrayal is vitally instrumental to Christ's achievement.

The divine Bastard of Greek mythology is also destined at birth to be a saviour and thus an equal of the gods. Dionysus, Apollo and Hercules, all three the fruit of Zeus' adulterous relationships with mortal women, and therefore objects of Hera's relentless jealousy, are subjected from birth to a long sequence of tribulations. However their adversary's malevolence is no match for their resilience and they remain unvanquished, invulnerable and unscathed. (As in all mythical tales the heroic formula must be reversed to achieve full significance: the hero does not survive miraculously because he is a god; he is acclaimed as a god because he survives). Thence the power he is granted to regenerate humanity (Dionysus), to bestow health and wisdom upon it (Apollo), or to deliver it from the monsters eternally reborn to hinder its progress (Hercules). For although heroic deeds vary in circumstance and setting, the story's basic message is always the same — a message above and beyond ethics, whose moral is that a hero becomes a super-human being insofar as, stemming from a murky source, he has had to forego from the start all those family ties which maintain ordinary mortals in perpetual mediocrity and sap both their energy and their freedom. Put to the test on account of his doubtful extraction, he is promoted by means of the test to the rank of conqueror, healer, legislator, founder of civilisations, giant-killer or prophet. Thanks to his shameful birth he founds cities, empires, moral laws or even that Kingdom which though claiming to be in another world has nonetheless left its indelible mark on this one.

Though the fairy tale is entirely based on the device of a dual family which is central to all myths, it is obviously in a different class from stories of legendary Foundling or Bastard figures who epitomise virtue or vice (or rather who are above either since supermen cannot be judged according to moral standards but according to their uniqueness, outrageousness and impressiveness). Prince Charming may well be born in circumstances apparently favouring his promotion to epic stature, yet he will never be Oedipus, Moses or Judas; he will never found Rome nor the Empire of Cyrus; he will not give his name to a hallowed site, a memorable action nor a quest accomplished in the name of humanity. Not that he lacks the necessary attributes to compete with such heroes: he solves riddles as well as Oedipus, thwarts his wicked step-mother's Machiavellian plans as cunningly as Apollo thwarts Hera's, beheads his dragons in true Herculean style and can even beat St Gregory the Stylite at his own game, since he thinks nothing of staying up a tree for seven years 'without smiling or speaking'. But it is not a matter of personal merit; the obstacle to his mythic career is simply the happy ending to which he aspires after his trials are over, and which proves that once his years of hardship and testing are behind him he will promptly rejoin the common herd. Whereas the true hero breaks with family tradition once and for all and thus is able to establish new social values on a higher level, the fairy-tale hero only seeks to 'live happily ever after' by founding a kingdom without history or stories from which he expects eternal bliss. He was not born for the great undertakings which require the mythic hero's utter selflessness and, more often than not, the sacrifice of his life. He has no desire to be put to death and gloriously resurrected, to save mankind at the cost of his life, nor to give up all personal satisfactions as an example to future generations. All he wants is a wife, 'a lot of children', wealth and, after his stormy youth, the peace and quiet of a cosy hearth. That is why when his reign begins, the tale must end; having chosen reconciliation rather than a final break, he has nothing more to do or say that is worth repeating; so he sinks into oblivion like all those who are cut down to the size of their private happiness.

Uncongenial to history and estranged from mythology by its romantic tendencies and modest ambitions, the fairy tale is confined to the sphere of pure Utopia where it is free to dispense with space, time, names and boundaries, everything in short which serves to co-ordinate reality. Thus it takes place 'in those days', 'once upon a time', 'in the wide, wide world', nowhere or everywhere, always or never, without providing a more precise setting for its action. Not that it aims at thus making 'another' world credible. On the contrary, it exploits Utopia, which probably accounts for its unmitigated popularity; for it denies the reality of experience, insofar as it claims to report everybody's experience; and it only stresses limitlessness the better to suggest the modesty of its aims and the ordinariness of its characters.

Consistent with the utopian rule it has willingly accepted, the fairy tale is always reluctant to name its characters (a further departure from legend and myth where proper names abound). Indeed, these are either completely anonymous or distinguished by some nickname derived from a peculiarity or deformity which only seems to enhance their absence of civil status (Puss-in-Boots, Tom Thumb, Cinderella, etc. are nameless precisely because they are nicknamed). It is further notable that nicknames are reserved exclusively for the younger generation (with the exception of Perrault's Bluebeard and Grimms' Faithful John and Beloved Roland, adults never have them), so that the King and the Queen are the first to suffer from anonymity.

Necessarily deprived of a civil status — Utopia abhors biography no less than chronology or typography — characters are simply the King, the Queen, the Prince and the Princess, the Father, the Mother, the Child, the Witch, the Dwarf or the Giant. Class is their main distinction — they are royal or servile with nothing in between. Sometimes however it is their profession, in which case they are Taylors, Peasants or Goldsmiths, Soldiers or Huntsmen, at least to start with. But of course the whole point of the fairy tale is to raise them above their rank. Although all such characters are more or less equally endowed with magic gifts, their human functions are not hard to distinguish: the contrasting principle is readily provided by an ordinary inventory. Thus the King is opposed to the Prince and the Princess, the Father is opposed to his Son and his Daughter, the Stepmother to the Stepchildren, the Mother to the Father — though this last opposition is much less obvious. In this way all the characters without exception can be divided into two contrasting categories, one social — the powerful and the humble — the other according to generation — adolescents and adults (who are generally parents and children and who provide a further subdivision when they are accompanied by the Good and Bad Fairies, the friendly animal and the Ogre). Apart from tutelary powers, unclassifiable insofar as they are ageless and dispense their favours to the eminently underprivileged, age groups and social groups tend to overlap. Thus, in fact, the tale's basic contrasting groups can be reduced to two: the oppressors — who are powerful, adult and wicked — and the oppressed whom the tale favours. Here again its democratic tendencies transpire in spite of its fundamental snobbishness, for although it is always ready to grab a throne for its favourites, aristocracies of age and power are its perennial butts.

The fact that the conflict between generations is regularly associated with social conflict — albeit a latent conflict, half-heartedly suggested in the final reversal of circumstances — tends to focus our attention on the King who, in all fairy tales worthy of the name is at the hierarchical summit where for better or for worse he reigns as total despot. He is, as we noted, 'the King' or 'a King', without further distinction, whose kingdom is the nowhere and once upon a time of utopia. Oddly, this King — whose omnipotence is continually referred to — has only the vaguest and most conventional attributes: unlimited wealth, vast territories, superhuman control over people and things. But he is never seen actually or remotely exercising his functions, never, in fact, shown in the act of reigning. Neither the way in which he orders his affairs, his relation to his subjects, nor even his exploits on the battlefield, play any part in the story. Thus, in spite of all his martial and royal trappings, he is singularly passive, indeed so detached from political commitments and all in all so insignificant that one cannot help wondering where his authority resides.

Judging simply from what we are told about him and his activities, the King has no other Kingdom than his family. Furthermore he exists only as husband and father, and when he happens to be childless his sole aim is to repair this terrible shortcoming. The King either has a wife or else he is a widower. This is the first thing we learn; if he has a wife then he has children from whom all the ensuing complications arise. For either he has too many girls and no boy; or too many boys and no girl; or the boy, according to a prophecy, will

murder him; or, after being childless and disconsolate for
many years, he is finally graced with an heir who pays for his
long-deferred arrival by an endless sequel of misadventures.
But whatever the family situation may be, the King only lives
and acts within the restricted circle of those to whom he is
related. And he is never unmarried. The tale is so explicit on
this point that it would be hard put to further elucidate its
notion of power, or the focus of its basic preoccupations.

Since the King is seen only as father and husband, the Queen
obviously has no other part to play than that of wife and
mother — real mother or stepmother, according to circumstances, and thus either the children's guardian angel or their
persecutor. No less indifferent to public affairs than her husband, her empire does not extend beyond the palace walls
between which she has her home with its responsibilities and
privileges. At her side Prince and Princess are the typical Son
and Daughter, with no other attributes than their minority and
their marriageability (marriage being their only means of
escape in the fairy tale, where boys never enlist in the army nor
girls take Holy Orders). Thanks to the obvious parallel there is
no difficulty in identifying what the fairy tale calls a 'Kingdom', thus conforming moreover to legal and colloquial
expressions ('head of the family', 'Queen of the Household',
potential mothers and fathers, husbands and wives): it is the
'next of kin' restricted to parents and children exclusively, that
is to say the human household seen through the child's magnifying vision and reduced to its elementary components which,
for him, are the only ones that count. Here aunts, uncles,
cousins and even grandparents are practically non-existent
(grandmothers occasionally appear in comical disguises as in
Little Red Riding Hood or Grimms' Devil's grandmother, but
even then their actual relationship is insignificant). Logically
the tale can and must ignore them since it does not deal with
the family as clan but only with the two beings who set the
child puzzling over the enigma of birth on the threshhold of
the conjugal bedroom.

With the extraordinary economy which characterises it, the
fairy tale posits moreover that if the King is Father, then the
father, however humble his circumstances, will be a king in
the end thanks to his rejected son's achievements. Whether the
son is born in a hovel or a palace, royalty is his due. Thus the

poor peasant, the craftsman or the labourer who abandons the offspring he cannot afford to feed, is granted the honours and riches on the day of the princely wedding that the 'happy ending' requires. The one difference between the father whom the tale identifies as 'the Man' and the one designated as 'King', is that the first is only wicked because poverty and weakness have made him so, while the second, being endemically evil, justifies the resentment he inspires. In other words the poor man is 'human' while the King, when he is wicked is more akin to the ogres he sends in pursuit of his unlucky child. The first is always forgiven, whatever his misdeeds, the latter always suffers the most subtle forms of retribution. For according to the age-old grudge of the underling which merges here with that of the Foundling, the powerful of this world are and will always be the Enemy, while the humble are never so utterly bad that they cannot be redeemed.

Thus the utopian cloud surrounding the fairy tale enables us to discover its actual location and to identify its intentionally vague landscapes, characters and events. It wilfully creates the hazy atmosphere it then proceeds to dispel, providing us with a clue here and there, accompanied by its solution. It tells us about Kings while presenting a typical father, about Kingdoms when describing an intimate household, about 'once upon a time' as it recalls the childhood incidents of that timeless age forever tinged with eternity. Whatever its claims it never departs from this small familiar universe. It may be evoking an imaginary replica, but in the end the replica itself turns into an ordinary household.

The fairy tale does not try to bewilder for the sake of entertaining. Its principal aim is to remind us that the most familiar things have an occult, forbidden content.[6] In fact the tale's peculiar skill consists in such shifts of illusion whereby a declared counterfeit serves to demonstrate the truth. Unlike the 'realistic' novel where invention must conform as much as possible to our general conception of plausible reality, it ignores credibility, vaunts its unreality, displays its unlikelihood, stretches, shrinks, distorts and perverts its components with the characteristic high-handedness of imagination's totalitarian rule. It is as though the anonymous writer declared: 'Such things do not happen nowadays. I do not believe in them and neither do you. I only tell them to pass the time, because life is so dreary and there is, alas, no magic wand to transform it'. Yet such an invitation to set sail on the treacherous seas of make-believe is really only an excuse for a more basic realism, a short cut leading to the physical origins of life and the first stirrings of intellectual curiosity. The great imitators of the fairy tale were well aware of this when, in all seriousness and with total irony, they created Utopias, Gargantuas, Desert Islands and Lilliputs: tall stories keep us on our toes.

Notes

1   The German term *Märchen* — from the archaic word which means 'tale' as well as 'folklore' — does not evoke the same sense of the wonderful as our 'fairy tale'. In fact in the German *Märchen* fairies are not gifted with the magic powers common to Celtic tradition; fairies are simply wise 'old wives' or indeed 'midwives' who, as guardians of the rites of birth, watch over the child they have assisted into the world and embody his destiny. Cf. Marthe Robert, Preface to *Contes de Grimm*, Paris 1959, and *Sur le papier*, Paris 1967.

2   E. T. A. Hoffman, *Der Sandmann,* quoted in Norbert Miller, *Der empfindsame Erzähler,* Munich 1968. The German Romantics all wrote *Märchen*, and many of them contributed to the study of folklore by publishing popular tales that were dying out. In 1913 Kafka wrote in his *Journal*: 'I would love to write *Märchen*. . .', but added: 'Why do I hate the term so much?'

3   Although Grimms' tales have some adult heroes — the Taylor, the Soldier or Faithful John the protagonist of one of his most beautiful stories — Perrault has only Bluebeard. Moreover the relation of powers is maintained since if the adult is not wicked and powerful then he is good but reduced to a state of dependence by his inferior circumstances.

4   Since the fairy tale ignores the emphasis which leads mythical and legendary tales to give to all family matters the proportions of natural or historical catastrophes, it is closer to reality and thus more explicit even in its tendentious distortions. That is why the mythological deposits we detect in it are so valuable. They do not, as the brothers Grimm believed, refer to ancient Aryan solar myths, but on the contrary to a precise social and psychic experience of which myths are themselves only a poetic exaggeration.

5   Otto Rank (op. cit.) applying the methods of dream interpretation to myth, sees the providential 'waters' wherein the new-born baby is intended to perish and from which he is invariably saved to fulfil his fate, as his birth. In the fairy tale proper, the water is always a spring or a fountain and never either the sea or a river, which probably proves that the story is less concerned with the biological process of birth than

with its psychological and social implications. Nonetheless the child, in this case, is not abandoned to the 'waters' at birth but 'lost' some time after (at the age of the Oedipus Complex and puberty), in the dark wood. Thus he is never saved from death by a fisherman but by a huntsman or, occasionally (notably in Grimm), by a kindly animal who feeds him, teaches him the magic spell and is always at his beck and call. The maternal aspect of such a providential beast is further stressed when it entrusts its own young to the hero in order that they too may assist him.

6   The Germans say *Unheimlich* to describe this *Märchen* atmosphere. We call it 'disturbingly strange' because we have no equivalent term based on word play. *Das Heim* is the home; *Das Heimliche* is the familiar as well as the intimate. The *Märchen* is the unrivalled master of the *Unheimlich* in that it stresses the occult, strange and ambiguous nature of what is familiar when seen by the specifically ambivalent 'Oedipal' child. Cf. Freud: *Das Unheimliche*.

II Nameless Land and Lost Paradise

Man was King before the Fall
Franz von Baader

Nothing has yet succeeded in healing
my heart, which is always homesick.
Gérard de Nerval

Tales of fancy or of wonder, curious, extraordinary, grue-
some and cruel tales — Romanticism is not short of names that
stress its relation to those children's stories which it sees as the
infancy of art, the golden, pre-literary age from which all
literature should draw its inspiration. For the true Romantic is
primarily a story-teller, and as such he aspires to imitate rather
than create, since he is convinced that the past illuminates the
present and that only by returning to the source can he attain
the truth. With his natural and theoretical taste for archaeo-
logy, his yearning for the lost paradise of individual dreams
and collective mythology, he tends automatically to see universal folk literature as the epitome of innocence and poetry.
The fairy tale represents for him more than a charming relic of
a past we have every reason to regret (which it evidently still
was for Perrault). It is the basic genre, a perfect model and the
repository of a hidden wisdom whose reflected light the writer
can only hope to perceive by rebecoming a child. Eminently
inconsistent in all other respects, Romantic thought's only
unity consists in this archaising tendency which characterises
its works over and above diversities of language and ideas.
And for the Foundling whose spokesman it thus becomes
nothing could be more appropriate.

Albert Béguin once wrote: 'Each epoch of human thought
could be defined by the relation it establishes between dream
and active life'.[1] Very true, so long as we remember that,
insofar as literature is concerned, 'dream' and 'active' life

cannot be immediately assimilated with the empirical phenomena so named, since dream like active life is not something which can be incorporated into the text, but simply a way of presenting imaginary data according to a conventional method. Literally there is no true opposition between the two states; neither are they directly opposable psychologically, since the novelist always writes in an intermediary state which is that of day-dream. Nobody writes in his sleep, not even when describing dreams; we all write more or less in a dream, even when the subject is active life. Maupassant is no less a dreamer than Jean-Paul, when writing his 'realistic' tales; and at the moment of writing his unrestrained fantasies E. T. A. Hoffmann is no more a dreamer than the most staid novelist bent on limpid representation. It is the outlook that counts, not the number of dream components incorporated in the text; and in this respect there are certainly two kinds of literature, two creative dispositions and, to use the expression in its most literal sense, two wholly contrasting 'world visions'. But the distinction cannot be reduced to such conventional oppositions, however convenient this may be for the historian. For it depends, more than on any aesthetic or ideological intention, on the two stages of the Family Romance, and on the two methods of coping with reality between which fictional literature is compelled to choose. Thus we are fully entitled to say that the stress on dream fantasies in a novel is crucial for our understanding of an intellectual age, and that, where intellectual creativity is concerned, the Foundling never evicts the Bastard for long without some inner motivation and the public's unconscious complicity.

Whatever the historical sources of Romanticism, seen as a movement, may be,[2] one thing is certain and that is that it is almost exclusively the Foundling's medium wherein he indulges the characteristic inconsistencies of his extremism and the relentless pursuit of his ends. As always, he rewrites his life in paradise because he finds life on earth unendurable; as always, he compensates for his humble condition by constructing an ideal kingdom out of nothing; and as always, he believes what he wants to believe and, thanks to his all-powerful imagination, proves the world's inadequacy. In a certain sense he goes even further than the proud little ghost who manipulates him, for he now sets up as a doctrine his contempt for reality, and rather than make a virtue of necessity, he finds honourable motives for his endemic faith in the super-natural power of thought.

It has frequently been observed that while we tend to consider Romanticism as a profoundly coherent movement, its various authors — not to say the various works of a single author — present such inconsistent and varied features that it is hard to define it in a single formula. Its diversity of opinions and beliefs, its miscellaneous and even incompatible aesthetic, philosophical and political attitudes are familiar to every expert on the subject. Yet despite obvious contradictions, those who contribute in one way or another to the Romantic manifesto have in common an unshakeable faith in the power of thought as such (the *Allmacht des Gedanken* which Freud sees as the essence of magic itself). 'Thoughts become laws' said Novalis, 'desires become realisations'. He extolled 'the ability to talk about imaginary things as if they were real things', and described the *magic idealism* by means of which man can 'become God'. Ludwig Tieck has the hero of one of his early novels, William Lowell, say: 'Everything is subjected to my discretion; I can give the name I choose to any phenomenon and any action. My whole life is a dream whose characters appear at my will. I am the sole law of nature and everything obeys this law.' And elsewhere: 'All that surrounds us is only real up to a certain point.' While Nodier asserts: 'Nothing is true but the counterfeit,' agreeing thus with Karl Philipp Moritz who posits the same notion in more scientific terms as '*absolute subjectivism*'. Indeed the Romantic credo is wholly contained in this singular assumption that subjective thought is real as such, that incommensurable subjectivity, precisely because it is objectively unverifiable and uncontrollable, can restore man's long-lost awareness of his own divinity.

Belief in the power of thought obviously involves the forfeiture of empirical reality which, to the poet who has glimpsed the inner glory, seems in comparison uneventful, dull and incapable of satisfying his unquenchable thirst for love and the absolute. Reality is either an illusion (*Dream is a world, the world is a dream*), or else a pure convention accepted for the convenience of human relations. 'Man will, on no account, be content with our universe,' said E. T. A. Hoffmann, speaking for all those who, like himself, prefer any nightmare whatsoever to everyday triteness. And Novalis, underlining the dualism which accounts for so much of the 'century's unease': 'The inner world is somehow more my own than the outside world. It is so *warm*, so *familiar*, so *intimate*. What a pity it is so vague and dream-like. Does what is truest and best have to seem so unreal?'.[3] At least Novalis gives some thought to the paradox which makes truth seem vague. Others do not even notice it. They turn a blind eye to what offends them and take refuge in a dream world; after which they proclaim man's ultimate reconciliation with his soul, with the Totality of Nature and of History, and with God. Or again, if the wound is too deep, they reject the world as radically as possible by opting for death or madness. Some, however, gradually come to realise that the dream obstinately continues to remain a dream, that the great spiritual revolutions their generation had prophesied have not been achieved other than on paper, and that reality has lost none of its concreteness (thus Ludwig Tieck, one of the movement's true pioneers, eventually lost faith in his Romanticism). These came to accept life while simultaneously betraying their ideal. And life seems to have rewarded them, for unlike the untractable Foundling, but similar in this to the legendary hero who generally dies at the climax of his triumph and revolt, they were granted the Romantic prerogative of an untimely death.

A proclivity to dream, an aversion for reality, and the idealisation of thought naturally converge towards a mystique of childhood, that pre-eminently magical age which ignores the distinctions of logic so that existence maintains its primal unity. All Romantics share the cult of childhood — not as a precise fragment of personal biography, but as a time before the Fall when beings, objects and animals still enjoyed a heavenly state of indistinctiveness. To be a child or to re-become a child is to dispense with the irreversible divisions erected by rational thought, to recapture the innocence, harmony and true understanding which fragmented knowledge subsequently preclude.[4] But a return to childhood is more than the end of exile. It is a terrible indictment of the adult's circumstances in a soulless world, torn by the incongruity of action and thought (Baudelaire's world where 'action is no longer the sister of dream'). 'I remained a child because I would not deign to become a man,' says Nodier, voicing the feelings of all those who translate their fear of growing up into an unambiguous condemnation of manhood. Indeed, such contempt for manhood inspires books and theories even when it is not proclaimed with so much ostentation (though this will continue to be done, notably by those Surrealists who are directly indebted to Romanticism). It may even be totally unobtrusive as in the ecstatic descriptions of a poet's rediscovery of his distant past. Thus Jean-Paul (Johann Paul Richter who, incidentally, makes a pseudonym of his Christian name as though to invite the public to address him as did his parents in the days of their long lost tenderness), recalls with emotion 'that childhood when I knew not individuals, not even myself, but loved them all; when I had not yet been excluded from the paradise we must forego and to which all possibility of return is prohibited by age, by the keen-edged sword of experience'. There can be no better description of the euphoric narcissism on which the Foundling thrives until 'the keen-edged sword of experience' forces him to discriminate between himself and others, between self-love and the love of humanity which flows spontaneously in paradise. Jean-Paul, who also wrote 'Nothing ever moved me more than Jean-Paul Esquire,' has moreover, a greater awareness than most people of the basic exultant egoism from which stems the bliss of those early years.

To all the Romantics, whatever their differences, the return to childhood represents a re-integration of the self which is the only way of countering the effects of exile. Maurice Guérin writes: 'Like a child on a journey my soul smiles unceasingly at the beautiful landscapes it perceives in itself and will never see elsewhere.' As soon as the poet is back within himself — back home — he participates in the whole cosmos where he discovers its wordless language and the secret of its origins: 'I dwell within the hidden particles of things, I retrace the starlight and the river's course to their mysterious source.' 'Nature admits me to the remotest of its sacred dwelling places, to the starting point of universal life.' Thus he who retraces his steps out of 'disdain' for mankind is amply compensated for what he forfeits in declining adult responsibilities: Mother Nature opens wide her double-bolted doors, welcomes him to 'the remotest of her dwelling places' and frees him from the burden of consciousness by imparting an unmediated vision of her sources which no intellectual wisdom can perceive.

Such blissful repose in the lap of Mother Nature, where the hero is initiated into the mystery of generation, obviously abolishes those distinctions which are indispensable to the workings of the adult mind. The Romantic's Eden is thus as ignorant of sexuality as the Foundling's and the Theologian's. And the mystery of universal generation is revealed precisely where sexual distinctions are abolished. 'At the start man is a sexless creature', Franz von Baader asserts, and he adds — in total agreement with the earliest version of the Family Romance — 'Man was King before the Fall'. Once again kingship is a natural consequence of sexual innocence (or more precisely of sexual amnesia, since the adult can never really believe he is sexless, however hard he tries); and the poet who becomes a child re-acquires the *sinless* omnipotence which enables him to pursue covertly his quest for infinity.

The major themes of Romanticism — magic, idealism, vindications of dream and childhood, return to nature and to a primal cosmic unity, myths of man's original androgynous state — all concur to fulfill the tremendous desire for omnipotence which consumes the Foundling even — or perhaps especially — when he appears most humble. For it is a fact that the Romantics often seem to oscillate between the belief that 'the self is everything' and the no less profound certainty that 'the self is nothing' — though actually the two faiths are not mutually exclusive: 'nothing' here does not refute 'everything' since it refers to a merging into the 'ebb and flow of universal life' which imparts to a being the most exalted form of power he can ever hope to attain. 'Nothing' converges on 'everything'; there is no distinction in this respect. The only point at which authors differ is that some think their dreams have already come true (everything is subjected to my fancy), while others believe they will come true, and try to find the means of achieving this end. According to Novalis, 'The one and only formula of the universe must be discovered which will confer unlimited power on mankind.' And Baudelaire: 'Nature, exiled in imperfection and striving to possess immediately, on this earth, a revealed paradise' is bent on finding a means of making us 'masters of the world' or of enabling us to 'lose ourselves in cosmic immensity'; which, in fact, is the same

thing in this perspective of conquest. Indeed, the Romantic
can only choose between being God or trying to become God
by exploiting the appropriate method which can be discovered
in the depths of his own being (but which can also be imparted
through initiation). However, one way or the other reality has
to be subjected to his will, even if it entails, when life refuses to
be overpowered, staking his all on the void.

Thus romantic desire is always torn between Promethean
ambition and a mystical communion with the 'World Soul' —
which is only another aspect of megalomania. But whether it
incites a Titanic defiance or a merging of the self with universal
being, it is never conducive to a man-to-man confrontation
and never aspires to personal possessions or a specific social
rank. It can be diabolic or angelic depending on the psychic
accidents that determine it, but it is always above human
preoccupations and thus protected from strife. Thus the hero
is more given to speculation than to action; he expects salvation from a possessive contemplation which will lay the world
at his feet. But he is the opposite of a man of action; he has the
dangerous privilege of being able to influence men's souls, and
to this end he exploits more or less scientifically acknowledged
supernatural methods such as hypnotism, magnetism and
telepathy, which have come to take the place of magic. Angel
or beast, chosen or lost, and sometimes both together, but
always doomed to excess, he wanders in infinite space deprived alike of friends and enemies.

A tremendous show of power in a formidable contest which
is always the Great Gamble;[5] a proud, ostentatious aloofness
which makes him oblivious to identities and causes him to
shun all personal commitments and responsibilities; an unaccountable urge to transgress conventions — an urge which is
never satisfied since it is intricately bound up with the roots of
Being — all of these are what make a Melmoth or a Titan, but
also the seeker of 'Innocence'. They are the Heaven and the
Hell between which the Romantic shares his loyalties. For
vision replaces sight, possession is a substitute for communication, and description obliterates objects and turns people into
immaterial phantoms. Nothing could be more radically opposed to the art of the psychically maturer Bastard (though not
for that more true or better able to produce masterpieces — the
opposition is not hierarchical) who, compelled by the aims he

pursues to observe and to contrive, has at least one foot firmly set in reality.

The unity of Romanticism does not derive from its inner cohesion but from this contrast between two ways of confronting reality which gives rise automatically to two styles. This is what Albert Béguin instinctively realised when he compared a dream of Jean-Paul's to an identical scene in *Connaissance de l'Est* reported by Claudel as something which actually happened. Such a comparison is invaluable as an example of the two solutions the Family Romance can provide for the novelist.

Jean-Paul's hero Albano is pleasantly swaying in the topmost branches of a tall apple-tree:

In his imagination the tree was gigantic, the tree of eternal life; its roots sank deep into the void, pink and white clouds suspended from its branches were flowers, the moon was its fruit, the little stars twinkled as dew-drops. Albano rested on its limitless crest, a stormy wind swayed the crest from day to night and from night to day.

Claudel too sees himself perched in an apple-tree, but a real apple-tree from whence he possesses the world by means of strict observation, through his calculating, penetrating gaze:

And I see myself in the highest fork of the old tree, in the wind, a child swaying among apples. From there, like a god on his stem, spectator of the world theatre, in deep contemplation, I study the earth's accidents and its structure, the disposition of slopes and planes; my eye steady as a crow's, I contemplate the countryside stretched out under my perch, my gaze follows the road which twice emerges on the crest of hills to vanish finally in the forest. Nothing escapes me, neither the direction of smoke, the quality of shade and light, the activity of field labourers, the cart travelling along the road, nor the hunter's shots. No need for a diary where only the past can be read; I see the present before me. The moon rises and from time to time an apple drops from the tree like a thought, heavy and ripe.

Two children swaying among apples, but what a difference between their aspirations! In one case the observer is so totally at one with what he sees that he does not notice a single individual object; only the universe, eternity, the boundless summit, the abolition of a time gap between night and day; the apple-tree itself is no ordinary tree; it is the cosmos in miniature, a memory of Eden. In the other case the child stares, all eyes, as if he were a god — obviously he has climbed so high for that purpose. He is the heedful god who carefully notes every detail of his own creation, who lets no fraction of the busy world escape him and registers even the gun-shots, symbols of its ruthlessness. On the one hand the cosmos and a hazy vision of a world reverting to indeterminacy. On the other the cosmos too, but inventoried with concern (in both senses of the term) as diverse objects to be included in a deed of possession. Jean-Paul's hero and Claudel's may both dream of power on the crest of the same tree, but they are nonetheless in two incompatible 'elsewheres', the one evoked by a nostalgia for myth, the other by a lust for the present. Moreover there is little chance of such heroes meeting in a book, unless the author happens to be one of those Bastards whose earlier compulsions have not been completely resolved; in which case it will not be to understand or reinforce each other but to wage an inextricable battle.

Such indeed is the lesson we can glean from a third account of an ascent reported by Kafka in a novel whose theme is precisely the conflict between Bastard and Foundling in the remotest reaches of the hero's psyche. Once again the ascent is successful but, instead of achieving Albano's ecstasy or Claudel's supreme control, it gives rise to a false hope, a delusion exposed too late and all the more dangerous since the hero sees it as a triumph when it is actually the cause of his undoing. K. the Land Surveyor is walking down a lane he mistakenly thinks will lead him to the Castle. He advances with difficulty in the deep snow beside Barnabas and Messenger who supports and finally almost carries him, when he suddenly recalls a childhood memory. Weary and humiliated by his weakness, he remembers how, as a schoolboy, he once accomplished the feat of pulling himself up on to the top of the cemetery wall. Till that day he had always failed in his attempts:

. . . one afternoon however — the silent, deserted square was bathed in sunlight, K. never saw it like that before or after — he had finally succeeded in climbing on to the wall with incredible ease at a spot from which he had frequently fallen back; this time he managed to get up straightaway, holding a little flag between his teeth. . . . He had planted his flag, the wind had unfurled it, he had looked down at the crosses stuck in the soil; nobody was at that moment as great as he . . . .

No apple-tree here, but a smooth, bare wall; not a tree, symbol of eternal life, but an insurmountable obstacle guarding the realm of the dead in the middle of an abandoned square; emptiness, silence, blinding light, representing, as always in Kafka, the absolute. By planting the conqueror's flag on the top of the wall the child triumphs over death, not life. That is why he sees only a few scattered objects in a dismal, bare landscape. The wall had taunted him, while in the two previous instances the tree had offered no resistence at all. Further, this conquest of the absolute is punished forthwith, for the schoolmaster supervenes and the child, caught in the act, hurriedly jumps down and hurts his knee in the process. Effort, struggle, fall and Oedipal retribution (appropriately inflicted indirectly by a substitute father-figure). Eden's bliss is lost once and for all. We witness the expulsion from Paradise and, in the ever-recurrent tragedy, not even Claudel's 'deep contemplation' will lighten the darkness. K. the Land Surveyor whose task it is to 'study the earth's accidents and its structure, the disposition of slopes and planes' (this is literally his vocation and his art) is too much of a Foundling at heart to resist the allurements of phantoms: instead of focussing on the difficult road he is travelling, he lets himself be waylaid by the absolute he once thought to possess. Thus he flounders deeper in the snow and will never reach his goal. Obsessed with the messianic narcissism of an earlier stage of development, torn between conflicting desires for the eternal Castle and for the respect of the mortal Village, so disheartening and moving in its actuality, he vainly tries to reconcile the two equally imperative requirements of his divided heart. In the end the Castle obstinately refuses to reveal itself to him but neither will he be able to exercise the legitimate, humble art of patiently measuring out reality. And ultimately, the eternity for which he foregoes his vocation to be a workman, is reduced to perpetual turmoil in a half-way region between life and death.

The Romantic hero who delves into the depths of his being not to know himself, but to discover a means of becoming all-powerful or else to lose himself in the Cosmos, is obviously immune to such humiliating failures. For he is not concerned with the trials and tribulations of existence; he commits crimes not errors, and if he fails Fate will requite him according to his rank: he will fall as angels fall, as an instrument of evil for whom Hell itself will be set in motion. Indeed the self-criticism at which Kafka's Land Surveyor excels is completely foreign to him: he takes sides against the world without trying to justify his inner motives for such an attitude. Just as the Foundling of the Family Romance rejects his parents ostensibly because they are not worthy of their function but actually because he longs to break away from them, so the Romantic hero accuses the world of common experience of the narrowness, indifference and inconsistency inherent in his own lack of maturity. Projecting on to the outside world the intra-psychic processes by which he is unconsciously motivated — an unconsciousness which, in fact, contributes to his clear conscience and his bad faith — he too defends himself by attacking society or the fate which allowed him to be born; he too belittles what he longs to possess and tries to regain his self-respect and prove his innocence in a relentless indictment which, needless to say, will be without rejoinder or appeal.[6] Parents are to blame; the world is to blame; because of them 'real life has vanished'; thus they are inexcusable. On the other hand, however, this has not always been the case. Once upon a time parents were good and strong, the world was a wonderland of harmony, real life was ever-present so that one could believe in eternity. Whence Romanticism's incessant oscillation between a metaphysical anarchy and orthodoxy, between individualistic rebellion and the need to conciliate — which was responsible for some of its most beautiful *Märchen*.

We said earlier that the Romantic is a teller of stories rather than a novelist. Now we can see why this is so and in virtue of what profound affinities. Indeed, for those who want to describe the 'mal du siècle' — or rather to evade it without feeling too guilty or running the risk of going mad — there could be no better instrument than the *Märchen*, for it is admirably precise and perfectly suited for the ventures — both subversive and anachronistic — of a rebellious literature. Every Romantic was instinctively aware of this. Whatever his nationality, he sensed his affinities with a genre that tolerated the most flagrant inconsistencies. Thus it became a weapon for the Romantics in the losing battle they waged against necessity in the name of the imagination. Thanks to them the fairy tale was welcomed into literature, ushered in by speculative lyricism. Fairies, witches and dragons were re-enlisted more or less undisguised. Sometimes they were called by other names and their magic paraphernalia brought up to date in an attempt to make them more credible. At others they preserved all their former terrifying or fascinating attributes. But whatever their appearance they always played the same role in the Foundling's tendentious apologia wherein he is the eternal victim of things as they are and the disciple of his own kingship.

Doubtless the Romantic tale can never totally conceal the rationality and worldliness which distinguish it from its archaic model. However it does so to the extent of maintaining the essential features of the fairy tale behind a necessarily modernised facade. Thus birth is still presented as an ineluctible concatenation of events in which individuals are either hopelessly trapped or break away at their own peril. Origins are no less of an obsession, symbolised here by a new-born paradise or an improbable genesis (since Romanticism cannot see the world as created it naturally indulges in notions of *original* languages, peoples and sin, and in a quest for beginnings in general). Furthermore we encounter the familiar idea of initiation, occasionally grafted on to the findings of recent studies in universal folklore (this is notable in the works of Tieck and Arnim, where ancient Israel and ancient Egypt are exploited, while others delve into the *Arabian Nights* and the Far East), without departing, however, from the traditional pattern: trials, metamorphoses, perilous quests for 'innocence', sylvan backdrops — even when the consecrated fairy-tale territory is replaced by the labyrinth teeming with grotesque and ominous creatures of Hoffmann's nightmare Berlin — and the inevitable dark midnight — the tale being the perennial nightmare where children and dreamers nurse their common melancholy — as well as the stratagem of the two families (one real, the other imaginary) to which, here too, the adolescent must resort in order to escape at least from the fetters of circumstance. In this respect nothing has changed since the Family Romance rejection, except that here the hero seeks a purely spiritual supremacy which will enable him to deny, besides his civil status, the very fact that he was born, all kinships and everything connected with the creaturely condition in which man is trapped. The reduplication whereby the Foundling was able to get the better of his fate by creating for himself an ideal replica of his own family, now threatens the creator in no uncertain way. For at an age when 'action has ceased to be the sister of dream', when the happy inconsistency of ignorance has become a deceitful 'as if ', to deny birth is to cripple life irredeemably. The renegade can no longer step 'through the looking-glass' unscathed, but only by splitting himself in two in such a way that neither power nor love can ever make him whole again. Torn between the here and now of the earthly family he rejects and the fiction of an impossibly ideal consanguinity, the *double* of Romantic fiction exactly reproduces the psychic dilemma which constantly threatens the child of no parents. And in this respect he is an invaluable witness. Yet he simultaneously refutes the theory by clearly demonstrating that an excess of magic idealism changes the most wonderful dream of unity into a nightmare and reduces dreams of power to the impotence of a split personality.

For the Romantic double, evolution and history do not exist. Everything always starts anew in endless repetition. Figures reduplicate themselves everywhere — not beings of flesh and blood but phantoms whose startling advent either enchants or terrifies. The eternal recurrence of identical phenomena and identical events does more than abolish time: it kills individuals leaving only their images, and dissolves objects into a mirage, vainly and irresistibly pursued till every form of conquest becomes nauseating. In such a universe, constantly perturbed by apparitions and metamorphoses, neither friend, enemy nor goal is irreplaceable to the reduplicated hero. There is not even a woman for him to love since he is incapable of distinguishing identities and only knows the Eternal Woman, always changing yet unique in her various disguises, who is embodied in every possible love-partner while none can equal her in perfection and innocence. In his quest for Eternal Womanhood rather than for any particular woman, for a mystic communion with an insubstantial vision, rather than a union contracted on earth, and for Love rather than for a beloved, the Romantic hero abandons once and for all the ways of traditional fairy tale adolescents who, realistic in spite of their unbridled imagination, overcame monsters and magic spells to obtain their 'true love'.

Because of the Eternal Femininity that makes all women desirable and deprives them all of distinctive individualities, the new *Märchen* turns out to be the exact opposite of the old.

For the Good Fairy, instead of being love's guardian angel, the tutelary, maternal divinity who watches over the youthful protaganists' mutual love, is now the object of the love-quest, the goal pursued through thick and thin, and all the more fascinating in that she is for ever unattainable. For the Romantic Good Fairy may still be a mother figure whom the tale continues to idealise, but her role has somehow been perverted; she obstructs rather than assists erotic fulfilment. Indeed she is the immediate cause of its failure, since compared to her all women seem worthless — and forbidden fruit into the bargain. There is only one woman — 'the thirteenth returns, she is still the first' — but there is no legitimate partner, all are equally forbidden. Thus Gérard de Nerval's visionary apparition can say in all truthfulness: 'I am one with Maria, one with your mother, I am besides the one you have always loved in all her disguises. At each of your trials I abandoned one of the masks that hid my features and you will soon see me as I really am.' She is indeed one, as every Romantic knows or dimly suspects when he confesses his need for absolute love and his inability to love.

Thus what is at stake in the magic trial is no longer a woman of flesh and blood who must be won from a powerful rival, but the eternal mother who reigns sublime and who only shows herself in some misleading disguise until the moment of death when she discards her last mask. The all-powerful feminine principle which finally reveals itself in a deadly union ('soon you will see me as I really am') involves no enemy to subdue, no material wealth worth coveting, no other exploit in fact than to perceive 'the saint's sighs and the fairy's tears' in the nameless land of melancholy. Bewitched and dreading more than all else to break the spell, the hero is condemned to wander in the labyrinth of his visions where he passes from adoration to blasphemy, from ecstasy to despair and from ardour to despondency. Because of the eternal absentee, haunting and ever evasive, he is indeed 'the sinister, the widowed, the unconsolable', the orphan hopelessly infatuated with a corpse (Novalis' mystical love for his little fiancée who died at fifteen is an example of this passionate cult) and incapable of falling in love because he worships an immaterial image (the *Statue of the Mother*, as a story by Brentano explicitly calls it). Woe betide this nocturnal hero if he becomes involved with one of the deceptive impersonations the deified mother assumes to seduce him. For then he will see the saint turn into a simpering demon, the fairy into a vulgar courtesan and the paradise of love will become a hell of eroticism where all his hopes of salvation are derided. Redeemed by love, lost through women, the Romantic Foundling is a foredoomed failure. Such is the grievance he voices in his writings, with the elegance and persuasiveness he has acquired on 'the other side'.

On the side of the Eternal Eve, related to primal chaos, Death and Night, everything is for ever out of reach, for if the one Woman precludes all women and exempts the hero from the responsibilities of marriage (this is what mainly distinguishes her cult, as Don Quixote realised when he decided to venerate his imaginary Dulcinea to avoid meeting a real one), she eliminates men no less efficiently, real men who possess women and thus acquire a social status. In the perpetually new-born world where nature spontaneously engenders harmony and where the Mother spontaneously gives birth, the Oedipal Father — the self-appointed custodian of women, the strict disciplinarian — obviously has no place at all. The inevitable consequence is that the father is as insubstantial as the beloved. He too is only a ghost, a magician emerging from darkest night to vanish at dawn after accomplishing transformations and wonders (like Hoffmann's fathers, grotesque, distorted beings no less comic than menacing, whose nocturnal pranks pursue the young lovers without otherwise affecting the plot). Neither husband, lover nor rival, he is summoned or exorcised but never openly confronted. He is the Enemy rather than the visible adversary who must be taken into account. He probably dwells in the regions where love's evil spells are contrived, and can thus be safely ignored by the hero bent on discovering Paradise. Marginal to the plot, to history, to the struggle for survival and the human couple's antagonism, this father, magically obliterated from childish dreams, can neither stimulate action, serve as a model in the business of living nor be overthrown on account of his tyranny. Since the dream-Queen has abandoned him he has lost the power to give shape and meaning to anything, and is relegated to a primitive anarchic stage where both love and rebellion ignore him.

The father's absence at the top of the social scale leaves

Romantic fiction stranded half way between the novel and poetry in an indeterminate literary sphere where art consists in by-passing the Oedipal situation rather than confronting it as an actual tragedy. (In Kafka's *The Castle* the 'Gentlemen' fill this role. K.'s rival 'Gentleman', aptly called the 'Commander of Women', represents the male principle from which the mysterious power controlling the community derives and ensures the coherence of a strictly hierarchical organisation.) Even when the length of the story might justify its claim to be a novel without overtaxing the reader's credulity, it is nonetheless affiliated to the fairy tale by its use of magic devices which enable it to avoid the basic psychic problem and the social conflict upon which Oedipal revolt thrives. The wandering hero of Romanticism may be in a state of grace or he may be a sinner; he may model his behaviour on Prometheus or on the mystic in pursuit of the Holy Grail; but he will never seize that which paternal authority claims as its due, nor does he ever attempt to supplant a superior or an equal (he disdains possessions and has no equals). He is mainly intent on wandering, not on founding cities, fighting battles or establishing laws. He never considers settling down nor would he ever utter the words of Rastignac when he sees Paris stretched out before him: 'To the two of us!' Born fatherless by a mother who belongs to no one and represents the essence of creativity, he does not aspire to particulars since everything belongs to him. He thrives on passion, ignores contingencies, dreams of total communion or total annihilation and breathes the peculiar air of his epoch. In his predilection for desert islands he is a Robinson Crusoe, except that he would starve to death because he could never fashion or manipulate a tool. Like Don Quixote he is always ready to fight chimeras and monsters, but his actions lack the ambiguity Cervantes' hero derives from his creator's pitiless rebuttal. He sets out on spiritual adventures, in pursuit of mystical or haunted castles but, unlike the Land Surveyor, he hopes to find eternal bliss within their walls because he is oblivious to the rule of the 'Gentlemen' and the degrading servitude of the human Village which ensues. As a visionary of the invisible, blind to facts, his obstinate defiance does indeed procure him a kind of eternity and the indisputable grace of childishness. The great end-of-the-century realistic novel will require characters of a different metal. Thus its inspiration cannot be said to derive from the Romantics — unless it be from those rare specimens who began to question the validity of denying reality.

Notes

1   Albert Béguin, *l'Ame romantique et le rêve*, Paris 1939.

2   Historical Romanticism is obviously only one aspect of 'eternal' romanticism that incessantly re-emerges more or less overtly in isolated works. Even in the hey-day of Romanticism this aspect co-existed with the militant movement without really being part of it. Neither Kleist nor Hölderlin were Romantics in the strict sense of the word, and there will always be Romantics who will remain isolated or be classified in different categories.

3   My italics. It is impossible to overlook the three almost synonymous adjectives so obviously stressing the parallel between inner life and the home.

4   This is one of Kleist's departures from Romantic attitudes. In his remarkable essay on *Puppet Theatre* he tackles the problem of spontaneity, so prominent in his day, but providing it with a dialectic solution which totally modifies its significance; perfect grace is the prerogative of the most primitive and least self-conscious organisms (puppets or animals), yet it is not inconceivable that man might re-acquire it at the end of a long digression through every sphere of knowledge (Kleist expressed this idea elsewhere: he takes us on a journey round the world to discover whether Paradise does not have a back door). Grace is the result of total unconsciousness or infinite knowledge, though the latter is in fact '*the final chapter of the world's History*'.

5   *Le Grand Jeu*, a periodical founded between the wars (1928) by René Daumal, Roger Vailland and Roger Gilbert-Lecomte on the fringe of Surrealism, was really the organ of that gamble against the world for a permanent transgression of the boundaries of Existence. Roger Gilbert-Lecomte's whole work was directed against 'the scandal of being born' and, with the unerring instinct proper to the Foundling (or the 'Lostling' which for the Romantics is the same thing), he called the posthumous book which was to have been his Summa *The Return to Everything*.

6   Goethe's well known aversion to Romanticism, which played a fatal part in the lives of poets such as Lenz and Kleist, might to a certain extent be accounted for by this feeling of bad faith, doubtless enhanced by the fact that Goethe himself was not entirely free from some strikingly Romantic characteristics. It would seem, moreover, that the most uncompromising critic in such cases is the Romantic who has succeeded in overcoming his tendencies or at least in satirising his addiction (Flaubert in *Madame Bovary*).

III   Crusoism and Quixotery

> The world only exists insofar
> as it appeals to us.
>
> Daniel Defoe

For the novel to leave the fairyland to which it had long been confined the Foundling had to acknowledge the Oedipal Bastard's more realistic requirements, that is learn to see the world as it is and to take an *interest* in what is going on. The birth of the novel coincides with that moment of suspense and conflict when, without entirely giving up his visions of paradise, he can no longer ignore his newly acquired experience nor by-pass necessity. Maturer if not cured, and forced to question the contrivances of his own magic, he still yearns for the wonderful adventures that only happen on 'the other side'. But when he lands on the desert island of his dreams it is only to undergo hardships, to become acquainted with toil and deprivation, indeed to be confronted with all that which had made him flee from reality. And although he is still, perhaps more than ever, the incorrigible wanderer dominated by the creations of his unbridled imagination, he is no longer surrounded by things that correspond to his desires but by a real world and a society which derides him and ultimately manages to make him admit his folly. He is Robinson Crusoe or Don Quixote depending on which of the two ways open to modernity he chooses, but he is usually a combination of the two, at times more lucid, at others bewildered, a Quixotic Robinson or a Don Quixote stranded for ever on the hopeless island where he has elected to cut himself off from the rest of the world. But one way or the other the novel can no longer exist apart from the heart-break he experiences — or at any rate it will no longer purport to be true unless it relates the hero's personal endeavour to cope with existence.

★

Of the two major works Western literary fiction rightly sees both as its source and its model, the more recent happens to have the more straightforward relation to the original pattern. And this is not really surprising since there is no reason why the genre's personal history should coincide with historical dates — though it frequently corroborates them. From the specific view-point of the Family Romance Cervantes' *Don Quixote* comes after *Robinson Crusoe* because its intentions are more carefully disguised — more care and thus more ambiguity and skill, if by skill we imply the ability to encapsulate the basic rejection in a totally new situation and thus make its identification impossible. Compared to this intentionally obscure work so cautiously veiled that centuries of scholarship have not succeeded in revealing its implications satisfactorily, Daniel Defoe's book is disarmingly transparent. From the first words it tells us what Cervantes took every precaution to hide, and so frankly that there is little point in seeking ulterior motives. Thus its place is among traditional children's books — not to say among fairy tales in spite of its newfangled realism.

Daniel Defoe, as everybody knows, presented *Robinson Crusoe* as a true story and not a novel — a genre he despised for its insipidity and the sickly sentimentality of its addicts. By 'true' he doubtless implied that the plot was plausible — indeed it was based on the adventures of someone who, according to a recently published account, had really survived a shipwreck and lived for many years on a desert island off the American coast. However he was probably not aware of the fact that his hero's odyssey involved a different kind of truth and one much nearer the bone. Daniel Foe (who added the particle to his name to give himself an air of nobility — a common practice among novelists — and was always dreaming of titles, riches and status) ought really to have recognised in Robinson Crusoe the happy and unhappy representative of his own ambitions, the insatiable upstart so avid for power that he can only find a situation worthy of his aspirations on the extreme periphery of the inhabited world. And indeed he probably did have some inkling of his affinities with his imaginary hero. That might account for the fact that Robinson Crusoe is for ever being lost and saved and that, after undergoing the many trials required in retribution for pride and betrayal, he finally achieves his ends.

Indeed the main theme of *The Life and Adventures of Robinson Crusoe* is the rejection of his family by an eighteen-year-old youth and his refusal to follow the profession of their choice — ostensibly because of his thirst for adventure, but actually in the hope of making a fortune and raising himself in no time above the humble circumstances his family would have him accept. With typical middle-class lack of ambition the youth's father is greatly perturbed by his son's wish to succeed by taking risks, a wish he considers impious and rash into the bargain. But neither exhortations, threats nor prayers are of any avail. Robinson will not be deterred from his plan and sails off one fine day against his parents' wish, secretly and with no other baggage than self-confidence and the will to 'arrive'. The shipwreck which puts an end to his first adventure forthwith sets the action on the field of transgression where the novel will consequently take place: the fall is the immediate retribution for the impatience and pride of those who reject their father in order to outdo him and thus commit in intention the major crime of parricide.

Robinson has now lost his innocence. He is well enough aware of the implications of his sin to heed the warnings of an immanent justice that never hesitates to execute the decrees of the Oedipal court. But he cannot turn back, for: 'An irresistible reluctance continued to going home; and as I stayed a while, the remembrance of the distress I had been in wore off, and as that abated, the little motion I had in my desires to return wore off with it, till at last I quite laid aside the thoughts of it. . .'. So he promptly sets out on a new journey of adventure which takes him further than anyone had ever been from the frontiers of humanity. Unlike the fairy-tale youth who only runs away the better to be re-integrated into the family circle, even unlike Ulysses, that paragon of seafarers and no less master of home-comings, Robinson breaks once and for all with those he has rejected. He will never again cross their threshold nor give them a thought. For him they died at the precise instant he left them and he cannot go back until their death which he secretly desired has become a fact. The punishment which later will cut him off from the world of the living is the visible manifestation of such a radical break: having wished to be nobody's son he becomes in fact completely orphaned, completely alone, the innocent self-begetter in a kingdom of complete solitude.

By escaping from his father in order to eradicate him from his life, Robinson gives vent to Oedipal rebellion and proves thereby that his psychic development is appropriate to his age. But in so doing he puts an end to rebellion — for running away is no way to fight, and once he is fatherless and free from all links with the past, he has no more rivals to overcome, no enemies to take up arms against. Thus he regresses to a pre-Oedipal stage where the absence of sexual competition precludes all conflict. His wanderings are motivated by defiance rather than by deep-rooted rebellion, so that his journey round the world is really a journey against time, a great leap backwards to the mysterious moment when life and death were still barely differentiated. His regression is proportionate to his desire to go forward, and this unconsciously sought regression entails a second shipwreck which brings him to the brink of annihilation.

Indeed shipwreck is not only a symbol for the retribution demanded of the rebel who destroys himself in the act of destroying the object of his rebellion. For the childish imagination it is a last resort against the necessity of growing up and epitomises the desire never to have been born and to start afresh in a new and innocent world. Because Robinson wanted to rise more speedily than the nature of things permits, he sinks deep enough to experience all the anguish of death — the waters engulf him, he emerges like a soul from the grave's dark and this time he truly believes it is the end. Yet he is safe and sound. Though he reaches dry land in a truly pitiful state, having lost all he possessed, he is entitled to see himself as a favourite of the gods since he is the only survivor. Thus the shipwreck of retribution is also an instrument of salvation, an overcoming of death, a purification and a rebirth where the dread of being abandoned is happily counterbalanced by the intoxication of a fresh start.

The sea that spares Robinson after threatening him with extinction is obviously the main feature of this irresistible, irreversible odyssey. The young rebel is at its mercy, it is full of potential dangers and hopes of salvation. Ever present, menacing, reassuring and unpredictable it plays the same ambivalent part Robinson might assign to his own mother, who also rejected him by siding with his inflexible father, yet who remains, nevertheless, a source of unstinting love and inexhaustible life. Evil, insofar as it is a place where manly undertakings are carried out — like the mother who submits to her husband's lust — the sea is friendly so soon as it has destroyed all other men. Then it becomes the pure female element wherein Robinson finds both refuge and exile — the prospect of reigning alone, protected from the trials of manhood. This youthful parricide by intent — he blames himself for the crime in his old age, saying that he killed his father as surely as if he had stabbed him — could have no better accomplice — the sea kills those who would contest his rights and surrounds him on all sides so that no one may disturb him in the exercise of his kingship.

A new Adam stranded on a virgin, uninhabited soil (no trace of Eve in this exotic Paradise, nor consequently of the serpent — the island animals are remarkably harmless), Robinson experiences the return to paradise for which he gave up everything. He is reborn at the age of twenty-six — the day of his birthday, in fact, so as to leave no doubt as to the significance of the event — in ideal circumstances that reproduce for his benefit the eminently natural state of original bliss. Naked, shorn of his past and thus washed clean of all his sins (his shipwreck is obviously equivalent to a baptism) he is as near as can be to the perfect Adamic condition, except that in his case Paradise does not represent reunion but total separation from the whole human race. Guilt and solitude begin at precisely the same moment with him, as he himself observes with astonishing insight into the mechanisms of the psyche which led him to the island of despair at the crossroads of transgression and rediscovered innocence. In fact he paradoxically enters Eden after the fall, at the very moment when the Biblical Adam was expelled. That is why at first he is unsure whether he is chosen or damned, miraculously taken to the heart of unsullied nature, or condemned to a hell of silence and oblivion. And he continues to vacillate between these two contradictory interpretations of his fate, favouring the first when danger seems to abate, and the second each time his peace is disturbed. For the desert isle is twofold like the desire which set it on the margin of civilisation: to the last it is an ambiguous paradise, the nameless site where the individual, lost to himself, experiences in turn original bliss and loneliness — or the price one has to pay for being aloof.

From the start Robinson is struck by the paradox of his
shipwreck which ratifies both success and failure. But though
he sees his story as a sad tale of unparalleled solitude, he is
never too dejected to savour its 'unparalleledness', and though
he often feels as helpless and abandoned as a new-born babe ('I
am lost! Lost!') he never fails to boast, even in his isolation, of
the fact that his survival is due to nothing but his own physical
strength and his resourcefulness. At his best moments the
pleasure of his undisputed sway over a kingdom whose very
existence is ignored by the rest of mankind incites him to
reverse the circumstances of his isolation — it is the world that
has vanished without trace ('I looked now upon the world as a
thing remote; which I had nothing to do with, no expectation
from, and indeed no desires about.') Notwithstanding his
plight this last-minute survivor feels fulfilled: there is no
elsewhere worth pining for, the world he has left behind is a
distant wreck, civilisation, society, history with all their
science, laws and relationships have foundered in the depths
from which he was able to extricate himself.

   Needless to say the island is a Paradise insofar as it is nature
unsullied by man and labour, and it is infinitely benevolent to
its first tenant. At first Robinson expects it to be hostile. He is
prepared for the worst since he is entirely unacquainted with
its fauna and flora. But he is soon reassured: none of the
animals on this peaceful island is fierce, they are all docile,
friendly, easily tamed and similar to those of temperate zones.
Thus they provide the main source of Robinson's nourish-
ment while the more evolved become his first servants and
subjects (the two cats, the dog and the parrot who come to him
of their own free will). As to the vegetation, though the plants
are not all edible, none is poisonous and the uncultivated soil is
not so refractory as to prevent Robinson from eventually
being able to extract from it enough to vary the monotony of
his diet (he even manages to grow barley in spite of the
climate, thanks, it is true, to a miracle performed by God for
his sole benefit). After a cautious inspection the island reveals
itself to Robinson as untainted by evil. Its innocence is so
complete that it remains uncontaminated even by the objects
of aggression it secretes (a knife, tools and coins which the
survivor promptly retrieves). Devoid of violence or any trace
of potential antagonism between its elements, the island is

submerged from end to end in blissful anarchy, it is like the starting point of creation and therefore the ideal site for a glorious rebirth.

Obliged to settle here whether he likes it or not, Robinson benefits from this primal peace at the same time as he unwittingly and inevitably disrupts it. For insofar as he is a Foundling who has chosen to be 'lost' rather than conform, he cannot dispense with his Eden; but insofar as he is a Bastard bent on obtaining here and now a substantial share of power and possessions, he cannot be content with passive day-dreaming. He must resist his romantic tendencies, renounce self-inflating insularity and disown the Wanderer of old and new fairy tales; he must in fact take an active part in salvaging his shipwrecked life rather than admit defeat as a sign of personal distinction. In this respect Daniel Defoe is perfectly entitled to call his novel a true story — it is true not, of course, in that its writing corresponds to fact, but because it breaks away from the convention of a purely theoretical *Utopia* where life is miraculously preserved without presenting any material problems. For the first time in fictional literature the land of dreams is a land that has to be reclaimed, reality can no longer be overcome by writing; tools, foresight and all the experience and patience of the craftsman are now indispensable. The novel is a genre that had always been distinguished for its idleness. It described fantastic contests, noble hunting scenes, thwarted love-affairs or the outrageous and amusing tricks of picaresque outlaws; but whether it was bucolic, sentimental or comic, nobody was ever depicted at work. Robinson put an end to such almost compulsory leisure which had contributed for so long to the genre's success in every social sphere (mainly, presumably, in the more aristocratic). With him work, labour and *need* penetrate the very heart of Utopia. We are no longer invited to deny the empirical world to spite it or make up for its barrenness, but indeed to turn it into a vast workshop where our hands as well as our minds are always occupied. In fact we are now invited to dream but, according to a much quoted formula, 'to take our dreams seriously' — to graduate from the utopian's unformulated rebellion to a first revolutionary step.

Predictably, modern criticism has attributed this practical Utopia to the conflicting aspirations which, in Defoe's day, led the English middle classes to lament their isolation while simultaneously glorying in it. Indeed by the end of the seventeenth century a rising social class had already become an unquestioned influence in economic spheres. However, owing to its lack of feudal or patrician traditions it was precluded from political power and strongly resented its social insignificance in a world where rank was entirely dependent on ancestry. On the other hand such a lack of roots provided its major chance of success. For although it had no share in tradition, neither was it hindered by antiquated rules and conventions. Thus its marginality favoured an incredible freedom of action and a new concept of liberty. Without ancestry, land or titles to bolster it in the eyes of a strictly conventional society, the English bourgeoisie of the period, forcibly kept on the fringe of history by an anarchronistic social system, lived, like Robinson Crusoe, in a no-man's-land of intolerable exile. Nevertheless its strength, resourcefulness, unstinting ambition and unquenchable self-confidence were soon instrumental in helping it to realise that its desert island, far from being a punishment of God for its humble origins, was a privileged situation, a Paradise to be exploited to its own advantage. Thus instead of indulging its resentment or forgetting it in fruitless day-dreams, it followed the example of that farseeing pioneer who, adventurous and obstinately inclined to 'reach for the moon' as he was, yet possessed a sufficient dose of realistic audacity to transform his exile into a means of achieving power and founding empires single-handed.

That the Family Romance should have first made its mark in modern literature by producing a middle-class novel — or rather a permanent model for middle class writers of the genre — is hardly surprising since we are well aware that the Romance only emerges from individual day-dreams when the transition from one social class to another is not obstructed by insuperable prohibitions. As a fantasy related to the individual's basic dissatisfaction with his inferior social status, *Robinson Crusoe* might have been imagined under any conceivable cultural circumstances, but it could only have been *written* in a fluctuating society where a man who has neither ancestry nor title has some hope of rising by his own endeavours — even if this requires a violent struggle against the surviving conventions that hinder his ascent. The sociologist's dictum: 'No theocracy = novels, theocracy = no novels' holds good in its positive form: there is no democracy without novels but no novels without democracy (if not in fact at least as widely shared aspiration). Daniel Defoe's genius consisted in realising the extent to which the novel form is essentially related to ideologies of independence and initiative, and especially in expressing it in a subversive fable whose edifying tone allows the bourgeois novel to pursue, unmolested, the aims of the eternal Family Romance. As a product of the transition from one version of the Family Romance to the other, Robinson was indeed a particularly apt representative of a rising social class as well as of the unrealistic rebel for ever in revolt against the fact of being born. Thanks to the truth he openly embodies in his dual aspect, he shows the adventurous bourgeois how to succeed by his wits alone and become an empire builder. But at the same time he gives the middle classes the one art form that is truly theirs, since it was generated by them, according both to their dreams and their practical requirements.

Revolutionary in his intolerance of restrictions, conservative in his yearning for a lost paradise and despotic in his tremendous thirst for power, Robinson invents a paradise where evil — or the necessity to earn his bread by the sweat of his brow which, in Genesis is the sign of divine displeasure — is introduced without in any way detracting from its perfection. For Robinson does more than simply prove that man can live alone — or that the bourgeoisie can create a productive world on its own — he shows that independent man is good, not necessarily by nature but because of the circumstances which constrain him to turn the threats of civilisation into *tools*. In the hands of the hermit baptised in the waters of shipwreck who, even though still weighed down by the guilt of sacrilege and parricide, is a new man, all that was previously evil becomes useful — the knife can no longer kill (except those animals unfortunate enough to be edible), money cannot corrupt, weapons do not inspire wars, for they are all regenerated together with the survivor and will contribute to his survival. The harmful or threatening objects still contained in the world's shipwreck — the ship, which has also run aground — have only to come in contact with the island's bliss to become useful or at least harmless. Since the master of the land is the only person they can serve, there is no danger of their being put to a wrong purpose by ill-intentioned people — the total absence of inhabitants makes sure of that. Unlike what happened in Adam's garden where evil was unknown, evil penetrates this paradise as flotsam from the civilised world and then, rendered invalid by the absence of a society, it is so completely subjugated that it assists well-being (Robinson's well-being, needless to say, since everything is seen in relation to him). In the dreamland of freedom and utility where life recreates its virginity, every evil is turned into a technical instrument of progress.

Thus with enormous patience and hard work and assisted by the fragments of a civilisation he has rejected, Robinson reconstructs a world unsullied by any other human presence, wherein he plays the different roles of society as though he had to re-invent each one anew. Step by step he retraces alone man's millenial achievements, with nothing but a handful of tools, weapons, rags and provisions salvaged from the wreck. True, this handful is plenty and, all things considered, it substantially improves the survivor's circumstances. So much so, in fact, that the misanthropic tendencies he frequently indulges seem more or less groundless. Robinson turns his back on civilisation when he would have more reason than most to be thankful for its blessings (that such hypocrisy passes mainly unnoticed is due to the fact that it is part and parcel of the plot. Defoe naturally fails to comment on it, and his followers likewise. But Jules Verne appears to have spotted it — *l'Ecole des Robinsons*, where everything happens more or less as in the original, except that the desert island has been acquired by an American millionaire for his children's pleasure and instruction, is an obvious indictment). Though the man who stands for the advantages of self-sufficiency sometimes thanks God for allowing him to survive, he does not seem to be particularly moved at the thought of all the intellectual and technical acquisitions from which he benefits. He is never even aware of the discrepancy, and indeed, how could he be when the whole object of his odyssey is to vindicate the merits of total solipsism? So Robinson does not waste much time paying credit to mankind. He makes believe he is starting from scratch and recreates every science, technology and means of mastering nature as if he knew everything without knowing where his knowledge came from (the extraordinary thing is that this hypocritical 'make believe' is precisely what renders his adventures so enthralling). First from necessity, then much later in order to get all he can from the island and colonise it, he re-invents: the calender, thus introducing time into the Foundling's chaotic existence; the art of building; carpentry and metal-work; hunting, breeding, agriculture, navigation, medicine and, of course, theology (this last rather late, when his material survival has become relatively assured). For many years — exactly as many as those he numbered on his arrival, since he only finds Man Friday after twenty-six years — he continues to develop the most varied skills in an endless labour, from which he alone benefits but which, with the passing of time ensures the progress and prosperity of the island itself. Selfish to the last degree and apparently equally productive, Robinson condenses into his admittedly very full life, centuries of struggle against bare necessity. He is man at every stage of his evolution: Adam bowed down, bewildered, beset on all sides by dangers, but succeeding by sheer tenacity in raising himself above inner darkness and environmental danger. He is kin to all those who laboured before him, but though he sums up their prehistory and their history he has the advantage over them of knowing where he is going and especially of working for his own benefit and without having to squander the slightest atom of energy on anybody else. Thus he accomplishes the unprecedented feat of representing the legacy of all humanity while illustrating the virtues of total individualism and the egoist's peculiar aptitude to become a benefactor, precisely insofar as he thinks of no one but himself (in this respect we can understand why Rousseau found he was the right sort of hero for his Emile). The island only begins to exist, to become prosperous and useful, because Robinson does his utmost to keep himself alive. Under such circumstances, therefore, personal interest coincides with the common good, the self-seeking bourgeois is an active agent of progress, and the Foundling can take his dreams seriously since now that he is firmly rooted on the magic island where his wounded narcissism landed him, such narcissism provides the surest means of ensuring his efficacy.

As first and only inhabitant of the island Robinson is well aware of having realised his over-ambitious desire to oppose the dictates of fate and rise above his situation. From the very start while still undergoing the greatest hardships and leading a precarious existence, he is more or less imbued with his sovereignty. He feels like a king among his courtiers when in the company of his dog, his two cats and his parrot: '. . . there was my majesty, the prince and lord of the whole island! I had the lives of all my subjects at absolute command. I could hang, draw, give liberty and take it away, and no rebels among all my subjects!' One might suppose that Robinson was being facetious when congratulating himself on such a paltry sovereignty; on the other hand if he is making the best of his misfortunes such an attitude is consistent with the Family Romance where kingly pretensions arise precisely when they would be least substantiated and when the imagination is our last resort against despair. Robinson clearly demonstrates that he is playing a childish game where power is directly associated with the right to kill, when he suggests hanging and drawing his pets; nothing could give better proof of the psychic level to which he has regressed since his first show of rebellion. However he does not remain at such a puerile stage. He toils for twenty-six years to emerge from it, patiently learning to overcome life's hardships so that his over-ambitious desire may one day be realised. When he will have grown up enough to assume the responsibilities of manhood, he will at last be able to rule over a repopulated kingdom.

The whole first section of the novel is an account of this systematic re-education which will enable its hero gradually to overcome the disastrous consequences of his immaturity (and benefit from its more congenial effects, since such is his peculiar talent). Robinson, who by running away and being shipwrecked has cancelled out his first twenty-six years, is kept as it were in quarantine for the next twenty-six. And during these years of both voluntary and forced retirement, he comes little by little to accept what he had rejected. So long as he 'reaches for the moon' he cannot break the solitude to which he is reduced by a largely anachronistic inner experience. Moreover his unbridled need for power will have to be content with purely imaginary satisfactions, feeding on his own pride within the childish 'make-believe' that delays his access to manhood. That is why Man Friday makes his appearance so late in the story when he might, in all plausibility, have arrived much earlier: Robinson can have no companions — or *subjects* as he calls them — until his apprenticeship to reality has been as near as possible completed. He can only become king, father and master when he has emerged from childhood and is sufficiently recovered from his dreams to establish his reign on a more realistic basis.

In the story of the island Man Friday opens a new chapter where language reasserts its rights and man his superiority over a primitive animal world. For until then Robinson had lived in perfect harmony with the simple animals who, as in dreams, fairy tales and myths, follow him around to help, entertain and serve him faithfully. This is the idyllic side of his ambiguous seclusion though he certainly deplores his pets' speechlessness, being still too intellectually motivated to be able to understand their dumb language (silence is the one flaw in his paradise, for which he tries to make up by talking to himself and, of course, keeping his 'Journal'). But although his yearning for conversation makes him resort to rather puerile devices such as teaching his parrot to talk while regretting he cannot do likewise with his dog, he enjoys nonetheless the honest companionship of his animals which, insofar as it is wordless, is devoid of misunderstanding and deceit as well as of questions and opinions which are ever a source of pain. Man Friday's arrival signifies the end of a basic communion with the wordlessness and honesty of animal nature, and thus inaugurates a more evolved era. For henceforth Robinson can put into practice what he has so painfully learnt during his long penance — he can instruct a human being and thus re-become human, which is precisely what was lacking for the accomplishment of his mission. Like all that is washed up on this happy, hopeless island, Man Friday has two conflicting aspects, one disturbing insofar as he brings on to the island that element of disquiet which is *talking* man; the other elating since he makes it possible for Robinson to realise that rebirth towards which he had been working since he made a clean sweep of civilisation. However once the first moment of dread is over — Robinson is always torn between the fear of solitude and the dread of seeing his solitude desecrated — the young savage becomes a wholly positive addition, not only because of the developments the story owes to him but mainly because he is such a perfect companion — the ideal tool which will enable the civlising hero finally to prove himself.

Man Friday presents Robinson with an exceptionally pliable and pleasant rough material to manipulate. Insofar as he is a 'savage' he is a piece of unadulterated nature, devoid of learning and furthermore impervious to the impact of corruption always threatening highly civilised man. In fact he is as virtuous as he is ignorant, a circumstance which, added to his extreme youth, constitutes perfect educatability. Robinson is not long in perceiving how well this particular windfall is suited to his role as protagonist in the arduous regeneration he has set himself as goal. Thus he starts by teaching him his own tongue (without a thought for the native's, since anthropology is not one of the sciences he has taken the trouble to reinvent). In this way human communication is gradually re-established and the secluded world where man and beast understood each other instinctively is taken over by pedagogy.

Now Robinson, despite his misanthropy, is a born pedagogue, indeed this is the most remarkable of all the talents which the island's rationale has forced him to develop. Self-educator and eternal apprentice (we must not forget that it takes him fifty-two years to overcome his immaturity,[1]) he is passionately fond of instructing and does so with utter dedication, in practical and ethical, as well as intellectual and spiritual matters, as soon as the chance presents itself (this is a distinction he shares with Don Quixote, another apostle of solitude who is also an enthusiastic pedagogue). In this respect Man Friday is truly a godsend — he has an upright nature, and is all the more malleable for being apparently completely devoid of knowledge to start with (the one exception to this total blank is religion: Robinson admits that he holds certain beliefs). With this young, docile, loving, singularly frank and devoted savage the island recluse can indulge, with a clear conscience, his taste for educating which is another aspect of his need for dominance. Thus as soon as Man Friday drops from the sky — or emerges from the sea which is here the receptacle of all that is unexpected — he is firmly taken in hand, educated and subjected to endless general knowledge lessons which he assimilates at an amazing rate, to become if not his white master's equal, at least an adequate companion for him. Once he has more or less mastered English, he learns all the manners, customs and ideas proper to civilised man. Thus he develops as his master had done before him during two years of total solitude, but starting from a state of innocence markedly different from the latter's 'fall'. For the two men undergo similar trials — Friday is 'lost' and 'found', separated from his father whom he believes dead and cast upon an unknown shore; only he is totally guiltless for he loves his father, never rejected him and is far from being a rebellious son. Indeed Robinson never tires of describing the endless attentions and extraordinary show of affection which testify to his filial devotion, when he finds his father safe and sound. So the story of the failed adult is re-enacted by the child-savage who must grow up and abandon his 'savage' state to become in due course a useful member of society; with this difference however that he is free from sin (the classical parallel between savage and child corresponds here to more than contemporary theory — it reflects the book's major theme, since Robinson's obvious childishness is presented forthwith as a return to savageness). When the rebel, regenerated by a long life of ascetic labours, educates Man Friday he creates a faultless child from nothing, a child who, combining innocence with intellectual curiosity, and docility with a lively mind, amply testifies to the excellence of his method. Whence the tale's exceptional popularity as reading-matter for children, as well as its ability to appeal to the young while recalling to adults the mysterious depths of their 'true' story.

Servant, disciple, work-mate and friend, Man Friday is all of these in his relationship to the man who, after saving him from a terrible death, uses him to his own ends. But more basically still he is an adopted son, Robinson Crusoe's spiritual heir prior to the physical heirs he will beget at the age of sixty in his native island. The perfect pupil is moreover a perfect son who, born of man and not of woman (he is a gift from the sea), provides one more element of the Family Romance plot. So long as Robinson remains on the nameless island he is too much a Foundling, or not sufficiently advanced on the Bastard's path, to be capable of begetting. Yet he must become a father. This is something he cannot forego if he wishes to outstrip his own father in power and sway. So once again he 'makes believe' and for want of something better he acquires a fictive paternity with the symbolic sea as partner representing his own mother and all the other women who never overtly trouble his thoughts. When he constantly calls the boy 'son'

this is not simply a manner of speaking; Man Friday is the ideal
son, the *dream* son with whom he can quench his thirst for
power while actually drawing him closer to reality. And
thanks to this boy he has brought into being and on whom he
practises his new-found realism, the shipwrecked mariner of
life can gradually retrace his steps to the civilised world: thus
he gets ready both to take his place among men and, as befits
this denizen of the fairy tale, to get married.

Man Friday's arrival marks the turning point between total
solitude and the peopling of the island which will become a
colony. In fact it dictates all future events — an additional
proof that the action's vicissitudes correspond exactly to the
inner process of adaptation which distinguishes this exceptionally clear and logical Family Romance. Robinson does not
encounter Man Friday until he has more or less recovered from
his misanthropy; but once he has stopped shunning the world,
the world begins to crowd in on him. Thus a single member of
the human race suffices to repeal the desert law and create as
though by magic the rudiments of a society. Equipped with an
adopted son who teaches him to think once again of other
people, Robinson can now provide for shipwrecked sailors,
prisoners captured by the savages, and pirates of all kinds who
ask him for shelter. Insofar as he is the first occupant who,
moreover has weapons, tools and a well-appointed 'castle', he
has no difficulty in imposing his prerogatives as 'lord and
master' of the island on the new arrivals. Thus he obtains the
kingdom after which he has never ceased to hanker since his
youthful rebellion and flight. And at the end of the first section
of his adventures he can say with the pride of one who has
raised himself to the heights of power, that he is like a king to
whom all the inhabitants of the island owe their lives and for
whom they would gladly give them up, and then go on to
confess that he takes some pleasure in treating them with a
certain condescension as though he were a monarch of old.
Robinson has undoubtedly got on in the world since the days
when his kingdom consisted of a few domestic animals — the
island now belongs to him, he can dispose at will of his
subjects' lives and he is the equal of those patriarchal rulers of
antiquity whose power and glory he used to envy. Simultaneously every one of his wishes has been fulfilled and all that
remains is to return home in triumph to flaunt his success.

Between his departure from the now inhabited island and his voluntary return to it some years later, Robinson decides to found a family, a real one this time, so that the cycle of his Family Romance may be completed according to the best traditions (a bit late perhaps, but then he has had to overcome an exceptional psychic regression). Concerning this part of his adventures, our ageing hero — the apparently inveterate hermit and bachelor who never once so much as mentions his love life during thirty-five years — becomes singularly reticent. He who was not habitually short of words devotes three lines to his marriage — after the event, moreover, when he is already the father of grown children and himself a widower:

. . . I in part settled myself here. For, first of all, I married and had three children, two sons and one daughter. But my wife dying, and my nephew coming home, with good success, from a voyage in Spain, my inclination to go abroad, and his importunity prevailed . . .

Marriage, births and bereavement barely take a minute between two adventures; Robinson dispatches the lot as quickly as he can so as to return to what has always been the heart of the matter for him. His wife is featureless, ageless and nameless. She dies no sooner than she has appeared and all in all we know hardly anything about her except that she has vainly tried, like all indulgent, motherly spouses, to restrain her husband's dangerous passion. The woman of flesh only emerges as a ghost; she has no substance compared to the overpowering dreams that obsess our hero each night (he dreams that his island is torn by internal strife and hears Man Friday call for help); but insubstantial as she may be from a general point of view, she has to die for Robinson to indulge his wanderlust. Thus she tactfully disappears, leaving him alone once again to face the adult world which at sixty as at eighteen still inspires the same aversion: he observes men either toiling for their daily bread or wasting their lives in excesses and vain pleasures, but all equally miserable since their aims are always unattainable. And, compared to this degrading existence in a corrupt, unmotivated society, his island Utopia is irresistibly attractive, combining as it does, happiness and wisdom. He remembers how in his kingdom he never let the growth of his corn exceed his needs, nor fattened more goats than he could eat; how his money had grown mouldy in its chest and had not so much as been looked at for twenty years. Robinson now reveals the basic idea which had guided him all along: the world is evil because it is dominated by pleasure, excess and money; his island is good because there, possessions are never hoarded, each does his share of work and receives in exchange no more than is strictly necessary to satisfy his needs (in this respect it is not without similarities to the 'phalanstery' which played such a prominent part in the political Utopias of the following century). Thus the alternative is easily settled: having justified his thirst for power by this bitter social attack, Robinson can reintegrate with a clear conscience the kingdom of freedom and innocence of his childhood fixation.

During his extended absence conditions have naturally changed. The colony has prospered, the population has increased and its growth has caused violent conflicts, especially since the ex-mutineers who constitute the dregs of the colony soon took charge of the island's policy. Furthermore its formerly uncontaminated customs have sadly deteriorated; men and women live in a state of more or less general sexual promiscuity, polygamy is widely spread, marriages are no longer regularised which, among other drawbacks, deprives the women and children of legal protection. In fact the new society is reverting to anarchy or to a savagery hardly less odious than that of the neighbouring tribes whose members occasionally come over to attend endless festivities. Robinson never actually witnesses any of these alarming occurrences (his nature is incompatible with sin and he has only to land on the island for evil to get immediately under control), but he hears about them and no sooner has he done so than he puts an end to the disgrace without wasting time bewailing it. In twenty-five days — his second stay numbers as many days as the previous one years — he re-establishes order, punishes the culprits, organises the division of labour, shares out the land, legalises marriages (it is he who marries his subjects, showing more enthusiasm for this activity than for his own betrothal), censures morals, converts the pagan and brings the Christian backsliders back to the fold — in short he combines the functions of judge, minister, doctor, priest and police officer, not to mention of course that of army commander-in-chief. Once again the island owes everything to him. It reverts to the

simplicity, moral integrity and puritanical frugality it possessed in its primitive state, and rebecomes the active paradise he
had first intended to create, but with this far from negligible
difference that by increasing its productivity it has developed
into a source of incredible benefit for its owner (this notion of a
profitable paradise is unquestionably the novel's most brilliant
invention). When Robinson decides to leave and indulge his
wanderlust one last time the island is flourishing and unequivocally pacific. Moreover if it is often in his thoughts during
his journeyings — he crosses Europe and Asia from end to
end, trading in all kinds of goods, including slaves and opium
— he never dwells on the difficulties he underwent but always
on the formidable concentration of power which crowned his
endeavours in this seemingly most unpropitious site.

His aim is power and he achieves it so totally that he is truly
entitled to boast, as he does to a Russian lord he meets in the
course of his peregrinations, that he was once in his own
kingdom a greater prince than the Tzar of Moscovy. When the
Russian shows some surprise he adds that he disposed of his
subjects' lives and their fortunes and that in spite of this no one
ever complained of his rule nor resented his wealth. Neither
Peter the Great nor any other ruling monarch can claim such
success; no potentate can assert with Robinson Crusoe that all
his subjects were ready to lay down their lives for him; and no
tyrant — he does acknowledge himself as such — has ever been
so universally loved and so terribly feared. He, who some little
time earlier had accused himself of parricide and who admits to
having wanted to be a tyrant, now contemplates with a clear
conscience the unequalled reign he established singlehanded,
precisely as he had planned to do when he invented his Family
Romance. And whatever the share of satire and self-irony
contained in such a justification — Defoe does not spare
himself here — we cannot deny him the merit of having
carried out his plan with exceptional perseverence and taken
his dreams of grandeur and despotism with the utmost
seriousness. Faithful to all the implications of his troubled
adolescence's 'resourcefulness' he took upon himself the dis-
graceful Oedipal crime and, thanks to such a transgression
which he was able to experience and, furthermore, to actively
exploit all his life long, he did indeed rise higher than any king,
past or present, acquiring greater power than any human

being — which was more than he had ever dared to hope.

Thus it is not only as a 'successful' man, nor is it merely as an ordinary king, that he gets ready to retire from the stage, but, as becomes his transendental position, as a divinely elected superman.

*

For about a century Crusoism was greatly appreciated as a genre and widely cultivated by translators, imitators and publishers. There was hardly a country in Europe that did not have its national Robinson and in America there was even a Robinsona. Desert islands were mass-produced and no adventure story worthy of the name lacked a shipwreck. Indeed Defoe's masterpiece became common property and as late as 1805 a *Bibliotek der Robinsone* came out in Germany in five avowedly incomplete volumes. Doubtless such imitations rarely attained the standard of their model; usually they simply retold the adventures already familiar to their readers, sometimes supplementing them with variations and a touch of the exotic, but never modifying the Family Romance Defoe had created in response to his own personal requirements. The new Robinson was always the Foundling partially imprisoned in his own magic who, though old enough to turn his dream island into a workshop, could only accomplish his apprenticeship by avoiding women and sexuality. He too resorted to pedagogy at which he excelled (Campe's German *Robinson* is accredited with having inspired the great geographer and explorer Alexander von Humboldt's vocation), yet if he had become little more than a pretext for educative moralising, he continued for a long time to be a favourite among children and something of a middle-class hero, simply because, for the growing child as for the rising bourgeoisie, he vindicated the most subversively realistic undertakings without sacrificing more than a minimum of illusion to such budding realism.

Paradoxically, in order to be of some use to the Foundling — and thus serve as basis for the Oepidal social novel of the following century — Crusoism had to abandon the over-misanthropic or at least remarkably unsociable hero. For in fact it could not evolve so long as it remained entrenched in a paradise devoid of humanity where a single representative of the species does absolutely everything that has to be done including the specific functions of both sexes — in other words so long as Robinson, vowed to celibacy till the age of sixty, continues to be very dissimilar to the 'patriarchal monarchs of old' whom he hoped to resemble. The German writer Johann Gottfried Schnabell appears to have realised this when he introduced a blatantly Oedipal sexual element into the desert island theme — and, probably for this very reason, his book was almost as popular as Defoe's. Whereas according to the conventions of the story the desert island is presented as a bulwark against women, sexual temptation and dangerous passions (true, native women are finally included, but erotic passion is always banned: Robinson will have no truck with it), Schnabell's island — *Die Insel Felsenburg* — is seen from the start to be a highly eroticised locality where the inveterate hermit is replaced by a primordial couple capable of engendering on its own a new human race. So as to leave no doubt as to the meaning of this remarkable innovation, on the title page of the original edition the author introduces the Falsenburg patriarch in the following terms:

A native of Saxe, Albert Julius took ship at eighteen, was shipwrecked and cast up on a cruel rock/ discovered from the summit of the rock the most wonderful country in the world/ settled there with his companion/ founded through his marriage a family of over three hundred souls/ cultivated the soil most efficiently/ owing to specific circumstances amassed an amazing fortune/ was a benefactor to the German friends whose whereabouts he located/ lived hale and vigorous until the end of 1728, that is till the age of one hundred years/ and is probably still alive at present.[2]

As we can see from this summary the story — or rather sequence of loosely connected episodes regularly interspersed with sections of the patriarch's biography — derives equally from the traditional Crusoism and from the fairy tale. Among the traditional themes we find the adolescent runaway, the shipwreck, the desert island and the founding of a prosperous colony. Whereas folklore contributes an orphan persecuted by his cruel stepmother, the discovery of hidden treasure and, predominantly, marriage constitute the basic action from which all further events arise. The book is made up of a collection of tales relating, for the benefit of future residents,

the lives of the principal settlers. Each tale refers to a different
Family Romance corresponding in every detail to the standard
model, the most circumstantial being of course that of the
patriarch Albert Julius without whom the Island of Felsenburg
would never have existed. According to his own words the
sequence of events which led to his running away are intimately related to his exceptionally unhappy childhood. An
orphan, adopted by a shepherd who is promptly widowed and
remarries, young Albert becomes the object of his adulterous
stepmother's hatred when she catches him spying on her for
his adoptive father. Since this woman has vowed to destroy
him he runs away from the one home that could still provide
shelter and wanders at random, getting along as best he can,
deprived of both affection and support. At eighteen — the
same age as Robinson Crusoe — he happens to make the
acquaintance of a young nobleman for whom he acts as
go-between in the preliminaries of a secret marriage. Thanks
to him the nobleman succeeds in marrying his beloved Concordia — such is the name of the colony's future mother — and
he is rewarded by becoming their servant and friend. Pursued
by the outraged parents' fury and obliged to run away once
again, Albert sails together with the young couple for an
unknown destination; but retribution catches up with them:
the ship is wrecked on a cruel rock and the three young people
are cast up on the isle of Felsenburg where they savour,
according to the best tradition, the bitterness of exile and the
delights of paradise (Albert recognises the site as the garden
from whence the angel expelled Adam and Eve). Thus the
hero, unlike Robinson, is not the sole survivor; his masters too
are safe and sound as well as a certain captain who, being in
love with Concordia, sows the seed of discord within this
miniature society (in fact he urges his companions to accept the
principles of sexual promiscuity, which, needless to say, they
refuse to do, less on moral grounds than because of the lofty
ends they are destined to achieve). Shortly after the four
survivors set up home on the island the young nobleman pays
the price of rebellion against paternal authority by falling to his
death; the captain (who among other misdeeds had been guilty
of raping his own sister) is now aptly eliminated as a punishment for his crimes; and so Albert innocently triumphs over
his two rivals without having so much as considered the

Oedipal murder (his success further represents that of the commoner over a corrupt aristocracy which, in the person of the captain, had profoundly humiliated him). Once rid of the father (in his twin role of good master and depraved lord) there is nothing more to prevent him from marrying Concordia and making her his Eve and the matriarch of this new Eden. He who had divided his foster parents, then united the spiritual parents that he had spontaneously adopted, now opportunely fills his master's vacant place, and the marriage, strenuously achieved in the face of Oedipal prohibitions, is the first step in a prodigious ascent never equalled since Biblical times. Albert Julius possesses the strength and the good fortune that always distinguish heroic survivors; but he has the further advantage over all other Robinsons that he fathers the three hundred souls of his future kingdom. Thus, having built his empire of flesh and blood, as it were, he insures against the hazards of power more thoroughly than a purely symbolic *Father of the People* can ever do. King and Father, King insofar as he is Father according to the basic fusion stipulated by fairy tale and Family Romance alike, the Felsenburg Patriarch has every right to the title of 'patriarchal monarch' which Robinson, in spite of his boasts, could only claim symbolically. Thus, notwithstanding all the Oedipal plotting and dissension constantly threatening to destroy his people, he is able to raise the island to the state of ideal Utopia where each one enjoys his life and his possessions in the midst of general well-being and perpetual peace.

So whereas Robinson Crusoe redeems himself by his labours and by shunning the sexual temptations tacitly associated with his defiance, the Master of Felsenburg finds redemption in the magic of sex and love (not that there is any lack of labour on the Patriarch's island, but marriage prevails over every other activity; it is every individual's main concern as well as that of society; indeed it guarantees general prosperity if only by continually supplementing the number of active members). True, the two islands are very similar, notably as they function in the same manner, both having the same ability to absorb the evil that comes from without and turn it to good use. However the evil to be transformed is of a totally different nature: in the first it is the tools of *aggression* washed ashore with Robinson that the island neutralises, while the second redeems the *sexual* transgressions threatening all those who happen to be cast up on its shores by some personal shipwreck (this contrast of basic impulses coincides moreover with a social and political contrast — Defoe's desert island is an *agricultural* colony, Felsenburg a *settlement*). On the one hand evil is represented by violence, brutality and blind destructiveness; on the other it derives solely from the basic ambiguity of sex and the diabolic aspect of love (two things which automatically vanish as soon as the island has mastered them). In one, killing for killing's sake — we must not forget that Robinson is equally skilled at hunting and fishing as he is at breeding — in the other, lewdness, covetousness, murder *for the sake of a woman* — or adventures rather than the great Adventure, erotic situations eventually leading to a mastery of the land. For the puritanical Foundling has a no less guilty conscience than the Bastard go-between and schemer, but he is not possessed by the same devil and does not break the same commandments.

★

But although the two utopian islands oppose and complete each other in certain respects, their literary merits bear no comparison. Nor can their role be seen as equal in the genre's evolution towards the 'slice of life' or the 'competition with the registry office'. Defoe's masterpiece occupies a prominent position in the highest spheres of world literature; in many ways it is a fundamental work which enabled novelists in the following century to explore new territories and influenced the very sources of creativity insofar as, having become almost from the start, a book read by children, it has been able to form budding novelists. All the novelists of the nineteenth century had been brought up on *Robinson Crusoe* and *Don Quixote*, and although the impact of such childhood reading is not always acknowledged, it cannot have failed to influence them unconsciously, were it only in developing their natural taste for certain forms of flights from reality. At first sight adventure stories, tales of travel and discovery or even science fiction may seem to be its direct descendants; but the Crusoism is not restricted to a choice of setting or of plot — it corresponds much more to a typical state of conflict that can be expressed in the most varied forms. From the point of view of the thematics of the Family Romance it could indeed be argued that Robinson is at the heart of any fiction which stresses the individual's alienation from society or which tries to evoke an apprenticeship, education or individual conquest to which the exigencies of the majority are opposed more or less overtly. In this respect Dickens' debt (half acknowledged for instance in *David Copperfield*) is no less than that of Jules Verne or Stevenson (who made no secret of it). Balzac is as close to Robinson in *la Comédie humaine* as he was in his youth when he wrote tales of piracy; Herman Melville is not Defoe's disciple only in that grandiose Crusoism, the epic of *Moby Dick*; and Kafka's early work *America* — where Robinson is reborn under his legendary name but in the highly ambiguous role of a European immigrant stranded in the New World — is far from being the only proof that he comes from the same stock. For kinship is much closer here than outward appearances would suggest: in an age when every novelist is torn between the individualism of his art and his desire to be part of a community, Robinson has become consubstantial, as it were, with imaginative literature. Thus it is not this or that specific work, but the novel as such, which sails off with him to discover the experience for itself the desert island's ambivalance.

Schnabell's book certainly has no such outstanding claims to the novel's gratitude. At most it is an odd work which, despite its immense popularity in eighteenth-century Germany, fell into oblivion without ever earning the critics' respect (already in 1828 Ludwig Tieck seemed almost ashamed of re-editing such antiquated suff). Though Goethe among others is known to have enjoyed it, *Felsenburg's Island* probably never enlightened or inspired anybody, and insofar as literature is concerned with upholding its standards there is no reason why it should be revived. However from our point of view — which presupposes at least a temporary disregard of rank — it deserves more than a modest place among other historical curios; for it exposes the intricacies of the novel's peculiar *craze for begetting* to which it is prone whenever life gets a grip on it. Albert Julius has one distinctive feature that also throws light on the problem of the novel's origins: in his capacity as father of all Felsenburg's inhabitants he is author of the fictional population whose activities provide the story. Thus he plays the part both of hero and novelist just like the child-author of the Family Romance. In this way physical procreation is a dual mainspring for literary creation; first it provides the material for the plot — which is no more than a sequence of love stories — second it supplies additional actors as the need arises (to the popular reader's satisfaction and the highbrow's disgust). Since all the characters are descendants of the patriarch (who in fact is the author of everything) their number bears witness to his virility. Furthermore the variety and wealth of episodes increases in proportion to their proliferation. Felsenburg Island is peopled with as many characters as its author and discoverer is able to procreate; moreover it is the subject of a story only insofar as it is fecundated, thus it constitutes an ideal literary site since *physical conception is equivalent here to creation*. Johann Gottfried Schnabell was so well aware of such an identification that he dedicated the book 'To Madam my Mother Tongue'[3] which confirms the main point of the work, but indicates furthermore an unusual insight into the essence of fictional writing and its intimate relation to incestuous motives. United to the German language which can reasonably be seen as representing his own mother[4] he innocently exposes the shameful truth, forgotten or carefully concealed by the more subtle Bastard: that every novel, basically concerned with reproduction, aims at nothing else than peopling some Felsenburg Island or other with an endless stream of its procreations and employing every possible means to make this new humanity plausible. The Great Families, genealogies, well-documented biographies and the active, prolific populations with which the nineteenth century was so concerned, all of these were more than simply an extraneous material on which each novel could draw as it pleased; they were that from which the novel was made before it ever was written. One 'makes' a novel in order to be the patriarch full of days and respectability guiding the course of history and psychology. All the motives writers suggest can be reduced to this one, and the more prolific a writer the more obvious it becomes. On account of this revelation, which *Die Insel Felsenburg* was perhaps alone in making at the time, it can be seen as the daring precursor of Zola's naturalism or Balzac's assertions in the *Physiologies*. And in spite of its unpolished naïvety, in spite especially of its total lack of ideological aspirations, it would be unconsciously imitated by many writers as soon as the Foundling was ripe for a revolution.

However revealing it may be for our purpose it must be admitted that Schnabell's book is far from attaining the aesthetic standards of its famous predecessor, for it is either overexplicit or unskilfully disguised. In taking as its only subject the various conflicts related to the reproduction of the species it restricts itself to the lowest fictional level — trite love affairs, gossip and stereotyped sensationalism — which expresses with a total lack of sophistication the Oedipal situation at its least evolved stage. Within its pages parricide and incest thrive, elopments, rape, abandoned or kidnapped children abound without in any way advancing the plot; crimes accumulate in monotonous disorder but provoke neither excitement nor horror (the only form of sublimation to have any prominence is the cultivation of the soil and the founding of a capital, otherwise the population has no thought for anything but gossip). Moreover such serious aesthetic shortcomings do not depend exclusively on clumsiness or lack of talent — they reflect rather a defective imagination. For Oedipal desire cannot be exorcised by evoking a sequence of forbidden acts. It has to preserve an aura of mystery, a margin of inexpressible dream, an irreducible trace of ambiguity, indeed precisely what art hopes to express and where it incessantly comes to grief. By expressing it in a mechanical sequence of 'realisations' which exclude such essential residues, a tale cannot fail to sink to the lowest fictional level where nothing new ever happens. Thus like most minor or popular novels which literary history has long been content to overlook, *Die Insel Felsenburg* follows the Oedipal plot too literally to be an inspired work. However, owing to the originality of its conception such a fault may be useful as a starting point for aesthetic investigations. For if it proves that the novel requires in order to exist a regression to the most primitive procreative instinct, it proves equally that every great novel must try to drive Oedipus back into his original darkness, encapsulating him in a vast network of symbols and allusions. Johann Gottfried Schnabell, who exploits the secrets of Utopia and *feuilleton* precisely because he is unaware of the secrets of desire, certainly failed to endow his mother tongue with the unperishable work he hoped to father on her. Yet he did

bequeath to fiction something more than a second-rate, out-
dated work: in fact he left a proof that art is never to be found in
the written word of children's tales but always between the
lines, in that margin of irrecoverable meanings where its
significance and perhaps the true secret of its beauty is unerringly fashioned.

★

Daniel Defoe was more than half aware of Robinson's debt to
Don Quixote; so much so that he based his defence of the
story's varacity — as well as a late summary of what he meant
by 'truth' — on such an affiliation. The summary, ascribed to
the writer and thinker Robinson has now become, is an attack
on the obtuseness of critics still quibbling over the authenticity
of his biography. The gist of the Preface to *Serious Reflections*
which he devoted to this subject, is that certain critics overtly
accuse him of inventing, whereas he has in fact interspersed
imaginary stories with true facts; however, imagination which
can only be expressed in images has nonetheless its own truth
— it reports intimate facts which, if they cannot be perceived
by ordinary means, have no less reality and significance than
the data of empirical experience. Thus the fear and apprehension Robinson experiences on seeing a human footprint, his
capture of the old ram, the object that rolls under his bunk and
startles him out of his wits, are true facts, as is the dream where
he sees himself taken by messengers (it should be noted that all
the passages he refers to as proof of this purely psychic reality
are closely related to the Family Romance, since they are all
concerned with the typical *unheimlich* quality of Oedipal fantasies). Here at last Defoe takes a positive stand in the contro-
versy of truth versus imagination: truth is not necessarily
similar to what is; it can perfectly well resemble nothing; it
frequently manifests itself as an exact representation of something invisible — an emotion, vague impression, superstitious
fear, dream or hallucination — experienced in the inner depts
of the psyche but which partakes of reality just as much as
anything perceived by all and sundry (all of which apart from
the implicit dismissal of conventional reality, corresponds to
the general Romantic theory). Henceforth Robinson can con-

cede the desert island's non-existence and that, although he has *frequently been shipwrecked* this was *rather on land than at sea* — what does it matter after all, since he has truly experienced the indescribable solitude the island exactly epitomises? When stranded on the island he was subject to many strange ideas, hallucinations, and so on. Everything he relates is a true account of a state of compulsory confinement symbolised in the story by his confinement to the island. It is quite as reasonable to represent one kind of imprisonment by another as it is to represent any real object by another non-existent one. Thus Robinson — or someone very close to him, we still have to discover whom — has experienced solitary confinement for which shipwreck, desert island and return to nature provided exact substitutes. This is the psychological reality his adventures must both conceal and suggest by means of a literary process which has already been used to depict a similar kind of isolation (not to mention the Family Romance whose system of representation is strikingly cinfirmed here). Indeed for Robinson *The Adventures of Robinson Crusoe* can find no better vindication than *The Fabulous History of Don Quixote* which, in the form of a story describing the activities of an extravagant being totally cut off from other people, reproduces an *exact image* of what effectively takes place in the inaccessible recesses of an unparalleled solitude bordering on the limits of human endurance. Robinson's life in a completely isolated *utopian* space, also translated into exact images, contains the same proportion of reality as Don Quixote's flight into the *anachronistic* space where he decides to imitate the heroes of his favourite books. Thus when a foolish and malicious writer acrimoniously alludes to Robinson Crusoe's Quixotism, he proves that he does not know what he is talking about, and may be rather taken aback when Robinson informs him that what he has said sarcastically is indeed the greatest of compliments. Nothing could have pleased the Don better than such a spontaneous homage from the first of his spiritual sons — even if it was provoked by derogatory remarks. Yet maybe Robinson's critic was not such a fool after all (if he ever existed — but even if he is only a rhetorical figure he is nonetheless useful since he inadvertently provides a valuable indication of the reputation enjoyed by the Book of Books during the second half of the eighteenth century), and in any case he comes in handy as a means of enabling our hero to say at last all he has to say. For by taking sides with the illustrious madman who, just over a century earlier had abolished literature's *ancien régime* at one stroke, Robinson does more than acknowledge the confused desires that instigated his reckless peregrinations — he carries the revolution of fiction a step further and reveals the significance of what henceforth will be known as Modernism.

Quixotic, Robinson undoubtedly is in every fibre of his wandering solitary being. He wanders through geographical space as Don Quixote wanders through the anachronistic world of his favourite novels, accompanied by a companion who, as his subordinate, servant and friend, is an exact replica of Sancho Panza. He loves adventure and the wide world, has unbounded faith in his dreams and in the reality of the 'other side', and yearns for a lost paradise. He is both misanthropic and bent on bringing happiness to mankind (by persuasion or, if need be, by force), a born reformer and educator, anarchistic to the core and simultaneously devoted to order, a vagabond because of his distaste for all that is established yet fixed in a single idea; thirsting for freedom and despotic to those who are at his mercy; he is moreover intransigent, hard-working, strict, chaste to the point of asceticism, blessed with an unparalleled physical endurance and immensely confident in his own intellectual abilities. In short he has all the qualities and defects, all the inconsistency and incoherence that contribute to Don Quixote's madness; yet of course he is not mad; for he is all the same better equipped for life, he is adaptable and amenable to development and improvement, all of which his model is obliged to reject. Thus though he embodies the militant quixotism of which he boasts once his adventures are over (he makes no mention of it before, for that would be too revealing), nonetheless he does not fight for quite the same cause but for a purpose more suited to his own pecularity and which bears, furthermore, the mark of powerful collective ingredients (language, nationalism, tradition and intellectual habits consistent with an insular existence, etc.). As a Protestant Englishman living in an age addicted to commerce and adventure, Robinson is unquestionably entitled to a good share of eccentricity; and he takes advantage of the fact during the fifty years he spends 'reaching for the moon'. But he can never go as far astray as his predecessor who, because he represents an extinct world he vainly tries to revive, has to live history backwards. Having set out as a Quixotic rebel against reality and doomed in advance to endless disasters, Robinson is the *survivor* of a death-wish induced by the inner despair of his early experience. However his Quixotic shipwreck only leads him to set his sights on a very concrete island, where he manages not simply to survive but rather to turn Utopia itself into an extremely profitable affair. Instead of coming back home as a failure forced to disown himself and admit defeat, as the sombre Knight has done, he returns as a successful, healthy, self-confident person prepared to settle down on 'this side' as a model for all self-made men.

Thus until he returns to the real world in order to overcome it, Robinson is like Don Quixote. After which, as we have seen, he follows the Bastard's more practical itinerary. In other words, he betrays Quixotic ideals, since Don Quixote, the Foundling totally unresponsive to experience and quite uneducable, is essentially someone who opposes all forms of progress. At the end of a long period of trial in the purgatory of his immaturity, Robinson mends his ways sufficiently to be able to pass gradually onto the side of reality and thus against Don Quixote, so that in spite of their very similar beginnings and their many common features, the two heroes end up as complete opposites. However if it is true that the former is a model of how to overcome the archaic tendencies of rebellious childhood, while the latter vindicates the absolute value of such tendencies whether or not the result is madness, this is also because their different levels of maturity correspond to two distinct stages of fiction where the relation between author and hero is very different. Indeed rigorous Quixotism stretches an invisible thread between fictive creature and creator so that, while their independence is taken for granted, they are in fact duplicates, or more precisely the product of a subtle form of duplicity. Defoe is always half aware of the possibilities such an illusion of impersonality presents for his project. Thus Robinson is not given as the homologue or disguised double he really is, but as *other*, a stranger leading an independent life and having no connection whatsoever with his author. Indeed, eccentric and exotic as he is there is little risk of Robinson ever betraying his true identity. He is readily taken for a purely fictitious character invented for impersonal ends and, owing to this false impression, it was a long time before anyone realised that the adventures of Robinson Crusoe were after all nothing but a disguised confession. However the general trend of the tale does involve a certain inconsistency, for Defoe does not merely want to confess — complain or console, avenge and justify himself like any other author of a Family Romance — through a resourceful adventurer who will symbolically settle his account with mankind and civilisation. He is equally if not more concerned with extolling the success of his fulfilled and cured Foundling self, which inevitably leads to his surreptitious reappearance on the scene — if only to occupy the darkest corner. Yet to enter the story and comment on the events is to contravene the neutrality accepted from the start as a premise (all the more binding insofar as Defoe presents himself as the 'reporter' of an actual occurrence); it would too force the author to supplant the hero and cast a slur on his own integrity. Indeed it is obvious that from the moment Robinson begins to speak with Defoe's voice and to eloquently impart his opinions and ideas, he has more or less abandoned his identity as the occult, *importunate* double who, till then, had been the true manipulator of events. Henceforth pleading his own cause too skilfully, too much as a speechifier and sage, he becomes the deifying *alter ego* and representative of what Defoe would have liked to be and might have been had his circumstances been different. We know moreover that in the circumstances that were in fact his he was never lacking in adventurousness. In this respect Robinson's worldly success is not entirely unprejudicial to his literary success, for he can only illustrate unambiguously Defoe's arguments by abandoning the dark spheres inhabited by his demons, but no sooner has he risen to the reassuring surface of the story than he falls prey to conventionality. All things considered it is the same in most cases of 'happy endings': a hero who is over-successful in a worldly way is in danger of being a literary failure. It is as if in the Family Romance there were some sort of secret pact between aesthetics and logic, stipulating that the Bastard can never betray the Foundling who survives within him without running the risk of a *literary* impoverishment — a loss of depth, ambiguity and poetry — and of losing at least some of the social advantages due to him.

To judge by the extent of his failure Don Quixote has certainly no cause to fear the loss of integrity Robinson suffers through becoming a mere pretext for dreams and confessions. For if he fails in everything, not just finally but all along the way, it is precisely because he is free to pursue his aims and, being as totally independent of Cervantes *in the story* as he wishes to be independent *in life* from temporality and necessity, nothing foreign to his whim can ever affect him or change his destiny. Insofar as he uncompromisingly scorns reality how can Don Quixote possibly have any truck with the author's *public* image, his official titles, qualifications, history and civil status which involve him *de facto* in a reality the Don has undertaken to oppose? On the contrary he must guard the frontiers of fiction in order to exclude from the novel any of those authorial anecdotes, historical passages, personal reminiscences, emotions or 'messages' usually taken for the trade mark of 'authenticity', and for that very reason abhorrent to him. Thus it is the consistency of his folly that obliges him to be, rather than Cervantes' likeness or interpreter, the strangest of strangers to him, a perfect 'unlikeness' dropped out of who knows what sky to the amazement of the crowds. For the illuustrious Knight is not only 'errant' in the sense of his favourite readings; he is essentially a displaced person, condemned to wander ceaselessly on the fringe of perceptible reality and to repulse from his vicinity anything remotely suggesting a worldly link. Compelled by vocation to live his life backwards, against experience and against common sense, it is easy to see why he is incapable of providing an identifiable image and can only represent the unreality of his Mournful Countenance, beyond the limits of space and time. In fact he represents nothing other than his own incongruous image, but just as he does not express anything concerning Cervantes' own personality neither does Cervantes specify what he wants to express through him. Thus in spite of centuries of scholarship and scholarly disputes, we still do not know what to make of his significant advent nor how to classify him.

Officially then (that is according to what the superficial context reveals) there is no sign of complicity between Cervantes and Don Quixote but rather a hiatus, a solution of continuity apparently denoting mutual ignorance or even positive antinomy. Don Quixote 'sets forth' because he cannot live in the ordinary world where Cervantes is quite happily settled. Conversely the reporter of his adventures has neither the inclination nor the ability to penetrate the magic circle the Don conjures up around him to restore the Golden Age. Thus instead of the 'and' implicit in every Crusoism and, indeed, in every autobiographical novel, we are faced with an alternative compelling the reader to make a choice. For if it is true that hero and novelist have no knowledge of each other, even apparently exclude each other, then it is useless to try and follow them simultaneously or associate them, with the help of some kind of compromise. We must resign ourselves to distinguishing their personalities and their aims while wondering what can possibly motivate such a strange incompatibility.

This has always been the attitude of critics who see Don Quixote as a pure and simple antithesis to Cervantes — which indeed he is at the *obvious* level of fiction — and believe they can reduce the Quixotic riddle to an 'either-or' which abolishes all ambiguity. Either Cervantes' realism is justified and then Don Quixote is condemned outright — he is nothing but a ridiculous, spurious madman who might even, considering his fanaticism, become dangerous — or Don Quixote is right to impose his lofty ideals on the wretched world about him, in which case he must be seen as a mocked saint and Cervantes, constricted by a sadly limited intelligence, as incapable of perceiving the grandeur of his own creation.[5] From the first point of view — far and away the most popular — *Don Quixote* is mainly a satire on a socially noxious vice. From the second it is automatically classified as a vindication or more specifically as a hagiography. Since both opinions appear to be reasonably well-founded and since, naturally enough, there is nothing in the text to provide an outright refutation of either, it is quite impossible to choose between them. But though there seems to be no way of conciliating them — Don Quixote cannot be simultaneously ridiculous and sublime, nor Cervantes a genius and a fool — they agree nonetheless on one point since, based on an identical delusion, they presuppose the hero's *otherness* and the novelist's *objectivity*.

Satire or vindication, according to the character assigned to its hero, Cervantes' novel might well be classified under either of these headings once it was established that it alludes to a specific moral characteristic sufficiently marked, and especially sufficiently common, to be worth stressing. For satire is never directed at a fault or vice completely devoid of statistical value, and neither are virtues vindicated which do not exist at least virtually. In this respect the two radically opposed genres are similar — they invent nothing but simply exaggerate features that may affect society at large, and thus set an example of something to be avoided or emulated. So how does Don Quixote's madness fit in? Whichever way we look at it one thing is certain, and that is that it cannot be diagnosed as an anomaly or virtue currently found among human beings — it is unprecedented and wholly improbable. Indeed many people have a distressing predilection for bad novels, many indulge chimerical hopes for a new Golden Age, and many dream of past eras and firmly believe in their dream, but not even the most deluded visionary has ever thought of forcing living people to behave like story book heroes, no one has ever been crazy enough to actually exchange his existence for printed texts. In spite of the use to which his name is currently put Don Quixote has nothing in common with the righters of wrongs, despotic reformers, mystical ascetics and dotty idealists whose patron he is assumed to be. What mainly distinguishes him from these is the inconceivable 'actually' which sets him beyond every locatable moral or spiritual attitude, at the extreme limit of what is human. Unquestionably eccentric, not as others are misers, liars or doubters, but in such a manner that no typology, no definition can epitomise his quest, the Don is set in the novel as a cipher from some unknown language or the symbol of improbability itself.

Thus insofar as he is a unique specimen of an improbable species Don Quixote belongs neither to caricature nor to a sort of Golden Age wherein, beneath its misleadingly comical appearance, his mournful countenance would be sanctified (indeed the author says from the start that 'Cervantes posits what he never proves', which implies that he refrains both from censuring as satire would require, and from glorifying according to the demands of an apologia). But if he is not drawn from a live model, if he is without precedent in history and unparalleled among describable beings, we must concede that, despite all precautions to make him unrecognisable, he is indeed a product of the author's subjectivity, since there is no other possible alternative for an imaginary creature. Thus we are led to consider the author's loudly proclaimed impartiality from a new angle and to ask ourselves if, well beyond the obvious data of description, the otherness of Don Quixote does not conceal something like a sinister, perhaps a shameful identity.

As we have seen, the novel itself remains obstinately unrevealing on the subject. Nonetheless the odd detail transpires here and there which despite its insignificance — or perhaps on account of its insignificance seems to make certain assumptions permissible. Thus when the narrator alludes to the fatal passion which leads Don Quixote to make his first 'sally', he tells us that the hero, had he not been driven by loftier more compelling thoughts would have liked nothing better than to become a novelist and contribute his share to the kind of literature from which he expects the salvation of humanity. This is a valuable indication which suggests the most intimate of relationships precisely where Cervantes is seemingly most anxious to show that none exists (moreover as a rule nothing reveals better the subjective derivation of a fictional character than his practice of literature or art, even when as in this case it is expressed as a simple desire). Were Don Quixote a thousand times more foreign to his spiritual father than he appears to be at any instant of his ridiculous undertaking, the books he dreams of writing would still abolish the distance and would suffice to stress the similarities and complicities so painstakingly eliminated elsewhere; more especially since these *abortive* books are not just an incidental feature of the tale, but the cause proper of the Quixotic enterprise which is precisely an *imitation* of books. Don Quixote dreams of writing and, for reasons which require elucidating, his dream never evolves from its state of timid velleity (once again in contrast to Robinson who is very much the man of action in such cases). Hence his decision to 'sally forth' and lead a life entirely consistent with his favourite readings — for want of being able to imitate the creators of fictions, the 'faiseurs de roman', he *copies* Amadis and his ilk, the 'famous heroes' he would have liked to extract from his imagination. In this respect he can be seen as the prototype of the novelist who feels that he has not been able to express a literary concept or experiences the frustration of thwarted aspirations.

That this is indeed his role — though the reader may have

some difficulty in perceiving it — there is evidence outside the context of the tale in what we know of Cervantes' attitude to books in general and especially of his secret predilection for the romantic twaddle so ruthlessly taken to task in his masterpiece. Indeed on his own confession the author of *Don Quixote* was a confirmed reader, positively a devourer of books (he says that he 'devoured even the scraps of paper he found in the street'), and in this he is most certainly a brother to his incomparable hero who was so intent on reading that he simply stopped living (Don Quixote is possibly the only character in fiction who could have said with the German poet von Platen on his death bed, that he had not lived his life but merely 'read' it away). Possessing an insatiable appetite for all written and printed matter — even of the worst kind — he has as well a passion for pure romance of the sort that emerges in every age and in all the diverse forms of escapist novel (there is little reason to doubt that he had read the vast number of books Don Quixote boasts of being able to quote from and probably many more he fails to mention). Moreover he was not content with enjoying the sort of book he presumes to despise, but finally let himself be tempted to write them, as *Persiles y Sigismunda* bears witness, where late in life, 'one foot already in the stirrup and experiencing the pangs of death', he gave his imagination free rein, almost as if to challenge his own realism. Written as a vindication of Don Quixote and in a style worthy of his hero, Cervantes' last novel impresses one as being totally inconsistent with his previous output. In fact it sets *Don Quixote* in true perspective, demonstrating, after the event, who the Quixotic demon really was and why he could never be exorcised.

If it is true that Don Quixote, because he never ceased to haunt his creator, came back in *Persiles y Sigismunda* to tempt him, forcing him into self-contradiction, we can see why Cervantes should have been compelled to posit what he never proves. For such a ghost admits neither refutation nor proof; it is impossible to argue with him, he must be either exorcised or accepted, but the best thing is to try and understand him by observing his behaviour (in which case, indeed, he is only 'posited'). Cervantes creates Don Quixote out of an element in his inner self which, being inconsistent, misplaced and totally incompatible with the definable part of his personality, must of necessity elude every attempt at intellectual and moral classification. It is in this sense that the hero is free — having to signify exclusively a split whose cause and gravity no one, not even the person involved, can know, he evades generalisation, assessment and rationalisation. Thus it is pointless to ask if Cervantes the novelist supports or denounces Cervantes - Don Quixote while exposing him to public derision; if he dreads or adores his shameful double; how far the higher processes of his mind are involved with his Quixotic demon, and if he considers him to be good, bad or simply ridiculous. The tale is told precisely to raise such questions without ever answering them and implies, moreover, that they are and must remain unanswerable.

Thus we have to return to the novel to see exactly how Cervantes organises his 'proposition'. Oddly the first character to be mentioned is not the Don at all but a certain Don Quixada or Queseda (or again Quixana — even the name is uncertain) about whom very little is known. Just enough however to enable us to reconstruct his features and circumstances approximately. He is a country gentleman, ruddy, lanky, with a thin face, an early riser and keen hunter who lives frugally on the produce of his unprofitable soil in boredom and idleness. A bachelor by choice or necessity — he was once in love with a certain Alonsa Lorenzo but never dared declare himself — Don Quixada has no other relation than a niece who, assisted by a housekeeper, keeps him reasonably comfortable, and no other company than the village curate and barber. Though poor he is far from needy and could go on living his restricted life devoid of tragedy or history until his death. Nothing, it seems, has ever happened to him; he has been excluded — or has excluded himself — from worldly events and should normally remain in this position since he is not really cut out for action of any kind. He possesses none of the attributes that make a hero interesting, nor is his life story worth telling; free from any notable vice or virtue a good fellow like so many others and like so many others wholly insignificant, Don Quixada is in no way the sort of person to play an historical role, nor has he the slightest chance of being remembered by his contemporaries. He has however one fatal singularity: his passion for romances of chivalry which, at the age of fifty or so makes him suddenly abandon his former existence and undergo a complete metamorphosis. Transformed into Don Quixote by virtue of the name he has chosen and the various attributes advertising his mission, Don Quixada condemns himself to oblivion (he will reappear only to die after Don Quixote has finally acknowledged his aberration). Thus the Don only exists through his inventor's suicide; engendered by death, death is his law, he is a phantom caught in the void whose every undertaking is fatally tainted with failure (in this respect he is the mirror image of Dürer's *Death and the Knight* but in a comic mood, since he only brings into the world an imaginary destruction the world derides). Don Quixote murders Don Quixada without being able to acquire in the process a true substance. Thus he is, from the start, an embodiment of pure imagination who, entirely free from further intellectual requirements, metaphysically murders life without benefit to the ideal or detriment to reality. On the other hand he releases in Don Quixada explosive forces which he would never have suspected in his former state; thus in the void where he must incessantly circle he nonetheless instigates rebellion and allows extremism to come out into the open, while his very existence is proof that the craziest dream is the most indestructible.

Don Quixote's advent reveals the omnipotence of desire — and the desire of omnipotence — peculiar to childish imagination. At fifty, the Don who has become the child he always was at heart, regresses to the psychic age of the little frustrated being, both loving and full of hatred and resentment, whose conflicting aspirations can only be resolved in a total recasting of his circumstances. We know nothing of his parents — he probably has none (the tale tactfully relieves him of such an encumbrance so that he may be free from the social and emotional directives to which the individual must constantly submit) — but all his undertakings reveal an unbending will to disown all kinship. Indeed he is an apostle of rejection, a being dropped from the sky who claims to be self-generated and without human kin (which does not stop him from enthusing over fictitious families whose actions are the subject of his beloved romances, nor, while disowning his ancestry, from relishing genealogies). Child of a supreme act of the imagination which created him out of nothing with his name, his Squire, his horse and all the epic 'apparatus' required for his strange crusade, Don Quixote realises stage by stage the Foundling's megalomaniac programme. But he does so as no other hero of world literature has ever dared, without making any concessions whatsoever to common sense or hesitating at the extreme limits of negation.

Indeed there does not exist in the entire history of the novel another such obstinately rebellious Foundling (even the fairy-tale youth is more realistic since his quest's inevitably happy ending forces him to finally toe the line). This completely unattached being on the threshhold of old age regresses to the most primitive thought processes and recognises none of the concessions fiction generally makes to credibility (the most fantastic story has to be credible, either by presenting, in spite of its absurdity, some means of identifying with the protagonists, or by encapsulating a 'symbolic' message in the absurdity of the plot). He will admit nothing but the 'make believe' of his hopeless ambition and the 'let's pretend' of childhood games. From the day he decrees that his favourite books are literally true and that he and no other has been chosen to accomplish here and now what heroes do on the printed page, nothing that he has learnt, experienced and perceived with his five senses can stop him from pursuing his ends. All that which lies before his eyes is foreign to him; he neither sees, hears nor understands anything that tallies with reality. Men are worth whatever he wants to give for them, objects are what he calls them and society is what he creates by distributing titles, distinctions, values and qualities. Even nature, now pliable to his will, becomes spontaneously unpredictable to prove his point. Within this identification of literature with life that rejects experience in favour of an *annotated reading*, every inn is a castle, the slut or the prostitute are great ladies and the worst bandit is a valiant knight — all these transformations are permanent, magically performed and unquestionable. Only the approach of death will succeed in cancelling them (though even then it is not easy to make Don Quixote renounce the crack-brained notions he clings to until his last breath). The spell-binder who binds himself to boost his wounded ego — not to mention further benefits he hopes to obtain — has the obvious advantage of being able to forget everything he has learnt, possibly at his own expense, during fifty years of a former undistinguished existence, consumed with rancour and humiliation. This is what enables him to bring the Family Romance back to its earliest stage of infantile innocence and, once fixated in this falsely uninformed pattern which superficially restores his purity of heart, to set out unrepentant in quest of supreme power and its attendant regeneration.

However much he tries to gloss over this aspect of his mission — the programme he has set himself never states it specifically — the desire to be a king is nonetheless the principal motive for his odyssey. He even admits that a single kingdom is not enough — he wants a great many which he will conquer in no time at all wherever the occasion may arise. To the servant he has promoted to squiredom he confides that in six days he might well have possessed himself of some kingdom with others subjected to it, which would come in very handy for the said squire who could be crowned king of one of them. Thus he wins the world in six days (implying that he will perhaps, like God, rest on the seventh). For he is not only intended for the highest honours but is also entitled to graciously bestow them, as befits the all-powerful dream master whose words have the magic power of becoming fact (let it be said in passing that he knows that one cannot invoke another's Family Romance but beguiles Sancho by showing him his own romance as if it were already realised). Even the Foundling never fostered such improbable hopes — but Don Quixote is really immoderation incarnate and thus is not content with wishing to reign immediately and everywhere, he must do so for the benefit of humanity.

As children make use of the stories they read to bolster and enrich the stories they tell themselves in secret, so Don Quixote bases his dream of omnipotence on the entertaining romances, part fairy tale, part heroic, which he devours as an antidote to boredom. At least in this respect he shows some discernment, for in his day romances of chivalry were a sort of fairy tale for grown-ups, a tall tale which from a certain point of view might even seem more disorganised, crude and retrograde than the simple folk tale. Whereas the fairy tale only uses supernatural devices insofar as they are required to enable the child to grow up, and never neglects the warm reality of human relationships nor the dignity of real objects, the romance of chivalry is remarkable for its total disregard for contingencies and for its taste for the monstrous hyperbole and the gratuitously supernatural which greatly detract from its literary value reducing it, more or less, to an intellectual self-indulgence.

By a stroke of genius never to be equalled in literature — though our best writers will always see it as a worthy example — Cervantes hitches the Family Romance of his ageing incurable child to the type of story best suited to further its ambitious cause. Indeed the two romances present striking similarities and might be seen as variations on a single theme — even to the chivalric notion of a liberating hero, righter of wrongs and protector of the downtrodden, which is not foreign to the daydreams of many normal children and neurotic adults.[6] In both cases the main point is to abolish an apparently odious present so as to restore a happy past. Not, of course, the recorded past of history, but a mythical 'once upon a time' which, for the individual is the puerile realm where wishes come true and, for society, the golden age of anarchy (the romance of chivalry is further related to the past in that, in Cervantes' day, it was already out of date and no longer read at all except by those who yearned for 'the days of yore')[7]. Amadis, Palmerin and their ilk who have completely turned Don Quixote's head are not called Knights Errant for nothing — they are indeed homeless vagabonds who wander through time and space, freed by special dispensation from the laws of society and of nature alike. Able to travel great distances in the twinkling of an eye and to take every obstacle in their stride, they are above reality in every respect, superior to common mortals, immune to fatigue, ageing and need. Never are they seen to eat or provide for their own welfare; their strength and courage are preserved in the worst possible conditions and they suffer the most deadly wounds without fatal consequences. They are miraculously exempted, moreover, from everyday cares, oblivious to labour and money. Since they are not affiliated to any established order or brotherhood they have no hierarchical superior to obey, and their vocation consists precisely in their freedom from any kind of authority. They own no land but the world is theirs. They go over hill and vale in quest of pointless ventures that earn them imperishable honours, and in spite of the fact that their exploits are of no use to anybody, nature defers its laws to enable a single one of them to overcome thousands and to throw himself at the feet of an equally superhuman beloved (unless he happens to be ranked among the 'baddies' from the outset, in which case his absolute power and all it involves is affected by a negative sign). In short they enjoy all the advantages, liberties and power their humble imitator so sadly lacks — whence the irresistable influence they exert over him and his faith in their ability to further his progress towards a status similar to theirs.

Unlike that of most fictional characters, Don Quixote's mind is never divided (division is not within himself but between him and his creator). No one could be less prone to self-questioning, to those 'storms in the skull' to which novels are generally so partial; where others come to life in the doubts, hesitations and shillyshallying accompanying introspection, he is notable for the unswerving determination with which he heads for disaster. Since his role is to impersonate a conflict that words cannot express, to be a gigantic 'pro' against the 'cons' he has rejected, he must of necessity be presented as an impenetrable block inaccesssible both to deep introspection and to the superficial fluctuation of thought. Since his personality cannot be split — being the product of an earlier split — he has to go straight for his goal without stopping to think or even to avoid the cruellest attacks aimed at him by the 'opposition'. True, such steadfastness inevitably leads to destruction, and his freedom appears to have no other purpose than to enable him to die in bitter disillusionment. But in the meantime he can clearly expose, to his heart's content, the huge fantasies born of childish pride which are never otherwise exposed to full daylight.[8]

Thanks to the total freedom he enjoys Don Quixote is ideally suited to become spokesman for the Foundling whose rebellion against the 'Thou shalt' of the adult world is motivated by despair and wounded pride. He espouses the same cause, expresses the same incapacity to live and the same refusal to change — except that he never shies at excess and that, rather than come to terms with reality as the young inventor of the Family Romance is inevitably compelled to do, he carries on regardless. We may suppose that during part of his life Don Quixote has imagined all sorts of triumphant revenges, but at fifty there is no time left for dreams (this physiological turning point is presented here as a returning point: the ageing immature hero finds his forward progress obstructed and can only turn back towards the past), he must either admit defeat or pass once and for all on to the 'other side' where his compensatory avenging dream completely obliterates reality. Whereas the child still hopes to win on both scores — regain his self-esteem by crowning himself with imaginary glory while simultaneously learning to live so as to acquire his share of effective power — the Knight of Impossible Utopia has absolutely nothing to lose. That is why his rebellion exceeds every conceivable absurdity, exceeds in fact the limits which even the most introvert Foundling, so long as he is not insane, imposes automatically on his daydream.

Consumed by shame and resentment for his insignificance, foreseeing that he must shortly die as obscurely as he has lived, Don Quixote unhesitatingly challenges the rebellious child's worst enemy: the present, the age of reason or 'Iron Age' as he calls it — a terrible age indeed which, characterised by the need to discriminate, calculate, define and acknowledge the boundaries of reality, constantly stresses the humiliating fact that he is a failure. What he decides one fine day as he sets out from home without informing anyone of his intention (understandably enough since such decisions are not communicable) is precisely to extricate himself for ever from the abominable present so that he may abolish once and for all, not only his pitiful personal history, but the whole history of mankind together with its suffering and toil. The Iron Age is evil, hard and trivial. It is opposed in every respect to the primal Golden Age when man, as yet unacquainted with necessity, sex and discrimination in general, was naturally good, just, unacquisitive, ungoverned by the laws of chronology and thus immortal. A happy time indeed, that Golden Age. All was peace, friendliness, agreement. The 'heavy blade of the bent plough had not yet penetrated Mother Earth's sacred womb', and she bestowed freely on all alike the produce of her fertile, capacious bosom so that the children who then possessed her might be sustained, regaled and inebriated. This idyllic vision of life on earth before the intervention of agricultural civilisation — peace, harmony and the communal possession of the virgin, fertile mother by all her children who effortlessly feed on her produce — is not a particularly original concept. It contains the commonplaces of a mythology of origins and the 'eternal' theme of Utopias where actual man — or adult man — is seen as fallen, guilty and corrupted by the so-called progress of a purely material culture (later it will be dubbed 'materialistic' but the indictments will be more or less the same). However if it is true that Don Quixote's Golden Age is entirely conventional Cervantes is misguided in saying that we could well do without it (infringing for once his pact of neutrality), for it is here, precisely, that convention is most revealing: it shows unequivocally whence the notion of Paradise derives and why Edenic peace is always associated with a lack of civilisation — just as innocence is associated with primal communality and beatitude with total inactivity. Judging from his long Hesiodic tirade on that 'happy time', Don Quixote is well acquainted with the Golden Age myth (or with its substitutes in a historical age): it is a time of ineffable bliss when the new-born child has still complete possession of an unclaimed Mother-Earth with her 'sacred womb' as yet unviolated by the virile plough. And the Iron Age starts with the reign of the active, resourceful father, labourer schemer and legislator rolled into one, who after daring to desecrate Mother-Earth has set himself up as supreme arbitrator for the distribution of women and land. Agricultural, sedentary and, because of the activities and notions it fosters, inevitably unjust, patriarchal civilisation is responsible for every form of violence and evil. It leads man astray and the more he is convinced of his progress the further he wanders from instinctive understanding and from what formerly represented the truth. Since Hesiod endowed it with a mythic formula, such a critique of civilisation — basic already to Biblical prophecy — is familiar to a long tradition of intellectual rebels. It is to be found more or less unchanged in the Utopian reformers, Millenarian agitators and Romantic poets who inveigh periodically against the present age or preach a return to primal simplicity (trade and industry may be the 'villains' instead of agriculture, but though the cause of evil changes, the fundamental concept never alters)[9]. However Don Quixote does not merely reformulate the traditional notion of two human epochs: he provides it with an explanatory note thus crudely revealing the Utopia's latent significance. For if the act of raping a mother is identical to that of violating the soil with the 'heavy blade of the bent plough' as

Don Quixote implies in his daring metaphor, then sexual act and agricultural labour are one and the same thing, and civilisation is cursed as the product of the generating father who set history in motion. It must be classed with sin and discrimination since, having forced upon the world the dual calamity — sexuality and the appropriation of land — it irredeemably dissolves the infant's union with the mother's 'sacred womb', that perfect union and sinless incest which, according both to collective myth and individual dream, stands for the communion of all with all and ensures universal love.

Since Don Quixote cannot make history regress to the first days of creation — which he would certainly not hesitate to do had he an adequate literary model at his disposal — he is only too willing to plunder the ample resources Knight Errantry has to offer. For if the Knight errant does not seem particularly apt to bring back prelapsarian peace, he possesses nonetheless, insofar as he is a totally marginal figure, all the features required as a righter of universal wrongs. Insofar as he is errant he is without land or wealth and has only his horse and the weapons he uses to defend the downtrodden orphan and widow. As a knight he cultivates an ideology of love which forbids him to exploit women, and though love is the main interest in his life, he must remain single and worship the Lady of his dreams on bended knees in total submission and humility. His title makes it immediately clear that he is free from the two major sins which contaminate the actions of settled men. Thus he is peculiarly apt to repair the evils caused by sexual covetousness and its economic equivalent, acquisitiveness. Never mind if he then indulges his combative disposition — he fights the Iron Age with iron, which alone will heal its wounds — the one thing that matters is that, insofar as he is unmarried and possesses nothing, he should provide a readymade part for his imitator as that epitome of disinterestedness, the avenging warrior. In fact by assuming the role of infallible arbitrator preserved from sexual and economic guilt who redeems suffering humanity at his own cost, Don Quixote instantly acquires epic proportions totally incongruous with the nature of his ambition — he becomes for future generations the pure hero dedicated to a lost but sublime cause; absurd, maybe, but everlasting as the need for justice and noble as the endless quest for truth. This is doubtless the most successful aspect of his enterprise, for however much one may question his aims and purposes, whether one takes him for a madman or a saint, nobody is aware of the tremendous claim for power he disguises as ascetic idealism, nor that his legendary courtesy stems from a blend of very dubious emotions.

The antinomy between mythical and actual time which is the true subject of Cervantes' masterpiece might well have inspired him to write a classical satire exposing the hidden flaws of a given society seen through the eyes of an unsophisticated dreamer; or else the reactions of a rational, active community to an irresponsible visionary's onslaughts. However he takes the precaution to warn the reader that he intends to posit without proving — in other words that the novel involves a dual satire drawing us in two opposite directions and providing no moralistic guidelines. Since Cervantes allows his shamefaced double to repeatedly defy reality, he must also respect the antagonistic world's right to go its own way as it pleases and restore the balance as best it can ('In your conflict with the world always back the world' says Kafka in a paradoxical aphorism that plumbs the depths of all true Quixotism). There is nothing to stop Don Quixote from fighting against windmills in compliance with the clear dictates of his desire. But neither can the blows that rain down on him from all sides be avoided. The faithful reporter can do nothing to stop them; his task is limited to stage-managing the sequence of conflicts between the lonely knight and the world or, to adopt the tone of the novel, to be the 'magician' who sets the comedy in motion. Thus the two opponents continue to confront each other until the consequences of their antinomy are completely exhausted: Don Quixote is so constituted that he can concede nothing in respect to faith — he must accept every blow without a murmur, almost without noticing, since his sickness consists precisely in his inability or refusal to learn from experience. But the world is no less stubborn. It automatically chastises the recalcitrant, regardless of rights or wrongs, opposing to every onslaught its immediacy and, quite indifferent to moral standards, the irrefutable weight of living reality. Transgression here does not properly entail either retaliation or prosecution — it is punished by the blind apparatus of reality whose sanctions are never delayed. For between the self-deified genius's absolutism and the relativism of an opaque trivial, brutal present inaccessible to moral and spiritual arguments, there is really no possibility either of open conflict, of arbitration or of compromise. Each opponent must get on as best he can till the time when a choice becomes inevitable and when the evader of reality must pay *bodily* for the illusions of his inflated Ego.

The story of Don Quixote reflects in its very structure the comic situation (fundamentally tragic but having a comic effect, as the more recent writers it has inspired have realised), where an incorrigible visionary, armed with nothing but his own breath — that is to say with words — battles against the imperturbable course of established events that are, by nature, impervious to the recriminations of the imagination. The rebel trying to take evidence by storm ignores what confronts him, but the world scoffs at what is going on in his addled brain and simply *corrects* him (in the double sense of rectifying and punishing), by setting in motion the mechanisms which enable it to function and thus to last. (Don Quixote is further *corrected* in that through his blunders he comes in contact with what is most abhorrent to him: he avoids physical love and is knighted by a prostitute; he despises physicality and is continually reminded of his own body by the blows he receives; he loathes substance and has his nose rubbed in the most objectionable substances). Such automatic corrections of uncorrigibility dominate the structure of the story from start to finish — Don Quixote inhabits a no-man's-land he peoples with imaginary beings and objects, while the remainder of the fictional population occupies normal space where the ripostes, trials and countertrials of reality get under way. The two systems do not communicate, each asserts its superiority and believes it is itself a sufficient refutation of the other up to the point when their violent collision puts an end to all the hero's adventures without, however, reducing him to repentance. For Don Quixote can no more renounce blurring the frontiers of dream and reality than reality can halt for his benefit the inevitable sequence of its events. Thus the novel, which consists not in a series of progressive episodes, but in a system of duplicates having identical meanings, incessantly turns in its inexorable circle of repetitions. Here the narrative is split up to suit the meaning: having to express the split which the eternal recurrence of the same unattainable dream creates in Cervantes, the novel is split in half and, instead of progressing it marks time like its crazy hero who believes he can annihilate reality with the all-powerful weapon of thought.

Thus the bright Hidalgo's adventures are all made to fit the same pattern. None of them represents an advance in the action's development nor draws the tale into unforeseen complications. Be it his famous confrontation with windmills, his tussle with muleteers, his massacre of Master Peter's puppets or his attack on wine-skins, Don Quixote always begins by assaulting things and people — totally harmless objects and people who are completely unconcerned with him, going quietly about their business or simply having a good time — with a violence which casts some doubt on his alleged gentleness and kindness. For we tend to forget — and this ability to induce oblivion is typical of fanatical idealism — that Don Quixote the Good, as he calls himself in the end, is on every occasion the unscrupulous aggressor and brutal trouble-maker who, though frequently compelled to plunge his sword into thin air, inflicts nonetheless considerable damage to persons and their possessions. He really and truly slays the two muleteers whom he does not hesitate to strike down because they dared approach his weapons in order to water their animals — at least there is no mention of their ever rising again, and the Good Knight has not so much as a thought for them. Neither does he ever think of making amends for the havoc his heroic interventions create (logically he has no cause to worry, since real objects do not exist for him it makes no difference whether they are whole or damaged). He never pays for his board and lodging, treats Sancho live a slave and considers the honour of enduring what he does for such a master sufficient reward. In fact he is generally assured that everything is due to him simply because he makes so much fuss about his own disinterestedness (his argument is that of the uncompromising idealist confronted with materialistic demands: money means nothing to me so it can mean nothing to you and therefore I do not have to repay you). Brave — or rather a braggart — in words, Don Quixote is a coward when faced with positive danger — the faithful Sancho is molested under his very eyes without his doing anything to protect him, and he who joyfully challenges whole armies of Giants is routed by the sound of a treadmill. He is good, noble and generous in theory but in practice aggressive, indifferent to the suffering of others and unbearably despotic. Though the very unreality of his aims renders him relatively innocuous and harmless, whenever he takes it into his head to meddle with positive events he invariably wreaks havoc (Andrew, the serving-lad he tries to save from his cruel master learns the hard way what sort of a righter of wrongs he is: he suffers such hardship at the Don's 'mercy' that he infinitely prefers the worst oppressor with whom at least the oppressed can have a realistic relationship insofar as his physical needs are concerned). Indeed all his ostentatiously angelic virtues have a fiendish side to them — or more precisely they are only another aspect of his fatal incapacity to cope with life. Thus he does not really represent the insatiable purity of ideality he is supposed to stand for, but on the contrary, a satanism achieved through a total dissociation of experience and thought.

Nonetheless if Don Quixote is far from being the innocent martyr we take him for, neither is the world that condemns him as blameless as it would have us believe. It lacks both the reliability and the irrefutable logic with which reality presumes to oppose the insubstantiality of dreams. Indeed to what sort of a world does this most recalcitrant of heroes finally have to submit, and what rights has it to back its self-assurance? The men and women who people it constitute a very mixed society sharing quite a few of the features that make the Don a laughing stock. Doubtless we have here the very criterion of reality which it is Don Quixote's mission to flout — in other words such people are able to weigh objects, calculate their price, date them, sell or buy them, thus apparently conforming at least in practice to the laws of logic. But in every other respect they are remarkably Quixotic — they are mainly adventurers (in the best and the worst sense) impelled to wander about the world for various reasons. The courteous Hidalgos, love-sick shepherds, unemployed soldiers, escaped prisoners and criminals on the run whom the Don encounters on his travels are no less imbued with romance than he is. Many — notably the Priest and the Barber who try in vain to bring him back to reason — share his disastrous passion for romances of chivalry. From one end of the hierarchic spectrum to the other, from the pandering

Inn-Keeper to Gines of Passamont the convict writer, everybody dabbles in Belles-Lettres, chance companions tell each other stories and sing songs together and so long as Don Quixote sticks to literature his eccentric ramblings are welcome to all and sundry. They all enjoy fine words and tragic tales of men who fight and die for love, except perhaps for the very few — muleteers, servants, farm-hands — who, in the novel represent the seamy side of labour. But then, as Don Quixote says, that is the point: for although this simultaneously refined and cynical society — refined in its upper spheres and cynical in the lower strata — adheres in theory to the Quixotic ideal of nobility and generosity, it has not the slightest inclination to practise it — indeed it subsists precisely by refraining from acting according to what it preaches. Adorned with words, phrases and highfalutin opinions no one wants to see practised, this society has no more truth than the natural share that all concrete organisms possess: it is physically true (Sancho Panza always coincides with his own truth even when he lies), but false in its attempts at moral justifications which invariably disguise its self-seeking intentions. High society, Lords and Ladies, slatterns, rustics and ruffians, indeed all those who come in contact with Don Quixote, believe in poetry, the Good, the Beautiful and the Ideal. But such a faith is in no way binding; it is good form to *cultivate* such entities while being careful to exclude them from the serious concerns of life. Thus Don Quixote, who actually wants to put into practice all those great hollow words that are so useful both as a sop to our guilty consciences and as a cover for our misdeeds, creates a truly impossible situation which compels the world to face up to its own hypocrisy.

Don Quixote's unreality is thus finally conducive to the truth since it reveals the basic imposture of all organised societies. But on the other hand society, behind the cultural ideological facade masking its selfish motives, is not entirely wrong since it exposes the infantilism and impotence of fanatical, idealistic insubordination. Alongside the discordant world in whose assumed idealism he believes Don Quixote doubtless stands out as a visionary (in the marvellous incident at Montesino's cave we see him actually spellbound by his own absurd and possibly invented visions, exactly like the prophet or poet every culture elects as spiritual guide). Which does not stop him from being in fact a dangerous void where the seeds of an eminently attractive — though nonetheless basically corrupt and historically doomed — spirituality abound. Such is the paradox on which Cervantes' admirable criticism of ideas is based and which, in that extraordinary summing-up, the Quixotic Gesture[10] is all he gives us by way of morality.

★

Cervantes' remarkable neutrality in matters where writers usually assert their opinions — the significance of life, individual and social ethics, political and religious beliefs, contemporary events — has always puzzled the critic. Why was he always 'in disguise', like the philosopher, so that after centuries of research even the most astute scholars are still baffled? Doubtless under the Inquisition writers necessarily tended to dissemble; simple self-preservation would require a certain amount of reticence in the expression of ideas, opinions had to be devious and only throve insofar as they succeeded in being so. But Cervantes was not content with dissimulating opinions that might be seen as subversive — which would already have been hard enough considering the religious tribunal's aptitude for detecting the slightest trace of heresy. There was not an issue he did not confuse, adopting in turn or simultaneously the most irreconcilable viewpoints as though he had the gift of perceiving at all times the relative truth of another's error and the relative fallacy of his own judgement. A strange tendency, indeed, pertaining both to humour — insofar as it is based on a casuistry of pros and cons taken to the limits of the absurd — and to a detachment probably unequalled by any fictional writer of significance (except Kafka to whom its systematic development finally proved fatal). Caution imposed by the Inquisition would surely not inspire such ambiguity; but how otherwise are we to account for the risky strategy he adopted of considering everything from a dual intellectual angle, which resulted in so many contradictions? It has been suggested that Cervantes had a natural taste for mystification, or that by expressing conflicting opinions without feeling the need to reconcile them he wished to confront his readers with the relativity of so-called weighty ideas, either to make them laugh at ideas in general or to lead them, through laughter, to an attitude of uninhibited enquiry. Or again this peculiarity is said to denote pure and simple inconsistency, not to say stupidity; which harks back to the old theory of the 'povere uomo', the simpleton — reactionary into the bargain — incapable of perceiving the significance of his visions.[11] Of late the tendency is towards a more subtle theory, unfortunately impossible to substantiate in the present state of documentation, but eminently plausible and sufficiently pertinent to require serious consideration. According to experts[12] Cervantes was one of those Christianised Jews who, in Spain during the Inquisition, lived under the constant threat of persecution, dreading denunciation and forced to resort to all manner of ruse and duplicity. There may be no single undisputed evidence of such a fact in his biography but on the other hand it would not be surprising if it were true. The convert — or Marrano — could only survive by trickery — first by falsifying his civil status and then by eliminating from his daily life anything that might reveal the 'blemish' (and any number of things could give him away at a time when to omit barding a chicken was proof that one observed Muslim or Jewish alimentary taboos). Thus there is no evidence one way or the other, for there is absolutely no proof either that the author of *Don Quixote* was of 'old Christian' stock. The certificate of 'unblemished descent' he had to produce in 1593 certainly proves nothing and nor does anybody suppose that it does. First because 'unblemished descent' is meaningless in scientific terms; and further because such certificates, required for the performance of any civil action whatsoever, could be obtained by privileged persons either with hard cash or by the intervention of a patron. It is obviously impossible to estimate the number of Muslim or Jewish converts who were able thus to foil Inquisitorial vigilance, but it was probably very great. At any rate foreign antisemites imagined it to be so high that they practically ceased to include Spain among European states (Erasmus said there was barely a single Christian to be found there). In such circumstances it is at least likely that Cervantes, as so many other undetected converts, was not entirely free from 'blemish'.

If instead of basing conjecture on doubtful biographical

evidence one examines Cervantes' own writings and the prominence he gives to the many dramatic situations arising from
a dual religious allegiance, scholars believe that the possibility
becomes indeed far from remote. Doubtless the vicissitudes of
converts and crypto-religions were painfully topical to a lot of
his contemporaries. They were mere platitudes in the literature of the time and fiction exploited them to the full, since
clandestinity, which is their main characteristic, provides all
sorts of fascinating situations and emotional complications
(for instance the thwarted or at least temporarily frustrated
love-affair). But in Cervantes' work they recur with an almost
obsessive regularity which seems to suggest a deeper and quite
other involvement than that of pure convention. For he does
not simply follow the normal trend and select some of his
heroes from the ranks of questionable Spanish subjects whose
private lives and public misfortunes were 'interesting' — he
provides Don Quixote with all the insecurity proper to the
pseudo-convert's existence. For example he pretends — not
without a certain drollery, but we know the nature of the soil
from which his drollery draws its substance — that he wants to
forget all about the village of la Mancha[13] where his hero was
born, thus assimilating the latter to the extensive class of
harassed individuals whose birthplace could not be mentioned
without revealing their shameful extraction and simultaneously exposing them to the most dreadful consequences. Moreover Don Quixote's civil status is riddled with anomalies, for
if his birthplace is a blank his surnames, on the other hand, are
legion — our hero can boast three: Quixana, Quijada,
Quesada to which Cervantes adds for good measure or perhaps inadvertently, Quixano. And in the end he exchanges his
questionable identity for a 'rare and significant' pseudonym —
that is to say a name with typically Spanish connotations 'like
all those he has bestowed on his equipment' — in order that his
real surname will have no chance of ever coming to light.
Furthermore among the three or four names that could be
attributed to him scholars have discovered that of a real Jewish
family, the Quijadas, whom Cervantes can only have mentioned wittingly since his own wife was related to them.
Associated at least indirectly with a certain Alonso Quijada
who was said to be unpopular in Spain because of his alleged
Jewish antecedents, Don Quixote has a further motive for

trying to cover his tracks: he is among those who have too many names because their real one is unmentionable and who falsify their civil status because otherwise their lives would be intolerable. Now we can see why the Don, usually only too ready to correct his Squire's blunders, holds his tongue whenever Sancho boasts about being an 'Old Christian' — which he is most wont to do, peppering his boasts with violent antisemitic attacks — and why he can only oppose high-minded generalities to repeated slanders against a race to which he is apparently linked. Thus he asserts that if blood is our inheritance, virtue on the other hand is acquired and therefore worth more — a democratic notion indeed, eminently subversive in the eyes of a theocratic society and, furthermore, perfectly consistent with the Foundling's wishes, but which, from a Don Quijada - Don Quixote betrays besides the revengeful, compulsively ambitious pariah.[14]

Insofar as Cervantes wants to lead his reader on to forbidden ground without, however, running the risk of being too explicit, he obviously cannot overtly implicate the Jews. Thus his converts are never Hebrews but Muslims and they provide an apt substitute for the compatriots he dare not mention. Nonetheless at one point he very nearly gives himself away, namely when he talks about the imaginary author of *Don Quixote* Cid Hamet Benengeli, and how he, Cervantes, had obtained the manuscript.[15] Cid Hamet, the Castilianised Moor who has long been acknowledged as a purely fictitous Arab, might well represent the Jewish convert to whom it would be too risky to ascribe the book's authorship — especially as Cervantes asserts elsewhere that he bought the manuscript at what seemed to him a very high price in a Jewish quarter of Toledo famed for its second-hand dealers and junk-shops. Since 'bought' in the context can only stand for 'wrote', the scrawl bought for hard cash in such an unorthodox neighbourhood leads one to suppose that the imaginary Arab writer is not there just for local colour but rather to conceal a real Jewish writer.

But I repeat, none of this is conclusive enough to warrant a definitive solution to the problem Cervantes, by choice or necessity, left unanswered. Neither the transparent allusions to Don Quixote's conversion, nor the satire overtly directed against the laws of unblemished descent to be found, for instance, in *El Retablo de los Maravillas*, nor even claims to freedom such as those pathetically expressed by the 'Captain' in the romantic interlude, prove irrefutably that when Cervantes dealt with such themes he was really referring to his own case and speaking in his own name or that of a clandestine group to which he belonged by birth and to which, in spite of the baptism excluding him, he still belonged. It is easy to imagine that, apart from any ethnic or religious involvement, he was one of the champions for the struggle against discrimination and intolerance who, in his day, had already begun to emerge all over Europe (although his inconsistencies — notably on the subject of converts and crypto-religions — cast such a veil of ambiguity over his opinions that some writers have seen him as utterly conformist or even antisemitic.[16] But the hypothesis of the converted Jew is, nonetheless, the only valid explanation for an intellectual stance that baffles interpretation and which we have always tended to shelve by seeing it either as a sign of his genius or as sheer irresponsibility. But a link between Cervantes and Marranism would provide a motive for the great tolerance of other people's opinions, the almost abnormal refusal to decide and to judge which enables the novelist, without overtly asserting his convictions, to see clearly while remaining uncertain of the validity of his intellectual choices.[17] Indeed the new Christian was necessarily divided between two languages, two faiths and two cultures, fully belonging to neither and never totally at one with his official status. A Jew by extraction and a Spaniard by the simple fact of being baptised, he could observe those who were still, in spite of everything, his kin with that mixture of aversion, suspicion and scorn proper to the Catholic he now was. On the other hand as a semi-'Castilianised' citizen he naturally considered his Spanish compatriots with the ruthless, undeluded clear-sightedness of the Jew whose trustfulness has been sapped by centuries of persecution. Because of this compulsory split his true individuality, such as it had been bequeathed to him by his ancestral patrimony, never coincided with the social reality historical circumstances had created for him. The former, whilst genuine, had to be disowned or at least concealed, the latter, exhibited for all to see, was at best no more than a legal fiction. The arbitrariness of such a predicament created a sense of unreality which pervaded his whole existence; but on the other hand it made him see everything under two totally conflicting aspects so that from the depth of his distorted being he could enjoy the somewhat doubtful advantage of utter impartiality.

Such a two-way existence fits in perfectly with what we know of Cervantes' cast of mind. But from our point of view it has this further significance of providing profound motivations for the Quixotic attitude. To a child born in the Spain of 1547 of certified or simply suspected Jewish parents, the biographical reconstructions customary to the Family Romance would exert a positively irresistible attraction; for in such a case invention would not simply be permissable; the instinct of self-preservation would make it practically compulsory. To disown parents who are in fact responsible for our humiliating circumstances and who have, even if unwillingly, themselves been guilty of a kind of disavowal; to invent a more impressive genealogy when we can see around us the terrible consequences of acknowledging our true antecedents; to take refuge in the irresponsibility of daydreams when reality is so absurd and threatening that it forces us to split ourselves in two — what could be more natural and what more tempting, especially when one considers mankind's innate tendency to make believe? In an age and in a society where everyone is obsessed with 'unblemished descent' and where the simplest official deed requires certificates and duly authenticated genealogical documents — historians can quote at least one occasion when Cervantes had to produce such a document — children, who at the best of times are powerfully intrigued by their own origins, would naturally feel more urgently than elsewhere the need to indulge their fantasies and continue to do so long after, in more normal circumstances, the mythomaniac age would have been outgrown. Confronted with a social system entirely based on racial distinctions, with the official creation of renegades enjoying a compulsory status and an ambiguous identity, and with all the fraudulence attendant on such a system, the contemporary Bastard, living in perpetual dread of being forced to the bottom of the social scale if he cannot reach the summit, finds himself urged in every way to pursue his Oedipal rejection to the bitter end; while simultaneously the unreality created by an all-powerful theocracy, blind both to individual psychic tendencies and to the practical requirements

of existence, would intensify the Foundling's total disregard
for what is, as well as his obsessive belief in the possibility and
the necessity of really reaching the 'other side'.

Whichever way the problem of Cervantes' extraction may
finally be solved, one thing at least is certain: his masterpiece's
Foundling, the innocent, the exemplary Don Quixote spontaneously self-generated so as to recreate himself and the
world as he would like them to be, could not have been born
elsewhere than in this world, itself disintegrating, itself made
unreal by its faith in bloodthirsty daydreams and itself guilty
of one of the most heinous crimes against rationality ever
recorded in history.

★

The lanky figure of Don Quixote casts such a powerful
shadow over the whole novel that we naturally tend to see
nothing else, as if all the rest were peripheral to the story — a
mere ornamental backdrop. In the critical perspective Cervantes provides, this is an optical illusion deliberately created
to isolate the Foundling (just as Defoe isolates Robinson
Crusoe till he has learnt to cope with life), and protect him
from the Bastard's corrupting influence. The barrier between
the Don and his various permanent or transitory companions
has to be impassible — primarily to ensure the continuity of
the story — but further because the narrative must follow,
from start to finish, the principle of dichotomy on which its
structure is based. Confronting a hero entirely made up out of
Cervantes' utopian desires — desires he wilfully exteriorised in
order to observe them impartially and thus neutralise their
fatal consequences — the characters we rightly call incidental
all represent the novelist in his capacity as social man, man
involved in the passions and conflicts of history, man in love,
ambitious, even somewhat idealistic, but basically realistic and
active. In other words, confronting the Foundling stranded in
his unrealisable dream, we have a milling crowd of Bastards
who come forward one after the other to recount their wars
and their love affairs, the hazards of fortune and the struggle to
survive. Cardenio, Chrysostomus, the Curious Fool who
wants to witness in person his best friend's sexual intercourse

with his own beloved, these jealous, unhealthily inquisitive characters, these soldiers pressed into the army, who all hold Don Quixote spellbound with their stories — without however inducing him to join their ranks — are devotees of the ambiguous Bastard whose tremendous vivacity Cervantes knew how to exploit. For the author of *Don Quixote* might, like many another — and as so many after him — have written the Oedipal story of 'sacred marriage couches flowing with red blood' — indeed he did so superlatively in his plays and short stories. But the major work he bequeathed to world literature written, as he says, as a solace for the melancholy and the distressed, bears witness to the insuperable horror he felt for all forms of desire because of the basic incestuous subsoil from which the roots of love, in all its aspects, draw their substance. In *Galatea* he declares that love is nothing but desire and that all passion stems from desire as streams from their source. Desire, he says, causes brothers to seek the forbidden embrace of their dear sisters, stepmothers that of their stepsons and, worst of all, fathers that of their own daughters. (It will be observed that he carefully avoids mentioning maternal incest, only referring to it in the attenuated form of a stepmother's attraction for her stepson, as though the most abhorrent and most forbidden act could not even be named[18]). This properly Freudian view of desire is the final clue to the strange Quixotic dichotomy and to the frenzied solipsism in which it involves the Don. For Cervantes, aware of his complicity with the Bastard whose guilt he shares, but too devoted to the truth and too realistic to feign ignorance, unravels before the reader's eyes the incestuous excesses, disguised parricides and 'primal scenes' which constitute the ordinary novel's main substance. These are, in the Foundling's epic, the 'incidental' or 'inset' passages representing furtive incursions into a forbidden fiction, a manner of cutting his losses. But no sooner has the Bastard intervened than he is silenced by the innocent hero who promptly draws into his own nothingness the sexual desires, intrigues and violence incompatible with his ideal (together with reality which is the prerogative of even the most impractical Bastard). Thus Don Quixote's role is, indeed, to free Cervantes from the murky desires on which all living men's thoughts and actions thrive. Needless to say he fails and can but fail (Freud would say that he goes much too far along the narrow path of sublimation — we can come to terms with our instincts but never kill them). However, thanks to this unparalleled failure he occupies an unprecedented and, to this day practically unequalled position in literature. For his Melancholy Countenance — wherein Cervantes embodied the inconsolable Foundling's melancholy with which he was only too familiar, as well as his own unquenchable light-heartedness — enabled the novel as such to rediscover its origins and thus to reproduce in an adequately structured fiction the complete history of the secret development so eminently conclusive to its public history. Thus he showed through that most self-confident of literary genres — the one most imbued with its freedom and potential significance — that fiction is a useless self-indulgence so long as it tries to correct reality — but that it can become truly effective if it succeeds in expressing in its inventions both the reality of its obscure desires and the incurable childishness of its delusions.

★

That the Bastard's zone of influence should be incomparably vaster, and consequently less homogeneous, than that of his predecessor in the Family Romance's implementation, is only to be expected in view of the two 'authors' ' very different attitudes to action and their contrasting outlooks on the imaginary quest for power. Imprisoned in his aloofness — or as the psychologist would put it 'introverted' — the Foundling inhabits a *sparse* universe where the intensity of his desires greatly surpasses the diversity and number of desired objects. His inventions correspond to the psychological insularity where he has established his kingdom: forceful and unvaried, they are all based on the 'me here, the world there' which is the narrative's main theme and its structural principle. The Bastard on the other hand is governed by no plan; having emerged from himself to take possession of as many objects as he can, tempted by every aspect of reality that writing is able to express, he freely produces extensive, plentiful, contrasting works, constantly exploiting the methods most apt to satisfy his need for action and change. The first endows literature with one or two perfect specimens which neither the dis-

covery of new subject matter nor the invention of new modes
of expression can impair (fairy tales, *Don Quixote* or *Robinson
Crusoe* are 'undying' in that, confined to the most archaic
psychological sphere their aim is to speak the unchanging).
The second produces a vast quantity of very diverse specimens, each representing one of the ways fiction can express
reality, but by no means denying the validity of all the other
ways. As a product of time and abundance, for ever compelled
to invent different means of satisfying his voracious appetites,
the Bastard thinks less of creating 'imperishable' models than
of acquiring as many real notions as he can so as to increase the
illusion of veracity he wants to give. Thus though his works
are invariably inspired by the same source of imagined reality,
they never possess the typical structure which makes the
Quixotic tale immediately recognisable. At their most characteristic they are never more than isolated instances, doubtless
sharing certain basic features but with nothing to warrant one
of them being used to represent the whole, nothing that
reveals some connection or homogeneity between apparently
arbitrarily inspired *oeuvres*. Since the Bastard is basically involved with every aspect of reality — it is his mission's 'make
believe' — he has no reason to confine himself to any given
technical device. He is free to tell his stories as he likes,
whatever the method, so long as they ring true and are
'life-like'. Thus in the 'slice of life' category each novelist
produces books that overflow with *human* characters — Balzacian, Proustian, Dickensian or Dostoevskian, etc. — but
devoid of *literary* character such as might constitute a typology. Unlike the Quixotic novel that presents an entity readily
identifiable in its most varied forms[19] a Balzacian or a
Proustian novel is not a type of novel but simply a novel by
Balzac or by Proust — that is to say an essentially atypical
work from which comparative analysis can draw nothing
unless it be an endless list of particulars.

Eminently individual products having now replaced types,
the Bastard's works can no longer be understood on the basis
of some generalisable feature. They must be examined sepa-
rately in detail, which reduces criticism to an analysis of each
author and thus to its most questionable level. The Bastard is
probably always the same, always the 'faiseur de roman' set on
using women to obtain success, an adept at combining love

and the achievement of his selfishly ambitious ends. But on the other hand he can only be understood through the totality of his production since he is forever inventing new ways of revealing and concealing his thoughts and, needless to say, such totality is inaccessible. Balzac's secret motives for endlessly writing and re-writing the plot of his Family Romance cannot be added to Zola's. For although, by and large such motives may have the same significance, they are translated into strictly incommensurable data. Moreover since it would be impossible to check all the occasions when they inspired an original work, we must resign ourselves either to taking them as a whole, together with their more or less congenital monotony, or to dividing them into infinite categories to account for the peculiar manner in which each writer stresses his need for evasion. In the first place we are inevitably obliged to repeat ourselves, and in the second we add considerably to the pre-existing confusion.

To mitigate the dual disadvantage of monotony and of confusion we could doubtless consider the predominant or overruling tendencies in the Bastard's writings, as some kind of criterion for their classification. Thus we would have the Oedipal Bastard, in the narrowest sense of the term, that is the Bastard who, because of his obsession with love-affairs, deals exclusively with the secrets of the heart and the bed-chamber, writing *la Princesse de Clèves, les Liaisons dangereuses, Adolphe* or *René*, with bedrooms as backdrops and the eternal threesome of thwarted love as the only actors; the popular Bastard who makes ample use of the mystery of birth and, going straight to the point, avenges all the downtrodden of this world, bearing them to the summit of success by means of true fairy-tale reversals of fortune; the Bastard founder of the great, imaginary family where births and deaths succeed each other incessantly, the creator of Physiologies and Human Comedies who engenders vast fictional populations, manipulates whole continents and can only be satisfied when he has achieved god-like omnipotence; the contender of paternal authority, potential parricide for whom the world only contains fathers and sons and who condemns himself in the guise of a fictional breed of devils; and lastly — if there is an end to such a sequence of metamorphoses — the inventor of the Trial without judges or witnesses where the sentence penalizes the hero for an unknown crime and for a sin which is as unquestionable as it is unconfessable. But such an extempore list is entirely misleading, for if it is true that every novelist differs from every other in his manner of exaggerating or belittling one of the dominant themes of the Family Romance, none of them restricts himself to a single pattern (unless it be at the simplest aesthetic level) so that the Bastard's works are always the outcome of more or less mixed intentions where the sociological, the emotional and the psychological are closely intertwined (whence the inaccuracy of former systems of classification; apart from the odd exception there are no 'analytical novels' which do not simultaneously tell a success story, or the story of an attempt to achieve some sort of power). The Bastard covets everything his imagination perceives in the world — this, as we know, is his peculiarity — and if he ruled alone in that place where the consoling dreams of an unresolved childhood are fabricated he would embody all his unbounded ambitions and betrayals in every book conceived for his vindication.

But notwithstanding his considerable popularity during the nineteenth century and the vitality that ensures his lasting success, he never reigns quite alone. He must always consider, to a certain extent, the demands made by the earlier self from whom he can never be free. As a rule the Bastard's realism is no more than a rational tendency, actively opposed by relentless sentinels from his past, a tendency which, however overtly it may assert itself can only be realised after a deadly struggle with the Foundling and his indestructible mythology. The Romantic literature of the nineteenth century reflects at every level of its output this latent conflict between two different psychic ages from which a work's significance and style derive, and which the postulates of aesthetics never take into account. A novelist's originality depends less on his way of tackling general Oedipal problems than on his *formal* solution of the ever recurring conflict between his two childhood tendencies. Or rather his original outlook is nothing else than the formal expedient to which a novelist ultimately resorts in this confrontation between his dual conflicting personalities, or in his attempt to find new ways of coming to terms with them.

Apart from a few novels conventionally known as 'analytical' and those popular versions of the Family Romance where the Bastard manipulates the plot unassisted, the nineteenth-century novel is the battlefield where two equally fascinating myths of omnipotence fight for supremacy, one enacting all the possible or simply imaginable conquests — of women, authority, wealth or other forms of distinction — and the other stubbornly reverting to a blissful lost paradise and utopian dream. Instead of a diligent Robinson Crusoe intent on freeing himself from the Foundling who cut him off from the human mainland, we now have a realistic Robinson Crusoe, accomplished and enterprising but unconsciously still at grips with the childhood wrecker he thinks he has shaken off. And the island's magic — a magic of words and phrases, of unfettered dreams — still shatters or disorganises the elaboration of logical theories. Either irrationality infiltrates the most deliberately prosaic themes and undermines their unity, or it spares the content and can only be detected through its insidious influence on the form. Or again it openly thwarts the Bastard's rationalism by subjecting him to terrible temptations and thus, tingeing the realistic tale with fantasy and humour, gives it the semblance of an epic. Or, finally, the Foundling's myth, no longer a source of conflict, becomes as it were encysted in an isolated work where it bears witness to an irreducible survival of rebellion and nostalgia. But whether he writes *la Comédie humaine* while dreaming of a *Quest for the Absolute*, or whether he switches from one to the other, endeavouring each time to enlarge the images he imitates till they fit the immensity of his visions, the contemporary novelist is entirely dominated by this dialectic between the acceptance and the negation of reality which is, for every significant work, not only the source of endless original ideas, but as it were the actual pressure of creation.

Notes

1   Defoe was sixty when he wrote *Robinson Crusoe*, about the same age as his hero when he returns to Europe rich, weighed down with possessions and still unmarried. Thus the author recreates his biography late in life and encounters a matured Robinson at an age when probably he unconsciously realises that he himself will not go much further.

2   Johann Gottfried Schnabell (pseud. Gisander): *Die Insel Felsenburg*, Stuttgart 1959, edited by L. Tieck (1828). The hero's extraordinary

longevity corresponds to the ironic formula of Grimms' fairy tales.

3   *Meiner Frau Muttersprache*. It should be noted that Schnabell, who baffled critics for a long time by using the pseudonym Gisander, was orphaned at the age of two and adopted by a close relative.

4   The native tongue is automatically associated with the mother who teaches it. Kafka, referring to this association which, for a writer is particularly significant, wrote 'Language is our eternal beloved'. Elsewhere he mentions the 'ambiguous embraces' he associates with creativity.

5   This is the opinion of Miguel de Unamuno in *Our Lord Don Quixote*. tr. Anthony Kerrigan, London, 1967. See also Marthe Robert, *The Old and the New. from Don Quixote to Kafka*, Berkeley 1977, where the more general interpretations of *Don Quixote* are examined. I shall not repeat myself here except to recall that most critics make the mistake of believing that Cervantes' impartiality is sincere, when it is no more than a technical device intended simultaneously to mislead the reader (which might be seen superficially as pure mystification) and to serve as an exceptionally efficient means of self-examination. Unamuno — one of the more consistent critics — is so convinced of the total dissociation between hero and novelist that he has written a life of Don Quixote, as though the latter had really existed outside Cervantes' novel.

6   The dreamer imagines a situation where he arrives just in time to avert an accident — frequently involving a horse and carriage (as in the daydream Kafka mentions in a footnote to an entry in his *Journal* as recurring during his adolescence: he saw himself rescuing a beautiful young girl by stopping her runaway horse). He thus saves rich attractive ladies — who can naturally do no less than marry him — or important persons who prove their gratitude by heaping favours upon him — and probably accepting him as son-in-law in the end. Such fantasies are obviously part of the Family Romance, and though Freud does not refer to them specifically in his essay he discusses them elsewhere, for instance in the *Psychopathology of Everyday Life* where he analyses the strangely ambiguous way in which his own rescue fantasy expressed itself: he thinks he remembers a scene in Alphonse Daudet's *le Nabab* where a poor accountant called Monsieur Jocelyn bravely throws himself in front of a runaway horse and manages to stop it. The carriage door opens, an important gentleman gets out and grasps his hand saying 'You are my saviour, I owe you my life. What can I do for you?' But when Freud looks up the passage in the text he sees 'to (his) great shame' that *le Nabab* contains no such scene and that the poor accountant is not called Monsieur Jocelyn but Monsieur *Joyeuse* (that is to say Monsieur Freud since Joyeux is the French for his name). He must then at some time or other have seen himself in such a situation and promptly forgotten it. The fantasy occurred in a period of great distress when he was wandering about the streets of Paris, lonely, penniless and humiliated and when, he says, 'I was in dire need of a protector until the day Maître Charcot welcomed me into his home'.

7   See *The Old and the New* where this aspect of Quixotism is amply discussed. The reader will find in this work a number of the themes I deal with here which, though considered from a different angle express the same opinions. I shall not always indicate such repetitions. They are inevitable insofar as the relation between áncient and modern on which my earlier analysis was based, necessarily merges with those I consider here between the primitive Foundling and the more evolved Bastard. Nonetheless *The Old and theNew* stressed the literary passion Cervantes makes central to his story, while here I am trying to unravel the more primitive passions Quixotism expresses far less overtly.

8   Children rarely talk about their Family Romance at home and still less do they actually try to enact it. However Melanie Klein reports the case of her own son who, at the age of five, decided to go and live with the next-door neighbours because he was convinced he was a foundling whose real parents were precisely these people whom he probably found grander and more affectionate. He would not be deterred from his plan and indeed went to live with the neighbours who were quite willing to humour him for a while and play their required part. Melanie Klein admits that she was very upset, in spite of the fact that she knew all about the motives for the child's behaviour. After trying in vain to reason with him she finally told him she would not love him any more if he did not come back home; at which he promptly complied, having scored at least one point — for if his enacting of the Romance had not brought him the power he dreamt of, it had at least served to prove that his parents loved him.

9   In this respect the neo-Romantic and neo-millenarian movements emerging more or less everywhere today have remarkable Quixotic overtones, if only because they are always associated with rebellion against sexual oppression and private property. For Don Quixote's obsession is ineradicable, but we lack today a Cervantes to enact simultaneously the obsessed dreamer and the realistic observer who dismantles the dream's infantile infrastructure.

10   The reader will doubtless have gathered that the Romance of Romances I suggest here cannot be submitted to a detailed analysis of those fictional themes — the biographical content of fiction, its historical references and symbolical significance — on which most historians and critics concentrate their efforts. Its purpose is to make possible a reconstruction of the basic pattern wherein the novelist outlines his original reaction to his personal inspiration and from which the mechanisms of all fiction derive.

11   Cesare de Lollis, *Cervantes reazionario*, Rome, 1924.

12   Notably Americo Castro, *Cervantes y los casticismos españoles*, Madrid-Barcelona, 1966; Salvador de Madariaga, *Cervantes y su tiempo*, Cuadernos, 40, 1969; and Dominique Aubier, *Don Quichotte, prophète d'Israel*, Paris, 1966. These three writers support their theory with more or less similar arguments. However, for Dominque Aubier, Cervantes' Jewishness had a direct influence on the form of his work, for as a Jew in Spain at that time he could not avoid being a Cabbalist. Thus his masterpiece would be a prophetic book, incomprehensible

outside the esoteric symbols which, by their very nature conceal its meaning from the uninitated reader (as they would from Inquisitorial censorship). I do not feel impelled to accept such a theory. If Cervantes were a Jew — and there are various reasons to believe he was — he might as well (why not?) have continued in the Talmudic tradition; have become indifferent or sceptical in matters of faith as rationalist critics once held; or else, feeling himself to be a Jew independent of any faith but simply out of solidarity with a people and a tradition, he could have used the absurdity of his condition as renegade — peppering it perhaps with Cabbalistic ruse — as basis for a radical critique of a culture and a society. In which case he would be the true instigator of the 'New Cabbala' to which Kafka was drawn in order to express a very similar situation (*Journal*, 16 January 1922).

13   Incidentally Cervantes never lived in this province of la Mancha immortalised by his hero. Dominique Aubier observes that la Mancha (mancha = blemish) might well refer — obscurely for us but clearly for those involved — to the hereditary blemish which the converts so much dreaded revealing by simply mentioning their birthplace (op. cit).

14   We might say, borrowing Hannah Arendt's terminology in her essay on the origins of totalitarianism (*Antisemitism*, vol. I p. 56, New York 1966 and 1968), that Don Quixote must choose between being either a *pariah* or a *parvenu*; all intermediary states are precluded. If he does not want to go on being Don Quijada the pariah society tolerates and will not leave in peace, then he must at all cost become the 'wily' hidalgo who, claiming to be the product of his own efforts, succeeds through his own skills in making a name for himself (as Cervantes wished to do on the battlefield and in literature).

15   For the pseudo-genesis of *Don Quixote* see Marthe Robert, *The Old and the New*.

16   Such was the case for Americo Castro in 1925. True the latter revised his opinion and, in 1966 even maintained the reverse, that is, that Cervantes was of Jewish extraction. A remarkable instance this, of the errors to which the most eminent experts expose themselves when they try to encapsulate Cervantes' ideologies in a given formula.

17   One is immediately reminded of Montaigne until one realises that there is one important distinction: for Montaigne the 'assimilated' convert, settled in a homogeneously civilised country (he had never seen a Jew till he went to Rome, for indeed, there had been none left in France for a very long time), was considered by everyone, including himself, to be no different from any French-born writer. Thus he could stand up for tolerance and open-mindedness without feeling any of the social and emotional ambiguities that inhibited the Spanish convert even in his inner self-awareness.

18   This whole passage on incestuous love makes the motives for the invention of Dulcinea quite clear and proves, if such proof were necessary, that Don Quixote and Cervantes are one. Or more precisely, that Don Quixote is the part of Cervantes which rejects blood relationships, birth and Oedipal predicaments, and in so doing, denies

the irreversible course of existence.

19   To quote only a few readily confirmed examples: there are remarkable differences between Gogol's *Dead Souls*, Flaubert's *Bouvard et Pécuchet* and Kafka's *The Castle*, but only one common feature suffices to create a close kinship between the three masterpieces: it is the technical concomitant of the Foundling's isolation in respect to the world of current affairs and intrigues.

III
SLICES OF LIFE

An innocent child, yes, that you were,
truly, but still more truly have you been
a devilish human being!
And henceforth
take note; I sentence you now to death
by drowning!

Kafka

I The Quest for the Absolute

I wish to rule in France.

Balzac, *Lettres à l'Etrangère*

Just as the arrival on the European scene of Don Quixote and Robinson Crusoe seems to coincide with definite historical situations — the first with the social and religious aberrations of a regressive theocratic government, the second with Cromwell's bourgeois revolution and the stimulus it gave to personal ambition — so the Bastard's success in the century of History and the novel would be inconceivable without the advent of Napoleon. The adventurer without background or fortune who, in no time, crowns himself, sets his brothers on the thrones of Europe he himself had made available and, from a nascent Republic of which he is barely a citizen, creates his own Empire, is in every respect a character of pure fiction. He is fiction from first to last, fiction that grows with the gradual infiltration of his power throughout the continent and which, for the first time since antiquity, is inscribed in letters of flesh and blood on reality itself. The insignificant little fellow who turns out to be capable of making his Family Romance into an instrument of historical power has indeed the right to say: 'What an epic, my life!' (and might have said with more reason: What a life, my epic!), for he is the Bastard incarnate, the perfect renegade who throws the world into confusion by scrupulously and remorselessly realising what others hardly dare to imagine. Thus for the contemporary Bastard he becomes an example, a master and an idol who encourages rather than overpowers his disciples, and for the modern novel the liberator whose activity, at the borderline of action and dream, extends the frontiers of the imagination further than they had ever reached.

Napoleon did not influence the novel as Alexander inspired the cycle of Alexandrine romances, by merely providing story-tellers with a vast store of pre-fabricated material; but rather by confirming the potential novelist's belief that anything is possible — that History itself submits to the all-powerful childhood myth once that myth is taken seriously, and that once the adventurer, uninhibited by the consequences of his criminal desires dares to transgress the Oedipal law, the world is his for the asking. On the strength of such an example the novel can evade the restrictions of conjugal bedchambers where primitive Oedipal curiosity tends to linger, and set out to relate the universal history of its conquests.

Obviously Napoleon is too much a man of his time, too much a Bastard in fact, to even think of assuming divine descent like the legendary Greek adolescent whose memory almost certainly obsessed him. Indeed circumstances made this unnecessary. He only had to take advantage (in all innocence since he was not among those who voted for or against it) of the regicide which represented for every Frenchman a collective parricide and, as self-appointed Emperor, automatically become the father of a guilty people. This enabled him first to do away with that loathsome, humiliating label, his real father's name, and then to redeem psychological and social guilt by restoring an Emperor to the parricide nation while continuing to be the child of a revolution whose father he was and intended to remain. His legendary illegitimacy — acknowledged by certain historians in order to account for his surprising admission to a military academy exclusively frequented by the aristocracy — satisfied the popular need to provide a practical explanation for his incredible success (we know that, according to legend and myth a hero cannot be born like everybody else nor enjoy a happy, uneventful childhood), while the usurper's enemies, motivated by an equally justified respect for concrete fact, could taunt him by bandying the name of Buonaparte, that irrefutable proof of the common extraction he vainly disowned. Thus one way or another a whole nation was enthralled by the Family Romance in which the conqueror of Europe was able, for some time, to achieve unequalled authority.

At each stage of his epic Napoleon contrived to realise in every detail, with unparalleled persistence and daring, the unconscious or semi-conscious programme of the Oedipally fixated Bastard. Once he had consecrated himself Emperor and thus freed himself from his real father who, here as everywhere, opposes both possession of the mother and the possibility of a noble birth (the fact that Napoleon was orphaned in early childhood made no difference to his antagonism), Buonaparte sets himself up as head and father of the family whose progress to the summit follows his own (an extraordinary circumstance in a Corsican family of the time where such a role would, in the absence of the father, naturally have devolved upon the eldest son). As head he weds his sisters to princes and obtains as many thrones for his brothers as Europe is made to concede to him — not by any means because he loves them or is moved by ordinary feelings of kinship (historians have generally stressed the poor opinion he had of his near relations),[1] but rather to fulfill, exactly as in the fairy tale, the primitive desire to beget a family of kings that avenges and consoles the rebellious child's anger at not being 'well born'. In this case however, though the fairy tale comes true in every respect, it cannot satisfy its hero's main ambition, which is to establish a true dynasty. For a profound unreality insidiously clings to the arbitrary empire established by a sequence of bluffs — the blood he sheds on all the battlefields of the continent can never wash away the blemish of his own plebeian blood: he will always lack birth and irrefutability of rank. Thus to obtain the royal issue without which his grandiose achievement — both political and personal — is ever in danger of collapsing, Napoleon has to repudiate Buonaparte's wife, render void his plebeian marriage and marry the heiress of a *legal* empire, a true empire founded on centuries of uncontested nobility. The Austrian Emperor's son-in-law and the father of the King of Rome having thus completed his Family Romance may hope to compensate for, or better still completely erase from public memory, the immoderation and fragility of his self-made Empire. But there he apparently went too far: with his last rejection his downfall begins.[2]

This adventurer of genius who sailed like Robinson Crusoe[3] from an island and, after setting a whole continent on fire, returned to another island to die, carried out the childhood myth so literally that he communicated to nineteenth-century fiction the most powerful impetus literature can receive from an historical event. Till then the genre had been confined to the bedroom where the scheming Bastard satisfied his desires and his curiosity. Afterwards the whole world was its stage, entire nations its heroes and its subject-matter involved all the problems experience raises, all the questions debated by a teeming civilisation in the thralls of doubt. But if Napoleon's example provided fiction with an unlimited perspective and an inexhaustible contingent of irrestistible adventurers, drawing-room Buonapartes, brilliant heroes infatuated with both power and freedom, dedicated revolutionaries, envious reactionaries, mean or ridiculous upstarts and narrow-minded snobs, it nonetheless condemned the genre to a guilty conscience (with some justice since it links the theme of social ascent to those reprehensible childhood passions whose stimulus makes success possible), and in consequence forced it to incessantly proclaim its innocence or at least its good intentions.

★

Napoleon's influence on the novel is mainly remarkable at the level of superficial narrative where the hero is characterised by a violent craving for success — achieved needless to say through women and in the shortest time possible — that will place him in a position of uncontested superiority strongly contrasting with the undistinguished, deeply resented circumstances into which he was born. This hero, usually an adolescent, is the child of poor or newly-rich parents, invariably lower class, whom he loathes and disowns simply because they thwart his ambitions. The more convinced he is that fate has treated him badly, the greater his determination to make a fortune and a name for himself rapidly and to become a great man — a great artist, scholar, nobleman, statesman or, if needs be, criminal. Indeed the outstanding heroes of the century share these various vocations between them and some even succeed in more than one — at the cost of sacrificing others or risking their own lives. Thus Julien Sorel, the son of a wealthy peasant, vows to die a thousand deaths rather than fail to rise in the world, and this vague but terrifying vow leads effectively to his downfall — not to a thousand deaths but to a single one on the scaffold where he comes to the sad end reserved since time immemorial to the rebellious son. The youth's ambition finds a strong incentive in the example of the plebeian Emperor, 'the man of fire' as Balzac called him, whose 'meteoric' career had just come to its tragic close. We are told that for many years Julien had probably not let an hour go by without reminding himself that Buonaparte, an obscure, penniless lieutenant, had become, with the aid of his own sword, master of the world. This thought consoled him in his misery — which he considered immense — and enhanced his pleasure when he had any. Rather than toil at the family saw-mill Julien reads the *Mémorial de Sainte Hélène*, that social climber's bible, consoler and vindicator of the ambitious dreamer. And his immediate reward is a double dose of sarcasm and blows from his mean, rough, miserly and cruel peasant father. For, needless to say, Julien is or thinks he is unloved, rejected and despised by his family. His brothers beat him, his father ill-treats him, he has no mother (that is why he is on the look-out for one whom he will be able to simultaneously possess and exploit for his sinister ends). Thus from early childhood he bears within him the bitter rebellion Stendhal (if we are to believe his literary double Henri Brulard) knew so well:

In the past, when people talked about the innocent joys of childhood, the irresponsibility of those years, the happiness of early youth, as the only true happiness in life, my heart would ache. I never knew any such thing. Indeed those years were for me a period of unremitting misery, of *hatred and vengeful but always impotent rage*.[4]

The object of his hatred and vengefulness is naturally his father, a father whose features are just as odious whether he is called Brulard or Sorel and whom M. de Rénal — the betrayed husband Julien doubly deprives of his wife since, not content with becoming her lover he then tries to murder her — exactly duplicates. The adolescent barely emerged from childhood feels such violent loathing for his father that he cannot believe he was really conceived by him and imagines he must be a foundling, thinking that 'this would explain why I hated him so.' Later those who take an interest in him believe him to be the 'illegitimate son of some rich man' and then, without any obvious reason apart from the irresistible urge to discover the Oedipal sources of any story, ascribe his birth to a certain Duc de Chaulnes — who never admits responsibility and who, for all the part he plays in the narrative, might just as well never have existed.

Thus nothing is lacking from the traditional plot. The humiliation of being for ever only the son of Sorel added to his impotent hatred of an 'unworthy' father obliges Julien to fabricate the myth of his illegitimacy, that childhood expedient which alone can account for unnatural latent desires and justify the cynical hypocrisy of rejection. The whole novel rests on this naïve and desperate fantasy, whose rationale, based on a commonplace news item,[5] rigorously controls the unfolding of the plot: Julien athirst for vengeance and esteem seduces an older woman, both maternal and 'well born', to whom devolve the multiple roles played by the mother in the incestuous Romance. This forbidden passion, justified moreover by the example of his idol, maker of fictions and Empires and no less determined to force his way by means of the weaker sex,[6] soon leads to crime — or more precisely to an abortive criminal act which expresses simultaneously his inability for action and his unconscious need for retribution. Thus just as Julien begins to live he has to undergo capital punishment which, besides being the fate reserved for him by fathers in general, corresponds to his intimate urge to expiate the transgression of sacred taboos. Ruined by the satanic covenant with love and ambition he has not even had time to exploit, he climbs to the scaffold as though it were the only way in which he could raise himself above his station — leaving as sole accomplishment and sole claim to nobility the illegitimate son he has, as it were, extorted from the aristocracy.

★

Only rarely will the great Western novel again achieve the somewhat terse simplicity with which Stendhal was able to express the strictly accurate and unabridged version of his own Family Romance. Indeed the genre was shortly to become more ambitious, that is to say that instead of depicting the complex network of conscious and unconscious emotions through which, against a relatively bare social backdrop, the Bastard had captured our attention, it succumbed to his urge to do everything, master everything, understand everything until the *ability to act* is identified with the *ability to write*, the latter even acquiring a mysterious priority. Whereas Stendhal still takes pleasure — and probably finds some genuine compensation for his wasted childhood — in reviving under the name of Julien Sorel or Fabrice del Dongo, the adolescent he once was in his private dreams, aiming no higher and not trying to encroach more than is strictly necessary on neighbouring territories, Dickens sees himself as a moral reformer, Dostoevsky as a visionary prophet, the saviour of the Russian people and Balzac aspires quite simply to 'rule in France', as though the successful Bastard's will for power were not merely part of the fiction but was automatically communicated to the written and printed text. In fact the time had come when the novel, far from being restricted to moving and diverting its readers through the intermediary of 'interesting' characters, presumed to exert an authentic influence by instilling into paragraphs, sentences, words, indeed into *writing as such*, the overwhelming vitality and grim determination to succeed which, insofar as they were elements of the hero's moral make-up, had until then been part of the *subject matter* with no immediate effect on the story's verbal structure. The character who selects adjectives and verbs and creates images is henceforth infected with the megalomania of the character whose story he is telling, so that form duplicates content, and the novelist simultaneously transmits two identical messages, one explicit, to be read together with the vicissitudes of the narrative, the other implicit, and transmitted solely through its material prop of phrases and words.

Amongst all those who allowed the subject matter's megalomania to infect formal structure, place of honour surely goes to Balzac, that unquestionably prolific Bastard and disciple of Napoleon who was the first to dare claim that the imagination's significance equalled that of those great wielders of power, leaders of nations, outstanding philosophers or men of action who achieved undisputed eminence on the strength of genius alone. Balzac, the Emperor of fiction, whose power derived from his inexhaustible inventiveness, saw himself as the equal — not of Byron or Walter Scott, whom he nonetheless admired — but of the statesmen, scholars and thinkers who were, for him, the true sovereigns of their age:

Here, in short, is what I am counting on. Four men (*sic*) will have had outstanding lives: Napoleon, Cuvier, O'Connell, and I shall be the fourth.

The first lived on the life of Europe, he infected himself with armies! The
second was wed to the world! The third embodied a Nation! And I will have
carried a whole society in my head! . . . .

Thus *la Comédie humaine*'s population has as much reality and
dignity as the historic populations Napoleon or the Irish
nationalist moulded. It constitutes a complete universe as
lively and rich in observable phenomena as the natural world
Cuvier describes and classifies. To contain such a population
in one's mind is no less a feat than the greatest conqueror's
exploits, the achievements of the greatest statesman or the
incalculable discoveries of the greatest scientist — it represents
a condensation of the very essence of genius. It even surpasses
the genius of all historical men of action, since however great
they may have been they were ephemeral in relation to the
absolute, restricted to a single sphere where moreover they
had to overcome the resistence of unpredictable forces such as
the laws of gravity and other natural laws. Thus according to
Balzac's assessment, the author of *la Comédie humaine* overshadows even the exceptional beings amongst whom he takes
his stand, for if he succeeds he will unquestionably reign,
unaffected by changes of circumstance, as supreme master
over humanity, nature, events and their repercussions, which
insofar as they have sprung from his own mind, can never
thwart him in any way.

Thus literary fame, despite its undisputed advantages, is not
Balzac's ultimate aim but simply a means among others of
attaining Fame itself which alone ensures unqualified, timeless
pre-eminence over mankind. Moreover Balzac does not follow his literary career in order to satisfy a basic need — he
writes to achieve the enormous power which an ambitious
man with the amount of foresight he himself possesses knows
he can obtain from it. Proust, who was intrigued by Balzac for
more reasons than one and considered him with the slightly
shocked indulgence a certain kind of pettiness always aroused
in him, was sharply critical of the fact that he 'set material and
literary success on the same level' — which he did, and which
may shock a scrupulous writer but is hardly surprising in a
man whose whole work expresses an unbridled will to power,
barely modified by a superficial 'sublimation'. 'The vulgarity
of his feelings is so extreme' says Proust, 'that experience

cannot refine him. The satisfaction of the meanest ambitions is represented by him as Rastignac's sole aim in life, not only at the early age when he is first introduced. Or at least such ambitions are so intimately combined with higher ones that it is almost impossible to tell them apart.' What shocks Proust is first that Balzac has grown old without learning anything ('experience cannot refine him'), and then that he preserves until his death the fatal association of love with ambition which, in fact, is the only subject of his books. A year before his death when he was about to marry Madame Hanska with whom he had been in love for sixteen years, he discusses the forthcoming event with his sister in the following terms:

Believe me, Laure, it is something in Paris to be able to entertain at will and to invite to one's 'salon' the cream of society which will be welcomed by a refined woman, imposing as a queen, high-born, related to the best families, witty, cultured and beautiful. *This represents a powerful means of domination* 7

It would be hard to find a more precise self-portrait of the Bastard. Each word betrays the social climber, especially the repetitiousness with which Balzac stresses the expensiveness and luxury of all that belongs to him ('a refined woman, *imposing as a queen, high-born, related to the best families, witty, etc.*). The letter which seems to have been written on purpose to illustrate our point, continues on the same cynical, naïve tone — cynical probably from excessive naïvety:

For me, whether I like it or not, this business, feelings apart (were it to fail I would be morally destroyed) is a question of all or nothing, double or quits. My heart, my mind, my ambition, ask nothing more than what I have been pursuing for the last sixteen years; were this great joy to evade me, I would be done for. You must not imagine that I love luxury. I love the luxury of rue Fortunée together with all it stands for: *a beautiful woman, aristocratic, well off and acquainted with the best people*8.

As Madame Hanska's future husband Balzac expresses himself exactly in the terms he ascribes to Rastignac, Lucien de Rubempré, de Marsay or any one of his imaginary social climbers. Which testifies to the fact that he himself will always be the social climber set on realising the elementary plot of childhood myths and that, since the urge to write is not more

imperative for him than the wish to perfect the Family Romance *of his life,* he will never have total access to the *separate*
world of literature.

Proust was well aware that Balzac's naïve and rather appealing pettiness, though inexcusable from the artist's viewpoint,
is automatically derived from the confusion of actual facts and
literary facts, against which Proust had hoped to secure himself (by means of a theory of writing which would avoid such a
confusion). But when he deplores the fact that this original,
vigorous genius should frequently be marred by such an
aesthetic blemish or infirmity, he is indulging the traditional
critic's tendency for antinomies (the inspired content against
the form adulterated by vulgarity). This detracts from his
perceiving that in this case genius and pettiness are two facets
of a single nature and that, far from mutually diminishing each
other they merge admirably into one and the same achievement: the competition with the registry office, which is a
highly fruitful means of exploiting the Family Romance but
certainly petty from an artistic perspective, because art as such
never competes with anything. Balzac was not a genius occasionally dabbling in pettiness — he was a consistent social
climber compelled to write by his psychic constitution for
want of a better means of achieving his ends. He was a Bastard
imprisoned in the pettiness of his dreams, stranded as Proust
says 'halfway, too idealistic for existence, too materialistic for
literature,' who as such, animates *la Comédie humaine,* transmitting to the text both his congenital misunderstanding of art
and his grandiose vision.

One of the main peculiarities of the Bastard who inspires the
Balzacian cycle almost unassisted, is that he does not write to
produce works of literary significance — indeed he seems
unaware that such significance exists independently — but
writes simply to communicate significant aspects of life itself
by representing them with as much variety and abundance as
possible. Unlike Flaubert, for instance, who only considers
reality as a 'store of describable delusions' he is interested in
literature only insofar as it can create a semblance of reality
capable of exciting or even of satisfying actual desires. Thus
the famous notion of 'recurring characters' — a fruitful notion
indeed, to which *la Comédie humaine* owes its eighty-five
completed novels and short stories — appeals to him because it

provides fictional illusion with a means of increasing its breadth and continuity, because it makes up for the isolated novel's inability to imitate consistently the persistence of living relationships and surroundings, and because it consolidates the novelist's influence over his readers by making them believe in the 'durability' and 'reality' of what they are reading. When the Balzacian Bastard thought of applying the principle of 'recurrence' systematically he never asked himself if such an innovation would provoke a purer, deeper and truer literary reaction. He merely felt that he needed it so as to extend the novel well beyond the word 'end' and create a fluctuating population similar to that of real society — a society where families are related by various ties of kinship, emotion and interest and as many conflicts as human families are capable of fostering; where he could generate characters and kill them off with all the sympathy of an eminently sentient witness and with all the indifference nature manifests to everyday tragedies. He needed it in order to hold each individual life he created in a network of supposedly unforeseen and unpredictable events. And he needed it more than anything else to satisfy his tremendous desire to dominate, by merging history with his stories and thus impersonate for the reader an all-knowing, all-powerful and divine creator.

Obviously the notion of 'recurrence' was a brilliant one, and it is natural that Balzac should have greeted it as a revelation (in this respect he undoubtedly served as an example for the most diverse writers, of whom one need only name Zola and Proust). For the characters of *la Comédie humaine* have indeed acquired a privileged place in international fictional literature. They 'emerge' from their respective novels (this is precisely where the novelist fails, but it is a failure the reader willingly puts up with if he is of those who enjoy books that are 'true to life') with the three-dimensionality, immediacy and humanity we associate rather with old acquaintances than with imaginary characters. We know Rastignac, Bianchon, Diane de Maufrigneuse, Blondet, Nucingen and Vautrin like old friends — or we believe we know them because their names recur again and again in the conversations of their imaginary set and thus establish a kind of genuine familiarity between them and the reader. However on closer inspection we realise that quite a few are little more than names, especially among the more aristocratic. Is anyone capable of describing the features of Desplein, Finot, Bixiou and so many others who are not ordinary people but persons of the highest rank in Balzacian society? And what do we actually know about Horace Bianchon — the doctor of whose fictional status Balzac himself is said to have been oblivious to the point of summoning him to his deathbed — apart from the fact that after being a half-starved student in the Pension Vauquer, he becomes famous and takes society by storm? Indeed a lot of people come and go through the pages of *la Comédie humaine* who do not really further the narrative in any way but only seem to be there because of their titles, their position in society or their more or less exceptional qualities. They are mere appearances intended less to exist than to serve as extras in a distinguished company, enhancing the character of a gathering, setting off prominent personages and increasing the number of eminences.[9] In general the recurrent appearance of one of Balzac's characters is not related to the preciseness of the vision that inspired him — for the Bastard can never invent too many important people, incredibly beautiful, fabulously wealthy and prodigiously gifted (if only for crime: the 'shark' Nucingen, known as the 'Napoleon of Finance', or Vautrin the 'Napoleon of convicts'). Be that as it may, we are always glad to come across these fictional characters whom the grandiloquence of description dissolves rather than exposes but who, nonetheless, are surprisingly able to impose their physical and moral presences. The vagueness of their features does not detract from their ability to provoke all kinds of reactions — a slightly irritated partiality for Lucien de Rubempré, admiration tinged with fear for Vautrin, pity for Coralie, aversion for Madame d'Espard — who takes such a mean revenge on Lucien — and just a hint of contempt for the Baron de Nucingen because, considering how much he talks he should have learnt to do so properly. Such perfectly natural feelings — the same in fact as Lucien or Rastignac probably have for their mistresses, sisters or mothers — have doubtless nothing to do with literature, but Balzac aims no higher, for they are exactly what he hopes to provoke in order to ensure the reader's credulity and thus relish one more proof of his own power.

These characters who circulate from book to book often

without any significant reason for their comings and goings, enjoy a further quite remarkable privilege which tends to make the frontiers of fiction vaguer still. Having already acquired the status of 'acquaintances' by reappearing in stories with which as a rule they have little connection but to which their reputation adds a certain glamour, they proceed to hob-nob with real celebrities as disciples, equals or rivals as if they were naturally on familiar terms with all the most important and outstanding personalities of their time. Not that we ever witness the encounters between historical and fictional characters — Rothschild's with Nucingen, for instance. Such associations are purely nominal but frequently referred to and unerringly stressed in order to intensify their significance. Desplein and Bianchon are Claude Bernard's, Dupuytren's and Laennec's peers; the names of Daniel d'Arthez and Canalis are mentioned together with that of Lamartine (whom Canalis in fact more or less duplicates in the *Comédie*'s literary circle) as the most prominent representatives of contemporary poetry; Nucingen, in his youth, had met the Baron de Rothschild and the desire to emulate or even surpass him is in fact what urges him on in his prodigious career; Corentin worked with Fouché — indeed he and Peyrade his acolyte played, in recent historical events, a part which for all its shadiness would explain a number of otherwise incomprehensible historical details:

It was in this unassuming apartment (Corentin's) that plots were hatched and decisions taken which would provide odd historical records and strange tragedies if only the walls could speak. Here between 1816 and 1826 matters of vast public interest were discussed. Here were sown the seeds of events which swept over France. . . .

(in other words the nation's history was not made by politicians *but by Balzac's characters*). Moreover the novelist is not alone in advancing such a theory; his heroes adopt it as an excellent means of appearing to be more than mere figments of the imagination:

When God so wills, [writes Lucien de Rubempré to Vautrin as he is about to commit suicide] these mysterious beings are Attila, Charlemagne, Mahomet or Napoleon; but when he allows his gigantic tools to rust at the bottom of a generation's ocean, they are merely Pougatcheff, Robespierre, Fouché, Louvel or the abbé Carlos de Herrera (Vautrin). Farewell then, farewell, you who with luck might have been greater than Ximenez, greater than Richelieu. . . .

Proust commenting on this extravagant letter, so characteristic of the obsessional background from which the great Balzacian fresco emerges, condemns the imperceptible way in which hero and narrator become one and the same person: 'Lucien sounds too much like Balzac, he ceases to be a real character distinct from all the others.' Which is only too true from an aesthetic point of view, but from the inevitably pre-literary Family Romance perspective Lucien is wholly entitled to use his author's methods. For he too lives in a world of exaggeration, he too must have only the best of everything — what is biggest, most beautiful and exceptional. If he has been unlucky enough to make friends and become involved with Vautrin — the lowest of the low — he must at least convince himself before dying that his shady patron was made of the same stuff as Napoleon or Richelieu and that, even while wallowing in the mire of crime, he can still be compared to the greatest rebels (in fact Vautrin deals with statesmen on equal terms and ends up, with everyone's blessing as a 'great' detective).

Recurring characters and the systematic confusion of fictional figures with their historical counterparts, incessant transitions from fictional to historical events and a proliferation of the most ostentatious emblems of power and wealth are so many means of enabling the Bastard to create an environment of undisputed greatness (whether good or evil) where he can patiently manipulate his peers — upstarts like himself and prepared like him to commit any villainy or fraud in order to obtain the wealth, standing and benefits of which nature has deprived them. For such indeed is the main theme of this story in eighty instalments — if not its sole justification — which will enable Honoré de Balzac to become rich, noble and famous (the high-sounding pseudonyms with which he signs his first books foreshadow the particle he later appends to his name when he is about to carry out his great scheme), while experiencing vicariously every conceivable adventure, from the humblest to those which occur in the highest spheres of society. Thus it is unfair to condemn him — as does Proust, always a stickler for consistency — for identifying with Lucien de Rubempré to the extent of giving him his own thoughts and even the tricks of his trade. Lucien is his own flesh and blood, he is made in the image of the charming youth Balzac longed to be — handsome, seductive, gifted, a poet, cowardly perhaps and weak as a child or a woman, but raised above ordinary men by the intensity of the fatal passions he inspires. Little wonder if such a character does not always express himself with the independence aesthetic rigour requires — he has not really got a separate existence, but only the inner reality of the fascinating double Balzac's Bastard for ever reinvents to compensate for his lost illusions.

La Comédie humaine is teeming with youths of such exceptional nature — unsophisticated provincials hoping to take Paris by storm, needy intellectuals consumed by pride, highly aware of their genius and of the fame which, thanks to it, they will some day achieve, hungry 'lions', profound, indolent dandies awaiting flashy careers as statesmen with scandalous private lives — whose sole purpose is to raise the potential of Balzac's ambitions to the highest possible degree — ambitions of grandeur surviving from his distant past, unrealisable dreams as convincing as ever they were, whose fascination neither age, experience nor adult rationality can ever dispel. The novelist is tireless in his invention of young upstarts, artless or cunning, amorous or cynical, gullible or blasé. But though he multiplies variants and modulations to disguise as far as possible the physical and moral make-up of the original model, his charming counterparts always betray their kinship by a suspicious similarity that, at times, makes them practically interchangeable. In the features of Henri de Marsay, Eugène de Rastignac, Lucien de Rubempré, Felix de Vanderness, Maxime de Trailles and countless other less obtrusive characters, Balzac was always retouching his self-portrait as though he believed that by indefinitely reproducing it he might alter the course of his destiny. Such repetition — together with the intense relish in day-dreaming to which the proliferation bears witness, and the no less profound frustration of unfulfilled dreams — is the mainspring of this cycle of stories sometimes called the Western *Arabian Nights*, and indeed may account for all overproductive novelists.

Henri de Marsay may be seen as the first of this generation of indolent and ambitious Bastards, compelled by circumstances rather than by nature to go to the dogs or to achieve the highest honours and the most responsible situations (de Marsay becomes Prime Minister under the July Monarchy, Rastignac is Under Secretary of State in his cabinet, then Minister of Justice). The hero of *La Fille aux yeux d'or* has precisely the family background and history his lightning ascent requires — this novelettish Bastard could not have written his autobiography otherwise had he been paid to do so, for everything happens to him according to the *convention* to which such literature conforms (Balzac's contemporaries were not entirely unjustified in classifying him with Eugène Sue: the novelettish aspect of a number of his stories could easily lead them to overlook the difference in quality and even influenced the judgement of such a distinguished and authentic novelist as Dostoevsky).

Lovely as the day, everywhere at ease, a thoroughbred with a schoolgirl's complexion, gentle and modest of appearance, slim, aristocratic and possessing beautiful hands, Henri is (let us conceal it no longer) a love-child, the natural son of Lord Dudley and the well-known Marquise de Vordac. . . .

In other words he is a genuine bastard whose characteristic inconsistency is given ample scope until he achieves a fortune and a government post which, at the time, was equivalent to Royalty. Henri's mother had been married off by her lover to an old nobleman called Monsieur de Marsay, 'a faded butterfly', who adopts the child 'in exchange for the usufruct of a one-hundred-thousand francs income automatically devolving to his presumed son . . .'. 'The old nobleman died without having known his wife. Madame de Marsay then married the Marquis de Vordac; but before becoming a Marquise she had not shown much interest for the child she had born to Lord Dudley . . .'. Here indeed we have a typical Oedipal Family Romance situation, what Dostoevsky called an 'accidental family' where everything conspires to enable the hero to create his own life unfettered and be able to transgress and transcend human laws. As a foundling who knows neither his mother's nor his father's identity, 'the only father poor Henri de Marsay was to know was, of the two, the one who had no obligation to be such. Monsieur de Marsay's paternity was naturally most unsatisfactory.' Moreover, first entrusted to the care of one of his adopted father's aged sisters, then to a learned, alcoholic priest, an atheist who was particularly interested in the one-hundred-thousand francs income into the bargain, this youthful Adonis grew up without ever feeling any 'dutiful' affection. And such a total lack of ties is precisely what makes his future supremacy possible. Unlike Don Juan, with whom he shares a complete lack of faith 'in men, women, God and the Devil', he will make everyone submit to his charm without himself having to pay for it in any way (it should be noted however that he dies young and, like Balzac, shortly after having taken the marriage vows).

If Balzac's highly-praised realism is not always as thorough as one tends to believe — indeed for certain psychological reasons we shall discuss later it is often totally inadequate — in this case, notwithstanding or perhaps because of the novelettish course of events, it must be admitted that he fully deserves his reputation, at least insofar as subjective personal realism is concerned. For this story, which combines extravagance with conventionality and where the most incredible clichés of Romantic folklore are heavily underscored, is absolutely true to life — not actually true, of course, but in its portrayal of an 'accidental family' such as that where Balzac himself experienced the ordinary, ever-changing tragedy of an unhappy childhood. With his distinguished father, generously distributing bastards throughout the neighbourhood, his notoriously unfaithful mother whose lover, a neighbouring worthy, was the official family friend, a beloved younger sister on whom he doted to compensate perhaps for the mother's neglect of her legitimate offspring, and a young brother (called Henri like the Comte de Marsay) whose illegitimacy was an open secret and who was the sole object of his mother's affections, the child Honoré would find in his immediate surroundings confirmation of the Family Romance's most daring inventions. First of all he would be entitled to believe that an illegitimate child is gifted with peculiar qualities that invite affection (both he and his sister Laure were very fond of Henri whom they never ceased to protect while trying to repair the havoc he made of his life). Furthermore, since he had countless brothers in the neighbourhood who did not bear his father's name and one under his roof who bore it without being his father's son, he had more reason than most young

Bastards to question the legitimacy of his own birth and to solve the problem without more ado to the advantage of his Oedipal dreams (since Henri bears my father's name without being his son, who can prove that I, Honoré, bear the name of my real father?). Thus on the one hand an illegitimate child enjoys almost magical powers that make his irregular situation particularly enviable, but on the other anybody may be illegitimate given the uncertainty which generally — and especially in this family — surrounds the notion of paternity and descent. With the help of a child's imagination, always ready at the best of times to add flattering touches to irreversible fate, Honoré appropriates the supposedly incalculable prerogatives of his younger brother, without renouncing the unchallenged rights of his own legitimacy. But the basis for the whole operation is the uneasy reality of a particularly suspect 'accidental family' which, seen through the eyes of a precocious, sensitive child, contributes to his fiction an element of realism and a partiality for the concrete and for verisimilitude which he maintains even in his most striking overstatements. (R. Judrin observes that 'a sane mind has never raved more wildly',[10] and conversely: never has a madman been so rational — suffice it to remember the German story-tellers). The youthful maker of romances who acts on the authority of a questionable civil status — always questionable but especially so in the Balzac family — to reinvent his biography *rationally*, will become the all-powerful novelist capable not only of creating countless existences but of competing with the one institution entitled to name individuals and legalise descents. Far from being a belated addition to art and intellect his famous competition with the registry office may be said to be an old habit, a familiar practice whose resources Balzac had exploited during the formative years of his intellectual pre-history, long before he was capable of formulating the idea.

Thus Henri de Marsay and similar young upstarts in *la Comédie humaine* illustrate the incredible luck of having claims to illegitimacy —a blessing for which the child Honoré could only envy his younger brother Henri who automatically enjoyed its prerogatives: incomparable charm together with more power and freedom. Henri and Honoré de Balzac, both raised to the peerage by the spurious particle the elder decided one fine day to affix to his name,[11] merge into the single figure of the irresistible charmer, gifted with a man's strength and the grace and beauty of a girl, who effortlessly captivates whomsoever he meets because, free from the emotional constraints of family ties, he *belongs* to no living creature. Having become in his own imagination the illegitimate child his brother really was, Honoré invents another Henri, a true Bastard this time, a favourite of both nature and society precisely insofar as, being born outside official relationships, he outrageously breaks off the sequence of generations.

He had grown up in mysterious circumstances which invested him with immense, inexplicable power. This youth held a sceptre more mighty than that of a modern king who is nearly always restrained on every side by laws and regulations. De Marsay possessed the autocratic power of an Oriental despot. But whereas in the East such power is squandered on besotted men, here it was supported by a Western mind, a French intellect, indeed by one of the liveliest and sharpest instruments of knowledge. . . . His imperceptible sway over society had invested him with a real but invisible majesty, unemphatic and self-contained. He saw himself, not as Louis XIV saw himself, but as the proudest Khalif or Pharaoh who believes he is of divine origin and appears veiled before his subjects because, like the gods, he cannot be contemplated face to face without causing instantaneous death. . . .

Invisible majesty, immense, inexplicable power, the awareness of being greater than Oriental despots — who indeed could not boast of having held sway over all Paris — all these prerogatives were de Marsay's as a result of illegitimacy and a neglected childhood which entitle him even to the most terrible of divine privileges, murder (he kills, unhesitatingly, anybody he considers has insulted him).

Among the extraordinary advantages derived from his hero's divine, outlawed status there is one Balzac refers to less frankly, even if in *la Fille aux yeux d'or* it is precisely what sparks off a sequence of strange events. It consists in the peculiarity of 'accidental families' such as Henri's to favour and even condone incest, because in them kinship is more obscure and hypothetical than elsewhere. Lord Dudley — similar in this respect to Bernard Francois Balssa, if we are to take Balzac's word for it — never bothered to 'notify his off-spring of all the siblings with whom he had favoured them', so that Henri is unaware of the existence of the sister he happens to meet when he is about twenty (incidentally in the most risky circumstances, since this unexpected sister is furthermore his rival for the affections of the golden-eyed girl whom she jealously sequestrates to prevent her from knowing the love of a man). Thus Henri might just as easily have fallen in love with Lord Dudley's daughter, in which case not he but his father would have been to blame for their incest, were it only because of his amazing frivolity ('Who is this handsome youth? My son? Oh what a nuissance!'). Conversely Honoré, were he truly the bastard he hopes and believes he is, might indulge his secret attraction to Laure, the beloved sister he incessantly pursues in the guise of all the Laures with whom he seeks to perfect his sentimental education and to find happiness (Laure de Berny, Laure Sallembier, Laurence de Montzaigle, Laure d'Abrantès, so many 'sisters' whose names foredoom them to revive a forbidden childhood inclination and, in the context of Oedipal transference, so many mothers won over from an abhorred father).[12] However Henri de Marsay does not commit the incest circumstances seemed to favour. He is precluded from doing so because the author had already concentrated on him all his hopes for a successful social ascent, and cannot therefore submit him to the supreme retribution automatically reserved for Oedipal transgression (Oedipus must be a king and full of honours when Fate strikes him down). Incest is thus averted and only occurs as it were by proxy, in the person of this strange golden-eyed girl who seems to be indiscriminately susceptible to the charms of all Lord Dudley's children, bestowing her favours simultaneously on the brother and the sister and thus creating an incestuous situation more compatible, doubtless, with the hero's lofty ambitions, if not with the requirements of ordinary ethics. The golden-eyed girl pays for this indirect incest she has innocently perpetrated, with her life — she is stabbed in the end, not by Henri, though he had considered killing her and been deterred at the last minute, but by Euphémie, who can easily be sacrificed since she has no role to play in Balzac's ambitious pilgrimage.[13]

Obviously *la Comédie humaine*'s Bastard can realise his plans without answering all the conditions 'accidental families' require. Rastignac, for instance (whose sister is yet another Laure), has an apparently spotless civil status. He is only morally a Bastard insofar as, humiliated by the mediocrity and penury of his background, he vows to become rich at any cost and to employ to this end the Family Romance's favourite method, that is love and the social influence of women. As a less fanatical and satanic version of de Marsay (he sets out on his career by becoming Delphine de Nucingen's lover, just as de Marsay has abandoned her, which raises him almost immediately to his model's level), he undoubtedly lacks the immense, inexplicable powers the true bastard receives at birth together with his illegitimacy. But he is far from inadequately armed for the bitter struggle for success — he has good looks, wit, a total lack of scruples and a cynical understanding of the machinations of society — all he needs to do to reach the top is disown the provincial youth he was on his arrival at the Pension Vauquer, reject his family and pronounce the famous words: 'Now, to the two of us!' which is his generation's battle cry. He keeps his vow, makes an immense fortune thanks to that obliging, mocked and satisfied husband, the Baron de Nucingen. Then, after being Delphine de Nucingen's lover for over twenty years, he marries her daughter and, still astutely combining love and his political career, he achieves power through a spectacular promotion. Count, Peer of the realm, Minister of Justice in 1845 and provided with 300,000 francs income, this great 'political manipulator' — whose similarity to Napoleon further involves marrying off his sisters to princes and making his younger brother bishop — has all in all a success more suited to his stature than that of de Marsay who, notwithstanding his Oriental despotism and 'immense, inexplicable power', has to be content with becoming Prime Minister in a constitutional Monarchy — which is rather a comedown for someone so extraordinarily gifted at the start — after which he dies prematurely, like Balzac himself shortly after concluding the rich marriage which should have finally established him. Wheras the ever lucky Rastignac, beloved of the gods if not of God, overcomes nature itself by simply surviving — as though his social conquests were not enough.

Lucien de Rubempré is certainly the most unfortunate of all the young blades who inhabit the pages of *la Comédie humanie*. He will have to pay for the major crime of changing his name with imprisonment and suicide (to the distress of Oscar Wilde who was probably aware of his own affinities with this charming and disturbed character). Where so many of Balzac's heroes succeed, Lucien is pre-cast for defeat, not so much on account of his shameful relationship with Vautrin — dubious indeed, or perhaps only too clear, considering the ex-convict's acknowledged homosexuality — as for his long-premeditated rejection of his father, Major Chardon, whose undistinguished background fills him with shame and humiliation. This wilful rejection which causes so much havoc is sufficient proof of his parricidal intentions and, since he can neither reconcile himself to the fact that his mother had married beneath her station, nor change his name without being stricken with remorse, it finally motivates his suicide at the precise moment when official jurisdiction is about to acquit him.

For Balzac Lucien's predicament is no different from that of all adolescents: 'He was in love and wanted to rise above his social station, a very natural predicament for young men whose hearts yearn for satisfaction and who must overcome poverty.' Indeed. But why could Lucien Chardon only satisfy his heart's desire and overcome poverty under the name of Lucien de Rubempré? Must he have a title to earn his living? Yes, says Balzac who knows what he is talking about. A title revives a 'humiliated soul' and, moreover, for a young man of Lucien's generation the need for honours, titles and wealth has become overwhelming since the advent of democracy which is itself the outcome of a parricide and a rejection, and for this reason stimulates all manner of lusts: 'By inviting all its children to partake of its feast society today awakens their ambitions from the first dawnings of existence' (note the terms: children, feast, dawnings of existence — here as in countless other passages Balzac puts his finger not only on the Family Romance's main emotional connotations, but furthermore on the intimate relation between democracy and romanticism in its wider sense). In the ruthless competition of which society has become a model, Lucien's mentor is the greatest contemporary hero, the upstart Emperor, the modern prophet of 'anything can happen' whom Balzac, notwithstanding his monarchist convictions will never cease to mourn: 'Napoleon's example, so momentous for the nineteenth century on account of the possibilities it suggests to so many second-rate people, presented itself to Lucien who, filled with self-reproach, threw all caution to the winds . . . .'. This handsome, irresistible youth is not however of the same metal as the Napoleonic Bastard. He is too conscious of the significance of his rejection and too critical of his cautiousness. Ambitious yet perhaps too much a poet to feel the cynical indifference of a Rastignac or a de Marsay, he finally lacks the strength to bear the weight of his guilt, and such weakness, unheard of in a hero, is the cause of his downfall.

Were it not for the woman who undertakes his social education it is doubtful if he would have dared to enter the Parisian rat-race. But Madame de Bargeton, as mistress, sexual initiator and motherly adviser, in fact as perfect representative of the Woman on whom the nineteenth century relies for the education and entertainment of its young males (consistent here with the Oedipal Romance), has no compunction in dispelling his scruples, reminding him of the harsh laws of the success on which his personal philosophy is based: 'She advised him to *boldly disown*[14] his father, adopt the distinguished name de Rubempré and ignore the protests that might result from a change of name which, moreover, the King would be sure to sanction . . .'. Indeed Madame de Bargeton encourages Lucien's Romance, reviving his revulsion for his humble extraction which the mere sight of the word 'thistle' (*chardon*) provoked ('His father's name written in this place where all the carriages circulated offended his vision . . .'), and helping him to overcome his faintheartedness. As accomplice of the Bastard she wants to make of him so that he will be a more worthy lover (and thus simultaneously the incestuous son of her own Romance), she instinctively knows that if he is to disown his father openly she must find him forthwith a father of higher rank in the person of the King of France — who alone has the power to sanction, and consequently assume responsibility for the sacrilege of this undertaking. With the King as his father instead of a common 'Thistle' Lucien will be free to do as he pleases — though in fact his status as writer has already set him above all moral taboos and responsibilities:

According to her, men of genius had neither brothers, sisters, fathers nor mothers; the great works they were destined to produce entitled them to a certain amount of selfishness, since they had to sacrifice everything to their self-realisation. . . . A genius depends on himself alone, he is the only judge of the means he employs, since only he is aware of his ends. . . .

And after evoking his 'profound awareness of the social vacuum where so many superior minds are obliged to stagnate on account of their humble origins and lack of means' the temptress uncovers her last card which is that 'He who takes his century by storm is entitled to risk everything, for everything is his . . .'. Indeed, armed with such advice that fits in so well with the machiavellian trend of his desires, the provincial youth leaves at once for Paris to take his century and the whole world by storm. For the Queen of Angoulême's suggestions obviously carry more weight than the rational objections put forward by David Séchard, Lucien's friend and brother-in-law who, though afflicted with an odious father, has nonetheless decided against such a rejection. David, another of Balzac's metamorphoses and prototype of the unsuccessful businessman he once was, will never emerge from the mediocrity consistent with his father's name and condition, his one compensation consisting in the foredoomed inventor's unquenchable optimism. Instead of writing his own books he humbly prints those others have written, just as Balzac had done in the rue Visconti before Lucien's surpreme ambition led him into more glorious ways (this is one of the minor vindications of *les Illusions perdues* — Balzac-David's failure as a printer is accounted for and compensated by the adventurous Romance into which Balzac-Lucien has had to launch himself.

Judging from the proliferation of Bastards in *la Comédie humaine* — they are all over the place, in Paris, the provinces, abroad, and of every description, status, age and profession — it would seem that Balzac identified uninhibitedly with such domineering, scheming individuals, part Don Juan and part Machiavelli, whose influence is achieved through a *practical* knowledge of the value of sex and wealth. Indeed he had a masterly understanding of them and the prominence they achieve in his satanic comedy enabled him to revolutionise an essential aspect of the novel. For thanks to their practical realism he could substitute the unobtrusive manipulation of social mechanisms which henceforth would govern every emotion for the sentimentality and violence still seen in the previous century as the only suitable themes for the genre. But if the Bastard within him was able to discover the enormous fictional resources which the black magic of finance presents to a modern observer — a magic powerful enough in his view to

overrule all the others including that of sex and ambition —
this does not imply that he was naturally a womaniser, a man
of action or a money-maker, nor that all the self-portraits
depicting him as such should be taken for true likenesses in an
ordinary psychological sense. On the contrary, there are
plentiful indications that the adult Bastard's supremacy so
loudly proclaimed in theory was based on 'wishful thinking'
rather than on actual fact, and that it enabled Balzac to pursue,
on a quite different psychological level, a much more primitive, obscure and dangerous battle on whose issue his very
sanity depended.

For in *la Comédie humaine* we find sections that would seem
to be at odds with the work as a whole, were it not for the
insights we have had into the novelist's general make-up (for
instance Balzac is reputed to have been both monarchist and
progressive, realistic and fanciful, idealistic and materialistic,
though no one has ever tried to explain the reasons for such
ambiguity). The relevant sections do not correspond at all
consistently to any particular one of the groups of stories he
published variously as Tales, Novels or philosophical Essays
— indeed Balzac's concept of 'philosophy' was far too vague
to constitute any kind of criterion, though it may help us to
appreciate the psychic level of his inspiration. However,
though the texts which clash most obviously with the rest of
his output cannot be classed in a specific category — some are
to be found under headings other than 'metaphysical', and this
category is itself heterogeneous — they are easily identified in
that the pursuit of success — ever the hero's overwhelming
obsession achieved with unmitigated relentlessness — has here
quite different ends and means. The ambitious hero is not the
calculating, embittered, sophisticated realist, the social climber who has pierced the mystery of social mechanisms and
patiently spreads his net while biding his time. Instead he is in
search of the Absolute, a solitary dreamer intent on possessing
an undivided Truth encompassing the One and the All (the
novel called *la Recherche de l'absolu* confirms our suggestion
that Balzac's titles are an unreliable criterion for classifying his
works, for despite the archaic oddity of his outlook Balthazar
Claes is a typical Bastard and his pursuit of the absolute is
hardly more concerned with spirituality than are the pursuits
of ordinary upstarts). The most famous of Balzac's pursuers of

the Absolute, the only one perhaps to deserve such a weighty title, appears in the pages of *l'Histoire intellectuelle de Louis Lambert*, a significant novel indeed, not least because the fiction here is a flimsily disguised autobiography.

The first person narrator — a stance not usually adopted in *la Comédie humaine* — has been on intimate terms with Louis Lambert since they were classmates at the Collège Vendôme (where Balzac himself was educated) and now, delving into his distant past, reminisces with nostalgic relish. Louis Lambert was born in 1797. His parents, poor tanners unable to 'buy him out of the army' hope nonetheless to save him from conscription by enrolling him in holy orders, and to this end entrust him to an uncle who is a parish priest (experts assert that in 1811 Balzac had a schoolmate called Théordore-Louis Lambert and moreover that before calling his hero Louis, Balzac had given him the name of his own younger brother Henri). At the age of five Louis is able to read and understand the Old and New Testaments which he comes upon by chance. After this he continues to read avidly and with an uncanny perceptiveness: 'His eyes took in seven or eight lines at a time and his mind grasped the meaning with a speed equal to that of his sight . . . . He had a prodigious memory . . .'. One day as this poor, almost ragged, tanner's son is sitting in a public garden immersed in one of his books, he is literally *found* by Madame de Staël, Napoleon's sworn enemy, who is instantly intrigued and not a little impressed by the small boy (she observes that he is reading Swedenborg's *Heaven and Hell* at the age of twelve!): 'Madame de Staël wanted to wrench him from the clutches of Napoleon and of the Church so that he could enjoy the fate for which she was convinced he was made; indeed she had immediately identified him as another Moses saved from the waters . . .'. The great lady of French literature who plays the part of Pharaoh's daughter or Fairy Godmother (they are interchangeable) sends her protégé to the Collège Vendôme in order to prepare him for the singular and dangerous future she foresees for this 'true prophet'.

Nobody would suggest that Balzac's choice of images is always particularly apt or felicitous, yet here we can but admire the wisdom, the unerring insight which makes him opt for one of the most secret of childhood realities. For Louis is truly a second Moses, a prophetic Foundling who, deprived of his parents and thus liberated from the strongest of human ties, can fully experience the Absolute in the terrible wilderness of his mind. Distinguished by the unfailing Quixotism of such callings, he is the exact reverse of the Napoleonic Bastard (even if, as has been suggested, the idea of having Madame de Staël *find* him is taken from Théodore-Louis Lambert's life story, it is nonetheless a stroke of genius). Not that he is less outrageously ambitious — indeed he is madly ambitious as well as plain mad, another of the author's more brilliant insights — but his aspirations are not related to society and its institutions (Madame de Staël saw to that when she alienated him from those two mainsprings of the Establishment, the Church and Napoleon). He aims beyond and above these so as to dominate them from the heights attained by the visionary through an arcane knowledge of Perfection. Thus his role is that of the lone contemplative who shuns women, men, friends and enemies, leading a life of total egotism in direct contact with the great spiritual prophets (' "Fame", he would say, "is sanctified egotism" ').[15]

Unlike Balzac's upstarts who see Napoleon as an adequate model, an incentive to attain status and honours, Madame de Staël's Foundling-Moses identifies quite uninhibitedly with Christ, Mahomet and Swedenborg, the supreme masters he believes he will have no difficulty in equalling so long as circumstances are favourable: 'Only nine out of Christ's thirty-three years are recorded; his unknown life paved the way for his famous life. I too shall have my wilderness!' Like every prophet he is a child prodigy who knows, understands and retains everything he has ever read, recreates past history from his personal inner experience and reinvents every philosophy. He is solitary and ascetic, has visions and prophetic dreams, recognises places he has never seen and instinctively comprehends the most incomprehensible phenomena. Like the prophets too and like the saints, he disowns without compunction his mother and father, secluding himself in a wilderness where he will encounter neither the consolations of friendship nor the excitement of enmity (two things the Bastard is well equipped to exploit) and renounces all human satisfactions so as to prepare himself for untold spiritual glory (and especially, of course, he shuns sexual experience).

Louis Lambert, the true classical Foundling whose power is

concentrated from infancy in the activities of inner life, is equally aware of his superhuman majesty and of his terrible shortcomings: 'I was too great and too small' he admits as every mystic does, thus revealing his saintliness. While constantly switching from one extreme to the other with the characteristic psychic instability of a true visionary, he never loses sight of his ultimate fame (the term is rather out of place in this context, but it is the one he uses), and in the meantime he indulges the ecstasies, visions and cataleptic fits which will enable him to achieve the most coveted of all revelations — that of the secret mechanism of the 'generation of thought'. Balzac adds:

But for some of these [Great Minds] is not such determination the result of their vocation? Do they not endeavour to concentrate all their energy in a profound silence *in order that they may emerge from it more apt to rule the world with word and deed?*[16]

Despite the interrogative form the child Prodigy's historian employs here — a pardonable rhetorical device since in fact Balzac is talking about himself — the purpose Louis is pursuing through meditation and experiment is never in doubt: it is simply to dominate the world, not by extorting from society such inconsiderable privileges as rank and wealth, but by equalling God in a total understanding of the physical and spiritual laws of creation. Thus is the Foundling in the habit of seeking his revenge — by substituting for the mystery of procreation he fails to penetrate a metaphysical understanding of the 'generation of universal thought'.

But Louis Lambert has not the Quixotic integrity to renounce the material world and disregard both instinct and reason in his pursuit of the sublime vision. The day comes when the desire for the Absolute can no longer keep him away from Paris, love, women, social rivalries and all the petty preoccupations of everyday life. So he abandons his 'wilderness', motivated apparently by more ordinary ambitions and the need to discard his primitive outlook and present society with a normal, or at least acceptable, Bastard. In fact he decides to move away from the 'Other Side' as did, we may presume, the adolescent Balzac in a similar moment of crisis. Paris welcomes him with the ruthlessness it inevitably deploys for

Balzac's young provincials brutally extracted from their normal habitat. For three years he survives on twenty *sous* a day, mingling with equally poor and equally ambitious youths, even presiding over their coterie, while trying to sort out his own ideas — a difficult task considering the extraordinary hotch-potch of science, mysticism and philosophy on which they are based — but without ever really obtaining a footing in this bustling and idle Parisian society where the mind and the senses are mutually inflamed. With his total lack of worldly wisdom, his spiritual fragility, prolonged chastity and all the other characteristics he has acquired in 'the wilderness', Louis is incapable of resisting such an onslaught of sensations: one evening at the Théâtre Français he finds himself next to a wildly beautiful, provocative, desirable and inaccessible young woman — she naturally belongs to someone else — and is seized with an irresistible desire to kill her. He manages only with a supreme effort to overcome this impulse but succumbs to a fit of murderous insanity which is the first symptom of his madness.

For Louis Lambert murderous impulses are intricately related to sexual prohibitions — prohibitions which the spirituality of his aims might explain superficially, but which correspond at a deeper level to a psychic immaturity, a pre-Oedipal stage of development where the conflicts of growing up have not yet sorted themselves out. This is further confirmed in his relations with Pauline de Villenoix, the woman he ardently loves and who, precisely by satisfying all his desires, becomes the involuntary cause of his madness and suicide. In the intoxication of first love he believes he is capable of being a man and thus coming to terms with existence: 'I shall stride towards fame and success where others crawl after them' (to stride instead of crawling is a further symptom of that excess wherein his inability to proceed on an ordinary level at an ordinary pace manifests itself). But the race for fame will not take place, though Pauline has all that is required to help him win it: beauty, wit, wealth and passion. Louis is doomed and Pauline unwittingly precipitates his downfall because, having seen her since the start as an angel, he cannot now perceive that she is a woman of flesh and blood without succumbing to his murderous impulses. On the eve of their wedding he writes to her:

Now I can confess that the day I refused the hand you held out to me so charmingly, I was experiencing one of those fits of madness when we contemplate murder in order to possess a woman. Yes, had I perceived the exquisite contact you offered me, as vividly as your voice echoing in my heart, I cannot tell where the violence of my desires would have led me.

Thus whereas the ordinary Bastard 'crawls' after fame but carries off the handsome trophy of love, Louis Lambert 'strides' but can only conceive possession of a woman as murder. Small wonder then that the imminence of his marriage should cast him into the abyss of terror in which he founders — seeing himself made impotent through his criminal disposition, or compelled to murder by the logic of his impotence, he contemplates, in his despair, resorting to the self-mutilation to which Origen believed he owed his genius, in other words to castration. His intention is naturally thwarted at the last minute — he will not even be allowed to sacrifice his virility to the accomplishment of his goal. Nonetheless he attains this goal in a roundabout way through madness, which brings him definitely back to the wilderness of his dreams and ultimately exempts him from marriage.

Were there no more than coincidences and correspondences between Balzac and Louis Lambert — similarities of taste (reading for instance) and of intellectual disposition — it might be unreasonable to speak of autobiography or even of an inner experience of the author's. But there is more. Balzac admits as much when he encapsulates his fictional character in his own body, giving him his own features, figure and size down to the 'short neck' whose significance was, according to him, so strangely confirmed by physiognomy (great men have 'short necks, perhaps because nature has decreed that their hearts will be closer to their heads'). Louis has

a remarkably large head, his hair, exceedingly black and thickly curled, adds an extraordinary grace to his forehead. . . . But his face with its rather irregular features, was more or less unmemorable once one had noticed his eyes whose range of expression was wonderfully varied and which seemed to reflect his soul. . . .

A large head (denoting genius), spellbinding eyes, extraordinary grace — everything tallies in this description where Balzac exhibits the self-satisfaction of a Narcissus captivated by his own reflection. For this is indeed a self-portrait and Louis Lambert is none other than Balzac seen through his own eyes — handsome, brilliant, as unhappy as he is admirable, and misunderstood despite his halo of glory — when he recalls, for his own benefit as much as for the reader's, indistinct visions of his passionate childhood.

The child prodigy contemplated from afar by the adult novelist with nostalgia and with naïve admiration, is the Angel who consolidates Balzac's ambiguous faith in the supernatural:

> With his peculiar combination of strength and weakness, of childish grace and superhuman power, Louis Lambert is the being who has given me the most poetic and the truest notion of those creatures we call *angels*. . . .

Despite his angelic nature suited for arid spiritual regions, Louis becomes a menace once he has given up the idea of *ruling the world by Word and Deed* and decides to make his mark as a man capable of possessing women, occupying a position, adapting to the times and patiently achieving his ends. Louis the unproductive contemplative, the unemployed expert of unutterable Unity, is and can only be a promoter of false glory — his dream of superhuman omnipotence[17] in which the Absolute is revealed in an instant of Grace beyond time and the struggle for life, automatically leads to madness, crime, death and, worst of all for a creator conscious of his vocation, to the vacuity of sterility (Louis Lambert leaves a *Traité de la volonté* which sums up and anticipates every philosophy but which is unpublishable and unfinished and, like all unknown master-pieces, will have no significance for posterity). He who tries to play the angel plays the beast and, according to mythology, the beast easily turns into the devil. Thus Balzac has no choice: if he wants to live, love, write and acquire through his writing the immortality Louis only achieves in his dreams, the angel-devil of his youth will have to be exorcised or, better still, annihilated.

We do not know how Balzac himself overcame the serious pathological tendencies — murderous, suicidal, self-mutilat-ing — he describes in his intellectual history with such clinical accuracy (this clinical precision has always been highly praised although no one has dared consider from what sources the author drew his knowledge). Yet we may infer it from the simultaneous centrality and peripherality of autobiographical data in *la Comédie humaine*, the gigantic work he extracted day by day, word by word from his own anguished and barbaric unconscious. When even the famous Esquirol gives up all hope of curing his madness, Louis commits suicide. This is the logical outcome of his disease, but it has a further positive implication since, from his tragic death are born all the prosaic Rastignacs with whom Balzac will henceforth identify in order to forget the baleful bliss of his lost paradise. In this respect *l'Histoire intellectuel de Louis Lambert* may be seen as the description of a sort of spontaneous cure. Having perceived in the nick of time the risk of pursuing his basic megalomaniac tendencies, he strove to reduce his ambition to more normal proportions. Now instead of trying to achieve total knowledge through a systematic 'disorder of the senses' (cataleptic states, visions, etc.) he endeavours to become the very wise madman who describes the world in detail at the risk of wearing himself out trying to represent every variety of being, every moral characteristic and every form of social organisation the human eye can perceive (this is in fact how he worked himself to death). But of course the cure was never complete. Louis Lambert's literary death could not suffice to achieve it — indeed in certain respects it seems to have had very little effect, for the Foundling is indestructible by nature, he is a ghost no one can reduce to total silence, a phantom well versed in magic who takes advantage of the slightest relapse to reassert his former dominance. Having died on the 25th of September 1824, Louis Lambert accomplishes the unusual feat of reappearing in *la Comédie humaine* in 1825 to expound his theory of life and the iconography of ideas. A feat due doubtless to an oversight on the part of Balzac — one of those made only too easy by his predilection for 'recurrence', but which has nonetheless the classical significance of a Freudian slip — it represents a compromise enabling the author to cling a little longer to the fallen angel he has had to destroy. So this ghost never ceases to haunt him. Despite the somewhat lapsed ideal he stands for, he will reemerge from time to time to direct or misdirect the course of daydreams.

Apart from passages where he recurs under his own name as, for instance in *les Illusions perdues* where his friends and disciples refer to him, Louis comes back more or less conspicuously each time his successor, the Bastard, is forced for one reason or another to make a tactical retreat or even to disappear temporarily. The story called *Le Chef-d'oeuvre inconnu* — a kind of tribute to his *Traité de la volonté* known to Balzac alone — is in part indisputably from his pen. He is recognisable in the features of Frenhofer, the mad painter and pursuer of the Absolute who is so intent on piercing the mysteries of art and its 'generation' that he leaves no proof of his genius apart from a few superb details lost in the complexities of an atrociously bad painting, and his inconsolable pupils. It is he furthermore who created *Seraphita*, the Swedenborgian angel who appears to women in the guise of a man and to men in the guise of a woman, who is immune to the laws of gravity and sexuality alike and whose brief incursion among human beings serves the sole purpose of enlightening the earthly Bastard as to the soul's physicality and the blessed timelessness of the flesh. And finally he recurs whenever Balzac's strict observer of reality weakens or abjures himself to the extent of turning opinions into intellectual fact and descriptive nuance into hard and fast decrees.

But by and large the Bastard does not often let him take over officially. However, if he is henceforth unable to play an active part in the elaboration of Balzac's writings — in the narrative structure, relationships between characters and aims pursued — he still has the power to substantially influence *la Comédie humaine*'s typical plots and especially its use of formal material. And where he cannot supplant the Bastard, Balzac's Angel is nonetheless able to *disturb* him. It is he who unobtrusively includes among stories of income and adultery the mystical visions of a Swedenborgian disciple, speculations on matter and spirit, physiognomical, phrenological and parapsychological professions of faith — indeed everything the Foundling has always and everywhere imagined to satisfy his ambition to be God. All this naturally distorts the strict observer's perspective, without however unduly upsetting him, since he knows that such angelic excesses can only increase the scope of his dominion.

The Quixotic element Balzac had tried to suppress — rather than give it free rein as Cervantes did in order to understand and control it — plays in *la Comédie humaine* the part of an anachronistic and importunate prompter. Thus when it can find no means of capturing the narrative in its system of self-deification posturing as doctrine — or when to do so would be totally inappropriate — it stresses the superhuman factor, resorting to an unobtrusive distortion of apparently commonplace sayings by the simple addition of the word 'all' or of that symbol of the Absolute, the definite article. Thus Balzac writes: 'And it was *all the* Woman. . . .' 'This last word was *all* the Woman, the Woman of *all* times and *all* places. . . .' 'The Duke cast on Madame de Camusot one of those rapid glances with which *the* great nobleman sums up *all* an existence and sometimes a soul. . . . Oh, if only the judge's wife had been aware of this Ducal ability!' Proust was greatly amused by this 'Ducal ability', in which he detected the rather appealing weakness of a novelist too easily carried away by his fluency and not quite strict enough with his style. But the 'Ducal ability' is not only amusing. It should be seen as a residue of that Angelic insight Louis Lambert had enjoyed long ago. For although Louis, the child prodigy, second Moses and fallen Angel, has all but disappeared from *la Comédie humaine*'s visible scene, he is still the active promoter of 'everything, at once' and of the 'all within all' which attract the realistic Bastard whether he likes it or not. Unobtrusive and condemned to the satanic underworld from which the novel draws its primal energy, he persists in being the all powerful visionary who demolishes with a single word the critical observer's patient constructions, the visionary threatened with madness who hopes to comprehend the universe in a glance, like God (or like the great noblemen who are God's representatives on earth), in fact the megalomaniac genius, incapable of moderation, who ceaselessly swings from the sublime to the absurd.

Notes

1   According to Chaptal who was part of his immediate circle at St Helena, he was frequently heard to exclaim: 'How sorry I am that I am not a bastard!', which proves that he would indeed have liked to be one, as we may also surmise from the abnormal persistence of the Family Romance's influence on his behaviour. Cf. *Le Dossier Napoléon*, Marabout Université, Paris, 1962.

2   Freud, in a different context (but nonetheless related to the Family Romance) noted that Napoleon's repudiation of Joséphine was a

significant psychic event. According to him Napoleon was emotionally fixated on the image of his eldest brother Joseph whose authority, according to Corsican customs of the time, was equal to that of their father. In the complex of infantile images the Emperor's career reflects, Joseph seems to be associated on the one hand with Joséphine — the beloved if frequently betrayed wife finally repudiated without compunction — and on the other hand with the Biblical Joseph, who became his brothers' benefactor after being sold by them into slavery (Letter to Thomas Mann, 29 November, 1936 in *Correspondance*, Gallimard, 1966). Incidentally in *The Interpretation of Dreams*, Freud attributes to himself this singular 'Joseph Complex' which, he belived, had influenced for many years the choice of his closest friends. Joseph, the infallible dream-interpreter, Joseph sold by his brothers because of the megalomaniac dream in which he saw sun, moon and stars bowing down to him, thus establishes an unexpected link between Napoleon and Freud. True they were both dreamers and both strong enough to make their dreams come true.

3 Indeed a comparison between the historical hero's epic and the adventures of the imaginary hero is most revealing. Both set forth from their native islands to succeed through 'enterprise'. But while Robinson turns his back on civilisation, is shipwrecked and cast up on an island where he atones during twenty-five years for his outrageous transgressions, Napoleon wants to be the organiser of the civilised world from the start. He overcomes the storm that rages when he sets sail from Corsica and only lands on the fatal island at the very end of his fantastic peregrinations, too late, in fact, for it to be of any use to him. Robinson, exiled during all his youth, has time to develop and learn to live. Thus once his exile is over, he encounters no more trials. Napoleon, on the other hand, who was immediately and overwhelmingly successful, remains at heart the disappointed, insatiable child he always was and ends his life alone on a rock at an age when Robinson is at last enjoying the fruits of all his previous efforts.

4 My italics. The same Henri Brulard expresses, moreover, unconscious parricidal affinities: he is overjoyed when he hears that Louis XVI is dead.

5 The fact that *le Rouge et le Noir* is based on a news item — the Antoine Berthet case — does not detract from the validity of such an interpretation. Antoine Berthet, as the evidence of the case presents him, is psychologically similar to Julien and realises his Family Romance for precisely the same motives. That is why Stendhal uses the case without feeling the need to alter the facts significantly. Which does not imply, as has been suggested, that he lacked imagination, but that he knew instinctively the way in which the universal Family Romance merged with his own and corroborated it.

6 Julien involves Napoleon in his plan quite consciously. In fact he seduces Madame de Rénal as Bonaparte seduced Joséphine de Beauharnais, a much older woman than himself and who, as the mistress of Barras and many others, helps him to climb the first rungs of the political ladder. He then has an affair with Mathilde de la Môle in order

to attain the highest sphere of society as Napoleon married into the
reigning Austrian family to consolidate his Empire. Finally he too has
a half-noble son whom he loves and has to abandon.

7   Cf. Proust, *Contre Sainte-Beuve*: 'Sainte-Beuve et Balzac'. My italics.
8   Balzac's italics.
9   It should be noted that Balzac's verbose descriptions of such charac-
     ters, the significant details he provides — physical appearance,
     clothes, incomes, dowries — reveal no more and sometimes much less
     than, for instance, Kafka's well-calculated vagueness and cruel reti-
     cence about the inhabitants of his fictional world. After all, *The
     Castle*'s Land Surveyor, possibly the most undescribed, uncharac-
     terised hero in literature, has a more exactly circumscribed physical
     and moral existence than many an 'eminent' character of *la Comédie*
     whose role consists mainly in swelling the lists. Lukács' theory,
     insofar as it contrasts Balzac's social realism — effective because based
     on a correct understanding of class relations — with Kafka's abstract
     imaginary world that denotes a selfish, asocial attitude, totally uncon-
     scious of real contemporary problems, rests in fact on the simplistic
     notion that literary data can be converted into experience. Indeed this
     was the delusion which sustained Balzac, who describes sumptuous
     apartments, heaping on signs of luxury and wealth as if the objects he
     describes had the value of material objects and could satisfy the general
     desire to possess them. With Kafka the few material objects described
     are there for the reader's literary satisfaction — with Balzac they can
     almost be used or consumed.
10   Cf. *Encyclopaedia Universalis*, under *Balzac*.
11   His earlier works, published under his own name were signed Honoré
     Balzac. When criticised for suddenly adding the particle to his name,
     Balzac defended himself by asserting that his father, member of an
     aristocratic provincial family, had decided to resume his legitimate
     title. (Cf. Preface to *Lys dans la valée*). However this is not very
     convincing. In the end he admitted that he called himself de Balzac just
     as Monsieur Arouet had called himself de Voltaire ('He knew he
     would dominate his century, and such premonitions justify every
     audacity').
12   R. Judrin (op. cit.) observes 'Is it not remarkable that most of Balzac's
     relationships with women were grouped under a single first name?'
     Indeed, very remarkable but also very understandable in an accidental
     family where circumstances favoured incestuous relationships and
     encouraged its members to collaborate in a single Family Romance
     (furthermore we know that Laure de Surville collaborated with her
     brother in some of his books and 'provided' him with plots). The
     author takes his suggestion no further but his conclusion corresponds
     to our theory: 'It seems obvious that in *la Comédie humaine* Balzac was
     inspired by this natural coincidence, *rather as Napoleon, less permanent-
     ly, set Bonapartes over Europe.*' (My italics).
13   *La Fille aux yeux d'or* is usually highly praised by Balzac enthusiasts,
     though the story itself is more melodramatic than tragic and the
     pomposity, overstatement and inconsistent similes (Henri rules over

1828 Paris like an Oriental despot!) border on the absurd. This is because Balzac, *a great novelist but not a greater writer*, has the knack of somehow dreaming right, like all those who have delved deep enough into their unconscious to be scorched by the flame of truth they find there.

14   My italics.
15   My italics.
16   My italics.
17   Were we inclined to doubt the literalness of such dreams of super-human power and immortality which always accompany the Foundling's self-deification, the assertions of some apparently more level-headed writers would soon prove that such caution is misplaced. If Maxime Gorky is to be believed — and surely his noted intellectual honesty would warrant this — Tolstoy, at an advanced age, would occasionally exclaim in the presence of his young secretary: 'What if nature were to make an exception for me?' (by making him immortal). Tolstoy was certainly far from mad, but the Foundling — repressed during his long years of Bastard literary activity — was finally triumphing and had come back to tempt him (which would explain the puritanical tendencies of his later works and his famous condemnation of fiction). In general the born novelist seems to be *preserved from madness* by the inner conflict between the Bastard, rooted in time, and the Foundling, stubbornly installed on the fringe of reality. Or to be more precise, he has to be mad soberly in order to become a novelist.

II Hatred of the novel

I who felt I was vast as the
world . . .

Flaubert
Mémoires d'un fou

When Flaubert (who both admired and criticised Balzac: 'What a man Balzac might have been had he known how to write!') first read *Louis Lambert* he had the strange impression of having experienced at first hand this 'intellectual history' of an exceptional genius suffering from an incurable disease. Such a reaction — somewhat surprising from this promoter of impersonality who considered artistic emotion to be quite distinct from the emotions of everyday life — was due neither to accident nor to a passing aberration. Indeed he expounded its motives at length in a letter to Louise Colet written a few minutes after finishing the book:

> Have you read a book by Balzac called *Louis Lambert*? I finished it five minutes ago: I am thunderstruck. It is the story of a man who goes mad from contemplating intangibles. It has caught me with a thousand fishhooks. This Lambert is, as near as matters, my poor Alfred. I found there almost word for word some of the things we used to say: the conversations between the two boys at boarding-school are those we had, or similar ones. There is an incident concerning a manuscript bearing the form-master's appreciations that is stolen by some schoolmates, which happened to *me*, etc. Do you recall my telling you of a (projected) metaphysical novel about a man who, by dint of meditation manages to have visions which lead to his friend's ghost appearing to him and deducing (ideal, absolute) inferences from (actual, tangible) premisses? Well, that same idea is broached in the novel; *Louis Lambert* is its preamble.[1]

Nearly all Flaubert's letter concerns his terrifying resemblance to Balzac's hero. He notes one by one parallels and coincidences that seem to turn his most intimate experiences into the materialisation and extension of this fictional life. As a child

Louis Lambert was drawn to the narrator of his story by the same passionate friendship and community of ambitions and ideas that had attracted Gustave to Alfred Le Poittevin, the child prodigy and ultimately brilliant poet whose premature death he still mourned (Alfred died in 1848, four years before this letter was written). Louis and his little comrade — nicknamed 'the Poet-and-Pythagoras' — did not mix with their schoolfellows — a cruel, stupid, trivial breed whose only reaction to superior minds was scorn and sarcasm. So too was Gustave isolated in his singularity at boarding-school, mocked by his fellows, misunderstood by his masters and dismissed as an idiot because of the endless daydreams in which he indulged ('I who felt I was vast as the world. . .'). Louis Lambert, inspired and reduced to impotence by the excess of his over-weening visions, wrote a *Traité de la volonté*, an unfinished and never-to-be-published masterpiece, which is the exact counterpart of *La Spirale*, projected but never realised by Gustave. But the resemblances are not restricted to this particular case: they are no less striking between the writings of Balzac and Flaubert, whose choice of subject-matter and manner of presenting it incomprehensibly coincide:

My mother pointed out to me (she noticed it yesterday) a scene in *le Médecin de campagne* which is *identical* to one in my *Bovary*: a visit to a wet-nurse (I had never read the book any more than I had read L.L.). It contains the same details, the same implications, the same effects, as though I had copied it — were it not, I may say without boasting, that mine is better written. . . .

   Louis Lambert begins like *Madame Bovary* with an arrival at boarding-school and they have one sentence which is *identical*. . . .

There is no question of influence in the normal sense of the word since Flaubert had not read *Louis Lambert* when he conceived *Madame Bovary*. It is a far more disturbing coincidence implying similar psychological directives in the two authors and, consequently, identical fears and temptations:

In the end the hero, in a fit of mystical folly, wants to castrate himself. I too at nineteen, during my hard times in Paris, had the same urge (I can show you a shop in the rue Vivienne in front of which I stopped one evening seized by the idea with overwhelming intensity) when I had been two whole years without going near a woman. . . . There comes a time when one would like to *hurt oneself*, torture one's body, throw mud in its face because it is so disgusting. . . .

And Flaubert, drawn by Louis Lambert deep into the intermediary region of the psyche where his premonitory dreams, vague ecstasies and anguished presentiments take shape, exclaims: 'Confound that book! It hurts me! How deeply I experience it!' — without apparently realising that such an unbridled confession might pain and shock Louise Colet his mistress.

From the stand Sartre adopts in *l'Idiot de la famille* in order to understand Flaubert by diligently compiling his 'existential' dossier, this account of the discovery of *Louis Lambert* is obviously of seminal importance. First because the book made such a profound impression ('it caught me with a thousand fishhooks') and further because it reveals the self-justifying, self-glorifying mechanisms Flaubert is in the habit of exploiting for his own ends. Sartre asserts that Flaubert's claim to have undergone at boarding-school experiences similar to those of the boys described by Balzac is pure make-believe: 'Alfred and Gustave did not become friends at school but at the Hôtel Dieu and they never experienced the delightful, clandestine relationship of two lovers contravening public opinion.' Moreover Alfred Le Poittevin did not go mad and was never preoccupied with 'intangibles'. And what can we make of the sudden transitions from 'he' to 'us' and from 'we' to 'I' in this wild letter ('Lambert *is* my poor Alfred . . . .'. 'I found . . . some of the things *we* used to say. . . .'. 'There is an incident concerning a manuscript . . . which happened to *me* . . .')? Just this: Flaubert has to identify the pair Gustave-Alfred with Balzac's two boys since, being considered idiots by their masters and school-fellows precisely because of their intellectual superiority they bring a welcome balm to old wounds and provide an honourable motive for his own 'idiocy'. 'He was by no means an idiot of genius as people tried to make him believe, as Alfred too, by simply existing, sometimes made him feel. He was a genius — he had breadth of imagination and profundity of thought . . .'. The same instinct makes him identify with his dead friend and thus appropriate the intellectual assets he thinks he lacks. Alfred, as the misunderstood genius Louis Lambert embodies so poetically, becomes a 'prop' for Gustave's pride. 'The survivor never tires of stressing the dead boy's merits so as to stress his own (the other's equal in the eyes of the world), and thus gain public approval at

the same time as a little self-confidence. . . .'. Thus for Sartre —
here, for the time being, his masterly study ends[2] — Flaubert
uses the parallel with Balzac's hero to the same self-interested
ends and with the same bad faith as characterise his intellectual
activity in general — he makes use of a fictional character and a
dead friend as means of inhabiting that unreality where,
incapable as he is of being a real man in a real conflict, he
decides to 'play-act'.

Even without referring to psychoanalytic theories, which
alone might enable us to estimate the validity of such an
interpretation and in particular of the judgements of value on
which it is based (Flaubert's passivity, his flight into the realm
of the imagination and his 'existential' dishonesty are overtly
condemned), we are entitled to suggest that if the letter to
Louise Colet has more affinities with daydreaming than with
logical rationality — which even Sartre admits when he refers
to make-believe and wildness — then it is hardly surprising
that the dreamer should see himself as different people and
condense various ideas into a single character or image. In the
intermediary state between dream and reality where he finds
himself after the overwhelming experience of reading this
book, Flaubert — caught by a thousand fishhooks and practically beside himself — acquires the ability proper to all
dreamers to be both himself and another simultaneously or in
succession,[3] to be therefore Gustave, Louis and Alfred, not to
mention Balzac who, having written almost word for word
the opening of *his* Bovary, constitutes with himself and beyond time and death, a mysterious unity. In so doing he
naturally distorts the truth since he is not mad, Alfred when
alive was neither mad nor a genius, there was never any
'Poet-and-Pythagoras' at the Rouen school, and Balzac is not
in any way his 'alter-ego'. But even if such tendentious
alterations mainly favour his pride, they are nonetheless real
from the point of view of his inner being which, in fact, is
really preoccupied with 'intangibles', the Absolute, the impossible and thus seriously risks disintegration. In this respect
he is entitled to assert that he is Louis Lambert (neither more
nor less than was Balzac who was not mad either and had
probably never tried to castrate himself), or more precisely,
that Louis Lambert represents that part of himself which is
simultaneously the best and the most threatening.

When Flaubert made use of Louis Lambert to 'fabricate' his Romance with the tendentiousness customary to such myth-making (Louis is the Brother-figure in league with him against all tyrannical, narrow-minded fathers), he betrayed his inner motives to a greater extent than he concealed or falsified them to satisfy his own self-esteem (and maybe impress Louis Colet who could not fail to be overawed by his similarity to Balzac). For Louis is not just another of *la Comédie humaine*'s ambitious heroes. He is a key figure, almost Balzac's double, an embodiment of that pursuit of the Absolute, that rejection of contingencies in favour of an unformulable mystical ideal, that dread of Woman and sexuality, that narcissistic obsession proper to those who are estranged from the world and prepared to sacrifice their virility in order to achieve creative omnipotence. Thus when Flaubert declares that 'Louis Lambert is me!', as he was one day to repeat in connection with Madame Bovary, he is not only indulging a tendency to paint his intellectual and physical shortcomings in flattering hues (though as a born novelist he would doubtless be prone to such distortions), he is also reacting to the terrifying discovery that he resembles the hero of a failed intellectual experience, a doomed Foundling-genius condemned to the Other Side where he will die a madman, leaving to posterity nothing but a handful of disconnected thoughts. Thus Balzac's pursuer of the Absolute stranded halfway between Moses' wilderness and a Quixotic nowhere, may contribute, as Sartre suggests, a certain imaginative breadth and intellectual depth to Flaubert's spiritual and social shortcomings, but in Louis Lambert such enviable attributes are only conducive to death and madness. They are precisely what destroys his creative ability insofar as they dominate him entirely, leading ultimately to a state of total solipsism and make-believe, or in other words to the void. And in fact Balzac could only write *la Comédie humaine* because he had been able, by sheer integrity, to rid himself of this destructive character or, at least, reduce him to neutrality by forcing him to compromise. Now, at the time when he discovered this 'terrible book' — he was thirty-one and had published nothing — Flaubert was as yet undecided whether, like Balzac he would sacrifice Louis Lambert to the *social* requirements of his life and work, at the risk of including some degree of imperfection in his writings so as to increase his output and popularity, or whether he would succumb to his urge to pursue the untrammelled paths of Utopia and thus perhaps endanger his creative ability. Indeed he was to remain undecided for a long time, and this dilemma, ever present in his writing, was the cause of his greatness and of his perpetual despair. It inspired the dread which made him tremble whenever he put pen to paper and, despite distortions of the truth he may have conceded to his vanity, the almost brutal sincerity of his confession.

Flaubert might further have convinced Louise Colet of the startling resemblance he had discovered between himself and Balzac had he told her that he too had written the story of a child prodigy. Not it is true, as a fully-fledged novelist, but when still barely adolescent. This was his *Mémoires d'un fou*, the first-person story of a disappointed man indulging, at the end of his life, his grievances against humanity. If he refrained from doing so it was not that this work had ceased to pre-occupy him — indeed it would seem that it was very much in his mind whenever he dwelt on old memories and emotions — at any rate he repeats, sometimes literally, some of its images and ideas, as though his inner life and self-knowledge had remained static for fifteen years. *Mémoires d'un fou* does not purport to be a novel. It is rather a lyrical confession, like many another fostered by the literary Romanticism of the period (it could be seen as the 'Confessions of a Child of the Century', minus the century), and although it reveals the numerous influences to which the adolescent author responded, it is certainly worth more than the half amused, half dismissive interest usually conceded by experts to the work of a novice. The youthful 'madman' who writes his memoirs before he has lived is most informative. First because, as Albert Thidbaudet points out, he says much which 'style apart, is totally consistent with what the author will write in full maturity' (indeed it is he who conceives the original version of *l'Education sentimentale*), and furthermore because he perceives with rare insight the fundamental Quixotism of his Family Romance, and thus reveals the basic cause for the adult writer's latent but tragic inner conflict — which left him no peace until he decided to overcome, or at least by-pass it by sacrificing his mundane existence to the cult of a deified Art.

Mémoires d'un fou is dedicated and 'offered' to Alfred le

Poittevin, the everlasting friend, spiritual brother and confident whose intelligence Gustave estimates so highly that he
humbly requests that he should think for him (the story was
published posthumously and it seems that, apart from Alfred,
no one but the Goncourts saw the manuscript during Flaubert's lifetime).[4] It is a monologue interspersed with exclama-
tions, interjections and invocations to the reader. The narrator
undertakes to 'set down in writing everything that comes into
my head, my thoughts, reminiscences, emotions, dreams and
fancies; all that takes place in the mind and soul . . .'. Thus
here, instead of inventing a sequence of events involving
various actors within a given space and time, psychic material
is freely associated, unconstrained by a pre-established plan,
and images are allowed to flow at random, with no effort to
sort them out, organise, improve or assess them (strangely
enough Gustave defines his method — setting down in writing
everything that comes to my head — in the precise terms of
Freud's 'fundamental' rule, that single, simple rule which
replaces, for the psychoanalytic patient all other obligations).
To write about everything related to his innermost being and
to write about nothing else — such is the highly narcissistic
purpose of the 'I' who sets out to tell his life story. For, as he
adds, 'my life is not events; my life is thoughts . . .'. Vague
thoughts possibly, as vague and inscrutable as the dream on
which they are nourished, but thoughts whose obsessions,
because of the peculiar property of dream, will nonetheless
emerge with a quite remarkable clarity.

The aged narrator first recalls all the things he loved in his
dream-infested childhood 'like a poor lunatic with no positive
ideas nor definite purpose!' (he appears to see in such a
confusion of thoughts and opinions an obvious symptom of
madness; nor is he entirely mistaken if by madness he means a
peculiar psychic tendency to give the unconscious free rein).
These are: water, the sea, storms, his mother, unconstricted
horizons, moonlight or bright sunshine — in short all the
requisite ingredients for the romantic elegy — to which he
adds 'carts, horses, armies, military uniforms, drumbeats,
noise, gun-powder and cannons drawn over the paving stones
of city streets' (he is already addicted to the long inventories
which will later contribute so much to the colour and rhythm
of his style). However, for some unknown reason this child

who was 'happy and smiling, fond of life and of my mother.
Poor mother!' finds his need for universal love unsatisfied: 'the
stormy sea of mankind' rejects him. So he shuns it and takes
refuge in reading and writing: 'I read, I worked with passion
and enthusiasm, I wrote. Oh how happy I was then! . . . I
possessed an infinity greater perhaps than the infinity of
God . . .'. Yet the divine ecstasy of writing is no more than a
vulgar delusion, for then 'I had to descend from these sublime
spheres to find words, and who can express in words . . .
gigantic thoughts under which sentences give way as a glove
that splits asunder around the powerful fist it clothes? How can
we climb down from infinity to the empirical? By what
degrees can poetry descend without being shattered? How
reduce this Titan who encompasses infinitude?' The poet is
king, he is 'vast as the world', greater than God (perhaps), but
the totality of his visions is shattered by the prosaic reality of
words, and the grammatical rules of language drag him brutally back to earth where his intentions turn to nothingness unless
he can discover the mysterious degrees whereby the infinite
can be brought into relation with empirical reality without
disintegrating. The fifteen-year-old lad is obviously too inex-
perienced and especially too impatient to answer such urgent
questions unassisted (he asks them nonetheless with more
pertinence than many a more mature writer, and with a feeling
for the right turn of phrase that would suffice to prove the
authenticity of his vocation). That is why, fed up with poetry
but as insatiable and as incorrigible as Bouvard and Péuchet
were later to be, he throws himself whole-heartedly into the
'field of meditation' in quest of a new Absolute.

And that is how he acquired his reputation as a madman
among his schoolfellows and masters. For in this respect the
Rouen boarding school was an exact replica of the one in
Vendôme where Madame de Staël's protégé had been the butt
of a self-satisfied, second-rate community:

The fools! To think that they laughed at me! Them, so feeble, common and
narrow-minded; me, with my mind drowning on the fringe of creation, lost
in the world of poetry, knowing that I was greater than all of them put
together, obtaining infinite pleasure and heavenly rapture from all the inner
revelations of my soul! I who felt I was vast as the world and that a single one

of my thoughts, had it been made of fire like the lightning, could have reduced me to ashes. Poor lunatic! . . .

Alone against all, greater than all and gifted with such power that he could annihilate himself in the flame of his own thought, this 'poor lunatic' does not attempt to identify with any given doctrine, as Louis Lambert did when he recognised his own philosophy in the works of the great visionaries. He is the beginning and the end of his inspiration which, having really nothing but himself as subject, dispenses with any kind of proof or foundation (in this respect he is the true 'mystic of no faith', the visionary without dogma or doctrine to whom Flaubert was for ever attracted). Such intellectual self-sufficiency enables him to dispense with the need to communicate his ideas and ensures his unmediated vision of infinity where beings and objects reveal their significance in the blessed chaos of an unviolated Eden.

Self-satisfied and dissatisfied with mankind — or self-sufficient in both senses of the term — the young 'lunatic' does not feel compelled in any way to account for his rapture. He feels entitled to indulge in self-contemplation and self-glorification without having to justify himself or provide the reasons for the haughty scepticism which has led him to renounce human relationships at such an early age ('And why such bitterness at such a tender age? How can I tell?...'). There is more to it than a simple aping of the Byronic, Goethian or Shakespearian hero whose aristocratic disenchantment has doubtless already gone to his head. He has deeper, more personal reasons which, with his customary unpredictability, he reveals in the second part of his memoirs — when, after a three-week break, he appears to have noticed that he had not yet stated the main point of his narrative.

The two sections of the text are connected only by a loose but vital thread: a dream (or two dreams, the context fails to make this clear) the narrator has one night and associates with other 'terrifying visions fit to drive anybody mad', which he reports unmethodically amongst his disgruntled reflections on life in general. First he sees himself in his cot in his father's house which is suddenly invaded by beings 'both big and small, thickly bearded, unarmed' except for 'a steel blade (each one is holding) between his teeth'. These ogre-like creatures

look at him with 'great staring, lidless eyes' and then begin
fingering the objects around him, leaving bloody fingerprints
everywhere. 'I then felt the house rise from its foudations as
though a lever were prizing it up.... And they began to laugh
with a sort of death-rattle...'.When they leave, the child has
the impression 'he has eaten live flesh' and hears a protracted
scream, imprecise and high-pitched 'like a strange song whose
every hiss semmed to tear my chest apart as with a scalpel'.

This horrific vision is succeeded without transition by another nightmare scene in a 'green, flower-flecked countryside'
(the two are so closely linked one cannot tell whether they
constitute a single dream or two separate dreams). The child,
now probably much older, is walking at his mother's side by a
river, when he realises that his mother, having just fallen into
the water, has mysteriously vanished: 'I saw the water bubble,
the circles spread and disappear . . . and then I heard nothing
but the sound of water flowing between the rushes and
swaying the reeds. . . .' In the end however he hears his
mother's cries for help but remains motionless, simply observing that an 'irresistible' force glued him to the ground: 'The
water flowed, limpidly flowed and the voice I heard coming
from the depths of the river engulfed me in despair and
fury. . . .' Thus the dream-child does nothing to save his
mother from drowning, and the adolescent author of *Mémoires*
merely reports the fact without trying to justify such passivity
and indifference. Indeed he promptly dismisses the subject to
revert once again to his gloomy reflections wherein he is able
to indulge his grievances while relishing his own distinctive
genius.

Dreams about men with daggers between their teeth and
drowning mothers might not seem to have much relevance to
the rest of the *Mémoires*. They are even somewhat incongruous, giving the impression that they have been caught by
mistake in the flow of half-forgotten reminiscences purporting to be those of a noble and melancholic being who, through
an excess of disillusionment has achieved a kind of serenity.
The nightmares, still imbued with the horror they once inspired (their authenticity leaves little room for doubt since the
fifteen-year-old writer would hardly be expert enough at his
trade to 'fabricate' a literary dream), and inserted amongst the
hero's mystical effusions, are in total contrast with the bitter,

complacent tone of the whole work — they appear to have been experienced or re-experienced while the pen was transcribing them. Or at any rate the anguish, violent revulsion and primitive terror of a helpless being are immediately perceptible, indeed all the childish emotion the narrator tries to suppress by assuming the persona of a man who has lost all his illusions. But despite the discrepancy — or perhaps because of it — the nightmares do not give the impression of being foreign to the story. Rather they fill the enormous gap where the 'mad' adolescent's response to men and to reality should have been inserted. For in fact they represent, with the customary displacement, distortion and condensation of dream images, so many fathers and mothers — seven or eight fathers[5] armed to the teeth, in whom the terrible generator's power is condensed and multiplied, and a mother submerged by the tide, condemned to death for an unidentified crime. Parents then, whose mutual relationship is evaded, but made all the more obvious through the unusual noise — laughter sounding like a death-rattle — the tell-tale stains and the tremendous quake that tears the house from its foundations. There probably does not exist in the whole of adult and juvenile literature a more suggestive and exact description of the *Primal Scene* — a nocturnal scene that has no place among daylight events, a love scene where the ignorant, fascinated child detects no love but only obscenity, a ridiculous paroxysm and an inconceivable outburst of savagery. Seen in this light the nightmares are indeed the *Mémoires* missing link. They account for the adolescent's 'madness' and his autistic refusal to participate in everyday life: having witnessed, or imagined this shocking scene which reduces his idols to bestiality, life's origins appear to him irretrievably sullied, and life itself — his own to begin with and then the lives of others — marked with a terrible stigma.[6]

True, the two dream visions are juxtaposed, so that castrating father and accomplice mother are not presented together. But if we accept the traditional Freudian interpretation of contiguity in dream images as an indication of their inevitable *causality*, then the mother's downfall is directly related to the presence of black-bearded men[7] whose contact alone suffices to shed blood, and her disappearance in the river waters signifies her punishment for the ignoble acts to which she has submitted (in the dream it is her son who punishes her). Thus the two nightmare sequences constitute a coherent whole and represent together *by default* the noose that anguish, desire and guilt inextricably knots round the adolescent's — and the grown man's — throat. The author of *Mḿoires d'un fou* has no hope of recovery (indeed, in this respect Flaubert was incurable).[8] Brutally confronted with birth and the irreversibility of being, disappointed in parents he had idolised and simultaneously experiencing disturbing homosexual and incestuous impulses of which he is deeply ashamed, he believes that his only means of salvation is evasion, avoidance of the world of men and 'empirical' things which are all more or less contaminated by the degrading truth. Thus he will try to cloister his diseased soul within that other dream he calls, not without a certain pertinacy, 'madness'.

The Foundling who writes his memoirs has been expelled from Paradise where sexual distinctions — and indeed distinctions in general — are incongruous, by the revolting act of which he has been the precocious and captivated witness. Henceforth he knows. He has seen or imagined (it makes no difference, experience here is no less fantastic than fantasy) the brutal violation of the flesh to which he owes his own existence. And on this score at least he will have to revise his former beliefs. For however horrified he may be by his monstrous discovery, or rather, because he has interiorised its horror, he cannot pretend it has not taken place; he can neither forget it nor tell himself that it was a nightmare vision with no substantial reality. Thus while Don Quixote manages very well not to know anything and Louis Lambert happily eliminates the primal cause of every form of curiosity from his mystical speculations, the child Gustave, probably predisposed to a certain permeability of the unconscious by his paroxysmal constitution,[9] is obliged to confront reality with anger and despair, incapable either of accepting it or of compromising with the horror of existing by pretending that real life is always on the Other Side. Disheartened by his irreversible knowledge yet still faithful to his Quixotically uncompromising ideal, he is torn between two incompatible and equally imperious urges: the one for Utopian irresponsibility and fantasy, the other, more realistic, for those 'positive' things most apt to excite his anguish, antagonistic disdain, fury and disgust. The only way in which he could cope with the situation was to find an outlet for his obsessions in his writing — by alternating between two contradictory forms of inspiration — and to try and overcome them by putting all his faith in the idea of Art as such.

By a coincidence due perhaps to an uncanny insight, the two sections of *Mémoires d'un fou* correspond precisely to what Flaubert would later qualify as his 'contradictory ideals'. It almost seems that the narrative's aim is to express successively the two versions of the Family Romance. Apart from the nightmares about aggressive fathers and a drowning mother the first section is about the Foundling who, because he feels himself to be 'as vast as the world', gives free rein to a narcissistic misanthropy where he finds a vindication of his own superiority. The second, on the other hand, written 'after a three weeks' break' for which the author provides no explanation, is an accurate account of the Bastard's reminiscences. It is a love story where the adolescent, partially liberated from his obsessions, describes a critical stage of his 'sentimental education'. At fifteen — Flaubert's actual age when he wrote this first version of his future novel — the narrator falls deeply in love with a woman met by chance at the seaside, but in such circumstances that he cannot or will not declare his passion. For Maria — or Elisa Schlesinger who later appears as Marie Arnoux in the final version of *l'Education sentimentale* — is married, the mother of a little girl and much older than him (Elisa was in fact twenty-six when Flaubert met her at Trouville). Thus his love seems quite hopeless, especially as these obstacles of age and situation are further aggravated by his natural faintheartedness — he has set Maria up on a pedestal and feels that even were he a few years older he would never dare declare himself. Protected by his adolescent devotion even more than by her circumstances, his beloved is and always will be out of reach (moreover he himself cannot decide whether he would rather possess her or be the infant she nurses at her breast). When the summer is over Maria leaves with her husband and he goes back to school bearing a wound 'from which he has bled' and that will leave 'a deep scar' for the rest of his life.

Such as it is described in the *Mémoires d'un fou*, Flaubert's passion for Elisa Schlesinger — a lifelong passion indeed —

presents certain features which are absent from *l'Education sentimentale*, or which pass unnoticed there thanks to the more accomplished writer's skill. Writing under the effect of emotions he has only just experienced, much closer to his instinctive desires and more prone than the adult novelist to submit to the conflicting impulses of a foredoomed passion, the youth crudely reveals what a more effective repression will later force him to disguise — the equivocal nature of the 'triangle' dominating his conception of love, and his ambiguous attitude to the object of this love. As wife and mother Elisa revives his infantile passion for the maternal initiator whom he once expected would reveal to him the mysteries of love. But she is married to Schlesinger — the man whom Flaubert later refers to quite explicitly as 'my father Maurice' — who symbolises the Oedipal father, the Lord venerated as a God, and the rival who is the object of every animosity because he has a right to possess women and to impose the sacred taboos. However the youthful hero of the memoires is already aware that he will fall victim to this primal couple who might have assisted another in the difficult transition from infantilism to maturity, for he already knows or at least suspects that they will become an insuperable obstacle in his 'sentimental education' and the cause of his failure to cope with existence.

For he is not content with pursuing his romantic ideal to the accompaniment of songs of praise to the inaccessible beloved. Submitting to the pull of simultaneous idealistic and rational tendencies he has furthermore to understand what love really is, from what it stems, what it signifies, wherein lies its evil and its good. To begin with he notes that love provides him with 'something mystical and strange like a sixth sense'. He feels 'bigger and prouder'. But on the other hand it is no more than 'Two beings cast by chance into the world and who meet and love each other because one is male and the other female!' Already the problem of love involves two responses: the Bastard's, to whom being in love suggests an extra sense and increased power, and the Foundling's for whom the lover's ecstasy only stresses the outrageousness of human existence — to be cast by chance into the world — and the no less monstrous difference between the sexes which leads to a grotesque union ('because one is male and the other female!'). In other words the Bastard makes a considerable narcissistic profit out of what the Foundling, humiliated by the fact of being born and by the manner in which he was born, can only see as an intolerable loss:

and so they come home, both overwhelmed by a singular passion, for the bodies attached to these two souls are violently aroused, and then they are at it, copulating amidst grotesque moanings and sighings, both intent on reproducing another imbecile on earth, a poor creature who will do likewise!

The Bastard is able to take in his stride — if he is not entirely unscathed at least he is not overly upset — these hazards of birth from which moreover stem the fatal difference of the sexes and the ineptitude of copulation. In fact they only worry him insofar as he is still unconvinced of his own virility, and if he scoffs at them it is out of spite, because the couple from which he is excluded inspires him with hatred and envy. But the Foundling who still surreptitiously influences his outlook has other reasons for rebelling against the natural course of events — for him it represents a constriction of the individual by the senseless chain of generations, and thus a crime against which he openly takes his stand.

Right through this autobiographical tale where fantasies loaded with forbidden desires readily overstep the threshold of consciousness — too readily to allow for a great show of talent — Bastard and Foundling alternately voice their complaints. The first expresses his impotent, jealous resentment towards the parental couple, while the latter recriminates against the blind fatality of birth that creates the illusion of life but condemns the individual to nothingness. Thus the Bastard first effuses over the object of his passion and then cynically describes the obscene visions his jealousy conjures up:

I began to sob like a child, for nearby, just behind the walls my eyes devoured, there she was, lovely and unclothed, imbued with all the volup-tuousness night can bestow, all the allurements of love . . . this man only had to open his arms and she complied . . . then I besmirched the two of them, I piled on them the most bitter ridicule, and these visions which had made me cry for envy I forced myself to mock and despise. . . .

Here the adolescent describes in Oedipal terms the Primal Scene his childhood nightmare symbolised. Except that the scene has become much more realistic, jealous rage and perversity have replaced fear, the voyeur masochistically recreates the act in all its details. For the father is no longer the ogre with a dagger between his teeth but the husband he wants to supplant. And the mother instead of being the drowning woman mysteriously engulfed by the waters, is a living, obscene and grotesque female, abasing herself to the rank of a prostitute.[10] Conforming to the secret law which stipulates that love must be dissociated from admiration in the later version of the Family Romance, the two parents are here degraded together. But whereas the loathsome father continues to be the object of unmitigated envy, even if he is the senseless instrument of procreation, the mother, deprived of her saintly attributes by conniving with gross life forces, becomes the lowest of the low. (In *Novembre*, the short story that some years later was to be an exact counterpart of *Mémoires d'un fou*, Maria becomes Marie, the young prostitute, and she in turn will become Marie Arnoux in the final version of *l'Education sentimentale*, thus proving further the indestructible link established in Flaubert's unconscious between the two contradictory aspects of feminity).[11]

The Bastard's biological heredity[12] constitutes another of his many grievances together with the moral constraints imposed by a society created before him, in his absence and against him:

Free, you? From birth you must suffer from your father's infirmities; together with your life you are given the seed of all vices . . . you will be told that you must love your father and care for him in his old age . . . you will be brought up to believe that you must beware of being physically drawn to your sister or your mother, when you, like all men, are the product of an incest . . . when the sun sets daily on whole populations who consider incest a virtue and fratricide a duty . . .

After asserting his natural right to commit incest (and parricide under the slightly attenuated form of fratricide) he proceeds to investigate the significance of birth.

Was it you who chose it? . . . You were doomed to be born because one day your father came home after an orgy, heated by wine and loose talk, and your mother took advantage of the situation, using all the tricks of a woman driven by the sexual instinct and bestiality with which nature provided her at

the same time as her soul, and she succeeded in rousing this man worn out by
his excesses since adolescence. . . .

Born by chance as the result of his father — rotten to the core
— having copulated with his bestial mother,[13] the child is,
from the day of his birth, the object of an irreparable injustice
he can only avenge by radically refuting the course of events
which constitute in themselves a limitation of his individuality. This is where the Bastard's sophisticated nihilism coincides with the innocent Foundling's metaphysical nihilism —
whether because of the taboos forbidding him to possess his
mother or because he has been evicted from his infantile
paradise by the knowledge of sexual difference, a human being
is 'had' and his life, however significant it may otherwise be,
will never possess more than the 'grandeur of nothingness'.

Because the *Mémoires d'un fou* happened to have been written
during that period of transition between childhood and puberty about which so many writers have reminisced but so few
have described while actually experiencing it, it is probably the
most remarkable document that literature has ever produced
on the Family Romance — that condensed story of the impossible desires that force men of all ages to jolt the world out of its
established order with every atom of imaginative power at
their disposal. Devoid of talent, undoubtedly (though not
lacking in inspiration) and thus all the more revealing as to
what it is that provokes the urge to write ('To write, oh, to
write and thus to possess the world!'), the narrative clearly
illuminates the two contradictory tendencies between which
Flaubert, without attempting to reduce them to a unified
ideology, was forced to divide his talent, while setting the
intangible truth of art above and beyond the 'positive' truth of
experience. Hence the significance of this text, still childish in
part but already loaded with the complex of emotions and
ideas the mature writer will spend his life describing (paradoxical as it may seem, he will never invent anything else). It is
a rough sketch[14] of all the confessions he would ever write
while forcibly excluding himself from his writings (for by a
further paradox this promoter of the impersonal wrote nothing but revised confessions). A very rough sketch indeed,
though complete in its way, and where he manages to answer
the riddle that was to intrigue and discourage so many of his

contemporaries and make him the least known of all famous writers —'or at any rate the least understood. Moreover it is the starting point of an unparalleled passion for literature, which explains why Flaubert, carried away like Kafka's country doctor in an earthly carriage drawn by unearthly horses, had no option but to become a novelist, and the no less imperious motives which forced him to write against one half of himself— in self-hatred and hatred of the novel.

★

A lot has been written about the way Flaubert alternates his themes and how this corresponds to his need for perpetual changes of environment, atmosphere and emotional or social tonalities (which is partly illusory, since in fact Flaubert has only two alternatives). After the rather cool reception of his first *Tentation de Saint Antoine* by his friends Du Camp and Louis Bouilhet, he worked for many years at *Madame Bovary*, the plot of which had been practically forced upon him by Bouilhet as an antidote to those 'hazy themes, so vague in themselves that you fail to contain them'. When Bouilhet criticised the vague and the hazy which he instinctively felt to be dangerous, he was not attacking a temporary defect. As a matter of fact for Flaubert 'vague exaltation' was the very purpose of art, while haziness, exaggeration and insanity were the significant core — or as he put it the 'nexus' — of genius. However he gave in (with a terrible cry of anguish we are told) and abandoning the teeming, colourful East of the famous anchorite for the uneventful world of middle-class Normandy, settled down to his long and tedious task.

During the five years it took him to transpose the story of Health-Officer Delamare — a news item that was still the talk of the town — into the story of Monsieur Bovary, he was, according to him, completely overcome by disgust and boredom at the triviality of the subject which made him literally squirm: 'Oh Bovary! I shall remember him . . . This middle-class topic repels me!' This book, the first to make him suffer 'stylistic pangs', is the object of bitter, violent recriminations, as though he could not forgive it for constraining him to live in daily contact with mediocrity and stupidity (two things of which he was not so easily to be rid). Thus one would have expected him to be relieved when, having completed this harassing task, he could revert to his beloved East and 'indulge in colourfulness' while writing his Carthaginian tale. But not at all. Despite the fact that he had chosen his subject to suit his taste — resurrection of the past, exoticism and loud barbaric vociferations — it was not long before he observed that the novel's title alone bored him to death. Thus disheartened by the *execution* of *Salammbô* as he always was when he had to stick to a given plan and conform to a narrative's logical sequence — two things the adolescent author of *Mémoires d'un fou* dispensed with but which Flaubert was now unable to avoid — he turned once again to the hopeless monotony of contemporaneity and the drab, petty beings who were the last to appeal to his desire for evasion. Then his original idea for *l'Education sentimentale* gradually began to take a hold on him and, while sorting out some old notebooks, he was seized with a 'strong inclination' to rewrite it and give it a definite novelistic shape. However, no sooner had he started than he was bitterly complaining once again: he did not 'like' his subject, the idea was not a good one and it was 'contrary to the aims of art' (indeed 'vague exaltation' had no place here), the intrigue was 'silly', the plot 'paltry', in short before he had finished it he was already vowing never again to undertake 'such a business'. In vain, as we know. For after the interlude of *Trois Contes* he launched himself into that incredible enterprise, *Bouvard et Pécuchet*, and the niggling, overwhelming task of compilation he had set himself was largely responsible for his utter physical exhaustion and final depression. Thus if he is to be believed — and he is indeed as we shall see later — this man who had turned to literature as others turn to religion and who saw art as the one thing which justified existence, got nothing from the novelist's trade but boredom and disgust.

With one exception, however, which (in a letter to Louise Colet where he tried to explain his aversion for *Madame Bovary*) he perceptively linked to a peculiarity in his character:

What comes naturally to me is what is unnatural in other people, the extraordinary, the fantastic, the metaphysical or mythological howl. Saint Anthony did not require a quarter as much intellectual effort as Bovary. It was an outlet; I found nothing but pleasure in writing it and the eighteen months I spent writing those five hundred pages were the most deeply voluptuous of my whole life.

And the fact is that in the whole of his correspondence there is not a single bitter or dissatisfied reference to this book which occupied his thoughts for twenty-six years. When he mentions it he invariably expresses his pleasure at feeling himself at one with what he is doing, utterly fulfilled and giving free rein to his imagination.

Indeed Flaubert's fondness for *la Tentation de Saint Antoine* undoubtedly stemmed from the book's peculiar nature. It is, as he himself admitted, an 'extravagant' work — he had even considered subtitling it *'The Epitome of Insanity'* — but a work which, precisely because it made no demands on him to conform to any sort of reality, allowed him to indulge his Quixotic aberration. To create a hermit in the wilderness to whom absolutely nothing happens, for whom there is nothing to do apart from thinking; to write a plotless story, a narrative without beginning or end enlivened only by the visions of a literally unbridled imagination — such an enterprise might at most be undertaken by a poet but never by a novelist unless he happens to be the guilt-ridden novelist Flaubert became as soon as he took up his pen. In such a case of course the extravagance of the theme is not only tempting in the milder sense of the word, it is, in the strongest theological sense, the most dangerous of temptations.

La Tentation de Saint Antoine, extravagant and insane as it indeed is, rigorously follows the Foundling's programme as we find it outlined in the *Memoires d'un fou* — it has no definite plot or positive idea — and especially in *Novembre*, the auto-biographical short story written between these two works, where Flaubert, barely emerged from adolescence, reveals both the *content* of his primal dream and the *technique* of the daydreams that were to become the baroque visions of his famous saint. The exercise of this technique could not be more unsophisticated.

I delved as deep as possible into my own mind. I scrutinised it under all its aspects, sank to the bottom, came up and started again; soon I was carried away in a frenzied gallop of the imagination, a prodigious leap out of reality, I made up adventures, told myself stories, built myself castles, installed myself there as Emperor, excavated mines of diamonds which I cast by the bucketful along the ways I would follow. . . .

Never has the Foundling of our Romance given a more

accurate and exhaustive description of what takes place in his
head when he *tells himself stories* in a *prodigious leap out of reality*.
Neither has he ever been more explicit as to their significance:

> I coveted the Emperor's absolute power, innumerable slaves, wildly enthu-
> siastic armies; I coveted the beauty of women so as to admire myself, let my
> long tresses fall about my ankles and contemplate my reflection in
> streams. . . .

The hero of *Novembre*, apart from his dream of kingship —
entirely consistent with fairy-tale tradition — surpasses even
the legendary Narcissus, since he covets the attributes of both
sexes[15] (we have already noticed that he was able to identify
with women, to be Marie as he will one day be Emma), so as to
recapture the totality of being he lost together with Paradise.

As Emperor he will experience the intoxication of absolute
power surrounded by his prostrate slaves and soldiers. As
woman his beauty will sway the world and he will be transported by self-love. As man and woman in one he will be
'King of the Indies, go hunting on the back of a white elephant,
watch Ionian dancers, listen to Grecian waves breaking on
temple steps, hear the night breeze whisper in the oleanders of
my gardens, elope with Cleopatra . . .'. Thus his *prodigious
leap out of reality* will instantly shatter the partitions of space
and time — he will be everywhere at once, in any period of
history, at the site of all vanished civilisations, he will be the
One and the All, the One elusive as Proteus, the All immutable
in its eternity.

Alone in the wilderness of intemporality, wholly absorbed
in the passive contemplation of the stories he tells himself,
skilled in a hallucinatory art that enables him to see the
changing creatures of his imagination as flesh and blood —
such too is Anthony despite his saintliness, or more precisely
thanks to his privileged situation as believer in the power of
thought. Doubtless insofar as he is an ascetic and a future saint
he aspires to Nothingness rather than All, but what we know
about the mechanism of his visions enables us to deduce their
significance, to imagine, that is, that for him such nothingness
is really All in disguise. Saint Anthony, known as *the Great*,
can satisfy his thirst for power without impersonating Nero or
the King of India. He only has to abolish himself as individual

and dissolve into a single thought — he is the visionary to whom the world appears against a backdrop of carnal and spiritual orgies. Nothingness sets him higher than the highest degree of power ever imagined by the ambitious frenzy of man. It raises him to the total void where individualities and categories break down leaving him alone before the Devil or God. In this respect Anthony's tragedy is very different from Faust's, although both see Helen of Troy and share an insatiable desire for power. For Faust made his pact with the devil in order to dominate mankind in every field of action, while Anthony is only a figure in the wilderness, a passive Don Quixote who has renounced action even in his dreams and who, sceptical rather than mad, must remain on the fringe of nothingness.

Like the child in the *Mémoires d'un fou* Anthony might say that he has no other existence than in thought. However, unlike him he does not recount everything that goes on in his head but *sees* it in a fantastic vision whose apparitions beset him, so that he is a prey to his own mind. In fact, throughout the whole story he is the projector of an exteriorised mental film, so that every passing thought takes body and he is transported to a timeless elsewhere in which he conjures up at will a turbulent population of phantoms. In this elsewhere he appears to be the captive audience — but in reality is the all-powerful producer — of visions that arise, unfold, emerge one from the other, tangle and finally destroy each other — they do not hold, neither do they uphold each other, for each one annihilates its predecessor. They flow independently, unconflicting and almost unrelated. For the Temptation is not restricted to the depraved hallucinations that overwhelm the saint — it consists furthermore in their absurd proliferation and inconsistency. Derived from the autonomy of a psychic process entirely unconnected with reality, it dissolves into perpetual contradiction, endless interruptions in the sequence of meanings, and senseless words directed at nothingness. It is deified thought 'tempting' itself, or as the Foundling whom it beguiles and vaguely disturbs aptly says, it is 'the epitome of insanity'.

The uninterrupted flow of images Anthony projects on to the desert sands — to recapture the world he has renounced and possess it together with its monsters, nightmares, insane

heresies and abominable perversions — does not reveal very
much about the development of the saint's mundane personality during his childhood among human beings. According to
the earliest version of the story it would seem that he was a
wealthy youth who gave all his possessions to the poor on
realising his vocation. One of his tempters reminds him of his
intellectual gifts and that, were it not for his folly, the vast
extent of his knowledge might have brought him world-wide
fame. There is no reference to this in the final version where,
on the other hand, Anthony is slightly more explicit about his
past which he sees as laden with guilt: 'I was blamed by all
when I left home. My mother sank dying, my sister made
signs to me to return, and the other, Ammonaria, the child I
used to meet at evening by the well when she brought back the
buffaloes, sobbed. . . .' Later when his 'thirst for matyrdom'
leads him to Alexandria — in vain as it turns out since 'the
persecutions had ended three days before' — at the Temple of
Serapis he imagines he recognises Ammonaria in a naked
woman beaten by soldiers and whom the Governor is about to
execute as a final warning to heretics. At other times, on the
verge of sleep, she appears to him in the guise of a seductive
temptress. Has Ammonaria been tortured to death for her
faith? Has she been reduced to prostitution by poverty and
despair? Anthony hopes she has not left his own mother
whom he knows, however, must have died of grief and whose
curses overwhelm him:

She will have cursed me for abandoning her, tearing out her white hair in
handfuls. Her corpse is lying in the hut, under the rush roof, between the
ruined walls. A hyena thrusts its head through a hole sniffing. Horror!
Horror! . . .

Between his visions of Ammonaria offering herself to him or
to all men 'her two breasts proferred' and the vision of his dead
mother rotting among hyenas, Anthony's life becomes an
abomination to him, and he wants to throw himself into the
precipice gaping at his feet. While he still hesitates to commit
this final sin an old woman whom he takes for his resurrected
mother appears. But instead it is Death come to extoll the
raptures of suicide. Then suddenly she is no longer alone but
accompanied by a lovely young girl whose features seem to

the saint to be those of Ammonaria. And now Lewdness tries to revive hís will to live by stimulating erotic desire. However the two figures finally intertwine and caper round him in a baleful dance which shows up their similarity: Lewdness has 'corpse-like attributes' while Death procures voluptuous thrills for the killer. Thus the mother and the beloved, from both of whom life and death are derived, belong to the same category of temptation — they have both made a pact with the devil who, for this reason, has conjured them up intertwined. True, the devil is on the wrong track, for Anthony has in fact truly renounced happiness and feels himself to be eternal.

Having called the devil's oldest bluff Anthony still has to undergo the importunities of two grotesque, hybrid creatures who represent the appeal of the Unknown and of the Imagination. But whether they are myth or fancy they have little effect on Anthony who is only moved at the last stage of his ordeal by the sight of an infinite swarm of beings crawling between life's folds. These are undefined organisms, neither animal nor vegetable, animate nor inanimate. They are rudimentary bodies and souls derived from ceaseless metamorphoses at the untold stage where matter is self-generated. Here, confronted with this genesis re-enacted for his benefit, Anthony is suddenly unafraid — wide-eyed, he perceives plants undistinguishable from stones, pebbles resembling human brains, limbs sprouting from limbless bodies, living organisms that are no more than an imperceptible vibration, and he is half-delirious with the incredible joy of being initiated into the mysteries of creation:

Oh joy! Joy! I have seen life emerge, I have seen the first stir . . . I could fly, swim, bay, bellow, howl. I would like to have wings, a shell, a crust, to blow smoke, have a trunk, to squirm, be divided into sections, be within all, penetrate every atom, descend to the depths of matter — be matter!

The nightmare is doubtless dispelled by the first light of day. At dawn Christ's countenance glows in the sun and Anthony resumes his prayers. Yet in one respect he has succumbed to Temptation: he has voiced the fantastic thirst for power from which his saintliness derives.

In this lyrical text, half-way between prose and poetry, in fact a hybrid itself, the 'epitome of insanity' is really the epitome of megalomania — to be part of everything, to be everything, *to be matter* — and Anthony, the novelist's spokesman for his most extravagant fantasies, represents his vindicating genius, the child's one consolation for having been born. It is not hard to see how this splendid 'overflow', which could accommodate all the things good taste and convention preclude from the novel, should have been for him the cause of 'stylistic delight' and incomparable satisfaction. But then why did he so often set himself tasks that were uncongenial to his unbridled lyricism? Why, more than any other writer, did he keep to strict plans, collect data and accumulate material in order to write books that would be as precise and as historically and sociologically accurate as fiction can ever be? Why in fact was he a realist, a founding father of realism, if as he says, reality was precisely what he hoped to evade through writing (he was impatient to get back to work on *la Tentation* so as to 'forget' his contemporaries)? The answer is doubtless to be found in the 'two conflicting ideals' to which he simultaneously aspired. For indeed such ideals were not mere intellectual superstructures but expressions of the inner conflict which made him incapable of coping with reality and from whence derived his profound pessimism.

The reason for which Flaubert abstained from writing nothing but 'insanities' — disguised as romances of chivalry or as fairy tales — should doubtless be sought in the context of *la Tentation*, that literary transposition into a religious mode of his own temptation as a writer (thanks to the term 'vocation' being shared equally by art and by religion: the artist too retires from the world, goes into the 'wilderness' to follow his 'vocation'). Now, although the text reveals almost nothing of the saint's biography it does report a significant fact, intimately linked to his spiritual experience — his mother's death and the curses she calls down upon him on her death-bed. At the story's simplest level the saint is cursed for his flight into the wilderness — he is a saint insofar as he is cursed and cursed insofar as he is a sinner (Anthony sees his mother's death as a consequence of his departure for the wilderness. But if we recall the child in *Mémoires d'un fou* who lets his mother drown without even the excuse of a vocation, and especially *Saint Julien l'Hospitalier* who murders his father and mother, we may suspect him of reversing the order of events. Thus instead of his mother dying as a consequence of his departure, he would have killed her and then fled to the wilderness in the hope of thus expiating his crime). Insofar as the great metaphysical 'howl' which is Flaubert's true vocation, is conducive to such terrifying tendencies as the rejection of the world, megalomania and matricide, it is obviously compacted with guilt and, to a certain extent, subject to prohibition. That is why, since he can neither readily indulge nor totally renounce it, he temporises by allowing it to lead a semi-clandestine existence in his work and only exploits it intermittently between two 'real', less suspect novels — or at least novels less entangled with the primitive forces deeply perturbing his 'saintliness'.

To contain All, be matter and thus able to understand its cause and its generation, acquire through self-contemplation the power to dominate the universe and thus be at the very source of existence — such was Anthony's demented ambition which presupposes the abolition of natural procreation where woman plays a passive but indispensable part. For this Foundling, who cannot bear the idea of owing his existence to beings of flesh and blood and therefore makes up stories in which he is his own generator (to be matter is to be capable of generating oneself at will) his parents are his worst enemies, since they restrict him to the narrow sphere of biology. Try as he may, the 'madman' of genius like the greatest ascetic of Christianity, will always be reminded who he is by his mother and father — in their presence greatness and sublimity are as nothing, dreams of perfection are shattered, fantasies of omnipotence are a pointless makeshift, a childish make-believe, the 'epitome of insanity'. Whence the necessity to murder them as did the demi-gods of mythology in the distant past, and as the heroes of civilisation, the founders and saviours of humanity who ensure progress are always doing.

But parents are not only condemned for metaphysical motives. They are further condemned because of their vile treachery, because they first presented themselves to the child as divine beings, when they are really irresponsible and libidinous, weak, ignorant creatures, wholly subjected to the darker powers of existence. Guilty insofar as they perpetrate a life of bondage, they are moreover despicable for the baseness of their deception which precludes any kind of reconciliation or forgiveness. For the desperately outraged Foundling the only solution is violent elimination — it is his sole means of revenge and salvation, the only atonement for the humiliation his glorified Ego has suffered through being born. 'Madman' of genius or saint — or for that matter artist — Flaubert's hero cannot and will not be free of the world except through the murder of those who placed him in it. The blood that binds him must be ruthlessly shed, his mother must expiate the dual crime of having cast him into a separate world and of having fashioned him in degradation and sexuality, he who is an equal of the gods! (in all Flaubert's writings concerning childhood there is always some more or less explicit reference to parri- cide: in *la Légende de Saint Julien l'Hospitalier*, that amazing short story where the novelist realises after a fashion his early ambition to write a fairy tale, the two parents are murdered together in their bed, while in the *Mémoires* and *la Tentation* only the mother is sacrificed).[17] In the primitive regions where the requirements of saint and author converge, art is not merely contaminated by its account of the primal murder, it is itself a criminal transgression for which the author cannot help being responsible even though it takes place in a sphere which is almost entirely inaccessible to thought. That is why Flaubert had to come to terms with the sort of writing which gave him the most aesthetic satisfaction — for its over-radical rebellion and exceedingly dangerous rejection would force him to proscribe it or at least restrict its output (he did so first in complying to Bouilhet's severe criticism which was obviously consistent with his own guilt).

Apart from their intrinsic primitivism the Foundling's works are equivocal insofar as they distort their own motives. For they make a great show of despising reality whereas their author has already outgrown such Quixotic innocence. At fifteen Flaubert was conscious of the true cause of his aversion for reality, and although he put up a certain resistance, the Primal Scene's traumatic effects, which had earlier sapped his self-confidence, had already convinced him that reality is unbearable precisely because it cannot be abolished, changed or dismissed by a simple intellectual act. In such circumstances negation is of no avail. Anthony may reject reality by electing to live alone in the wilderness, but reality overtakes him in the form of hallucinations and life continues, unperturbed. Thus the author who cannot unlearn his experience, is obliged to partially dissociate himself from the hermit saint whose revulsions and yearnings he shares. Since he cannot ignore a reality he perceives in its every detail, he renounces utopian visions and settles for an exact observation of actuality instead, which he undertakes with the same passionate enthusiasm he dedicated formerly to his daydreams ('details are agonising especially for those who love details as I do', he observed). This is the logic of his honesty — it obliges him, not to accept what he sees, but to love details in spite and because of the suffering they entail.

Devoured by guilt and, whether he likes it or not, no longer innocent, Flaubert's Foundling finds it easier than he would admit to accept the Bastard's prosaic outlook. For he is himself already to a certain extent a Bastard, at any rate sufficiently so to give a misleading impression with regard to his aspirations (in his letters to George Sand and others he tries very hard to make out that he is not a Don Juan but rather a sort of monk). He confesses in *Novembre* that what he mainly likes about women is 'the mystery of women outside wedlock' and considers the term 'adultery' to be the most beautiful word in the language. He dreams of 'the love of a princess or an actress which fills you with pride and sets you on the same footing as the wealthy and the powerful' and exclaims in reference here to his actual existence: 'Had I but an income of a hundred-thousand francs!' as if he asked no more than did Balzac's typical Bastards. Moreover he does not only indulge the social climber's materialistic ambitions, but admits that he dreams of being admitted to the highest social circles and of making his mark there.[18] He who secretly suffered from the fact of being born because birth is a descent into finite reality, now finds himself in the position of regretting that he was not 'well born'.[19] Moreover Flaubert was not above following up an aristocratic connection in his ancestry — he certainly considered doing so, though gave up the idea at once ('To think that I did not exploit such a connection as a means of making my way into high society!'). But he was really much prouder of his 'savage ancestress, a Natchez or an Iroquoi, I'm not sure which'.[20] In short he was fond of titles, fame, all that glitters, luxury and licentiousness; he loved money, Parisian high life, people of rank whose contact suffices to bestow grace and power, and princesses whose love makes the loved one noble.

And he could not, in all sincerity, eliminate from the world of his writing as he had done in his *Mémoires d'un fou* and *la Tentation* all that for which, in his youth, he had thought himself capable of striving — though it was highly distasteful to another aspect of his nature. However, if out of loyalty he felt obliged to bear witness to such tangible objects, then he would have to perform a crucial conversion in his writing — that is, he would have to switch from vision to observation, from pure erudition to 'field work', from the legendary to the romantic or, to use the significant titles of his two major works, from Anthony's Temptation in the wilderness to Frédéric Moreau's Education in the strictly limited material world where he tried to get on.[21]

By the time Flaubert depicted himself in *l'Education sentimentale*, which was no less than *la Tentation* the work of a lifetime (he began it when he was nineteen, returned to it at twenty-four and again at fifty-two, without probably ever ceasing to think about it in between), the Napoleonic or Balzacian Bastard had come to the end of his career — people had stopped dreaming of travelling-salesmen-Napoleons or of tradesmen and banker Napoleons either. They were not interested in men like Nucingen nor in those who gave the lustre of an historical event to their sexual intrigues. For the times had changed, History had turned about, a bourgeois king reigned in the Emperor's place and the fictional hero's scope was sadly restricted. Indeed heroes nowadays were most unheroic — they were either the embittered offspring of a disenchanted century with nothing but vague regrets and biting wit as spiritual baggage; or they were narrow-minded philistines, argumentative, busy, ambitious, certainly not happy but, as Rimbaud was to put it, contented. They embodied on the one hand dreams, nostalgia for past grandeurs, passion for passion's sake, art as opposed to the triviality of action; on the other hand, narrow conventionality, petty preoccupations, cynicism raised to the status of ideal and sordid everyday worries; but for the most part they were a mixture of the two, in a society that had not properly recovered from recent historical events and somehow managed to be both ferocious and drab. This is the realm of the average Bastard — romantic and philistine, rearing for action and incurably idle — whom Flaubert, resenting the fact that they had so much in common yet as clear-sighted as he was resentful, immortalised in a despicable 'bourgeois' paradise.

Frédéric Moreau is a charming version of this average Bastard on whom Flaubert had already taken his revenge when he invented Homais and Madame Bovary (there is nothing surprising in Emma Bovary's incarnating the male Bastard since we know that 'Madame Bovary is me!' and that Flaubert put all the effeminate, sickly sentimentality of his belated Romanticism into this character). Plagued with Rastignac's unruly appetites[22] but incapable of satisfying them, passionate but passive, still too romantic or, as he sees it, too much the artist, to participate in struggles and conflicts, but already too much of a bourgeois to risk giving way to serious temptations, Frédéric Moreau is a perfect product of the society of the century that was to see the budding and withering of revolutions. He goes round and round in the narrow circle of his exaltation and, taking this illusory motion for action, he systematically wrecks every chance he has of realising his immoderate ambitions. Thus he carries out the bitter prophecy Flaubert had scribbled in his youth on the last page of one of his manuscripts: 'My poor friend! You will always be full of enthusiasm for your dreams and disgusted by what you achieve.' And indeed he will always be intoxicated with himself and disgusted by his achievements — or rather by what he thinks he has achieved, forever the victim of his own wishful thinking.

But what are his dreams and what exactly is the nature of his disgust? As to his dreams they are very far from the impressive visions in the wilderness. They remain at ground-level, at the level of existence — an existence full of women, wealth and fame, of those tempting, easily obtainable things in short, which the dreamer lacked. For after *la Tentation* the significance of the word 'dream' was considerably diminished: Anthony's dreams were hallucinations, Frédéric's dreams are entirely consistent with his indolence — their purpose is not to create another world but to get out of this one all the wealth and advantages it can provide free of charge. In this respect at least he lays no claim to originality. He dreams of love — since love is the unlimited space which the unapproachable figure of Marie Arnoux inhabits — and then he dreams of rewriting his whole life, just like any other Bastard who banks on women

218 *Origins of The Novel*

for his success in the world. Indeed though he is truly in love, and sincerely prepared to give up everything for his hopeless passion, he can see no harm in simultaneously soliciting the favours of wealthy society ladies — why not, after all, since everything is grist to the mill of success? Thus after a party where he was at his best he dwells on the advantages to be gained from an amorous relationship with an influential lady:

First his appearance (he had admired his reflexion several times in various mirrors), [23] from the fit of his suit to the bows on his pumps, left no room for complaint; he has conversed with influential men, been in contact with wealthy women. Monsieur Dambreuse had been charming and Madame Dambreuse almost inviting. He weighed each significant sign. It would be devilishly fine to have such a mistress! And why not, after all? He was as good as the next man! . . .

When Madame Dambreuse is widowed he seriously considers marrying her, then forced to lower his sights and renounce such aristocratic aims, he sets his eye on Mademoisell Roque, the daughter of a fraudulently enriched peasant. Needless to say none of these plans is crowned with success (like Flaubert he might have said that he had 'much dreamt and achieved little'), but besides failing to conclude the match which was to have set him on the path to success he spoils everything — his chances with Madame Arnoux no less than his future social triumph — by contracting a liaison with a kept woman who has emerged from who knows what gutter. For some time he leads an idle existence — idleness is the one thing he gets out of his dreams — divided between his besotted love for a spotless woman and his desire for a street walker, so that the two images which share his emotional life finally merge and become interchangeable (consistent here with the fatal love to which Flaubert unconsciously alludes in his use of the name Marie). When the young man's passivity has achieved its aim he finds himself once again alone, probably doomed to perpetual celibacy and, like so many romantics who are too weak or too indolent to take their dreams seriously, definitively settled, without too much difficulty, in the role of a middle-class, middle-aged man.

The fame which was to have finally crowned Frédéric's

efforts fares no better than his love-life. As a schoolboy he had
already seen himself as a writer (the trouble with him is
precisely that he always *sees* himself as somebody) and aspired
'to be some day the French Walter Scott'. On leaving school he
imagined 'a plot for a drama, subjects for paintings, future
passions', while finding the happiness 'his exceptional mind
deserved' remarkably slow in arriving. But soon he passes
from enthusiasm to disgust — a recurrent transition which
always accompanies his attempts at realising his dreams.
When he sees that his literary efforts are clumsy imitations
rather than inspired creations he is disenchanted with writing.
But painting, which had seemed to him less demanding, does
not turn out to be his vocation either. However he is not
overly distressed — society life absorbs him and he becomes
involved in money transactions which, since he has no gift for
gambling, consume two thirds of his modest fortune. Finally
the '48 uprisings carry him along in their wake. He dabbles in
his friends' political intrigues and witnesses bloodshed. But if
he is moved in any way by these events, his emotions are too
shortlived for him to perceive their significance and be sufficiently convinced to change his outlook. Thus women, jobs,
honours, fame and wealth go up in smoke, not so much
because he lets real chances pass him by as because, wanting
everything *indiscriminately* and unable, on account of his indolent greed, to organise his aims according to a hierarchy of
positive values, he has only pursued an imaginary ideal and
this image has ultimately reduced him to submit to circumstances rather than lead his own life and be its author.

Flaubert was wont to say that in *l'Education sentimentale* he
had depicted the lost generation of young men who, between
1848 and Napoleon III's *coup d'état*, saw all their hopes collapse
and yet were unable to discard the Romantic delusions on
which their ideology had subsisted. This is true, for from a
significant perspective usually ignored by history, Frédéric
Moreau, Deslauriers and the youths fighting beside them on
the barricades are undoubtedly historical figures. But Frédéric
further provides one of the most authentic self-portraits — he
is Gustave, there is no doubt about it, Gustave portrayed with
the ruthless lucidity of one who knows himself inside out and
who sees himself as mediocre, unable to cope, pettily selfish,
ambitious and inconsistent (which he is in part and would have

been entirely had he not been redeemed by his faith in art).

Frédéric — who is incapable of enduring the extremes of the wilderness where the world can be possessed only at the price of an unpardonable crime and total destitution, yet who is also too fainthearted to follow the rebellious Bastard to the limits of depravity where he at least is prepared to risk even his life in the pursuit of his ends — wants everything so long as he can get it free.[24] He stands with one foot on the Other Side and one firmly planted in the regions where men contend for mundane success, and in this position, whose precariousness he fails to perceive, he is all set for the tremendous leap he never takes which would finally place him on a level with the one objective worthy of his ambition. But had he the courage to leap, even then his objective would evade, him, for its outline is vague and it dissolves into petty vanities as soon as it is constituted. Frédéric is in this respect no better than Maxime Du Camp of whom Flaubert observed with the true hermit's intransigence: 'Everything is mixed up in his mind, women, crucifixes, art, boots, they all whirl around at the same level and so long as they *excite* him that's all that matters!' Flaubert was sufficiently familiar with such a medley of desires whirling around in a pool of mediocrity to know how dangerous it can be. He loathed it for the intellectual slothfulness and especially for the lack of pride it denotes. Because for him there were two forms of qualitatively contradictory pride — one aiming at the so-called highest peaks, the other asserting itself in dismissing these as 'not high enough'. The hero of *Novembre* remarks: 'the most resounding fame would not have satisfied me because it could never be in harmony with my heart.' And Flaubert, writing to Maxime Du Camp who urged him to publish and *arrive*, asks:

Arrive where? . . . Fame is not my main concern. It can only wholly satisfy a very second rate form of pride . . . I aim higher: to be pleased with what I am. For me success is a result not an aim. And I have been heading for this aim for a long time, without, I believe, deviating an inch or stopping on the roadside to trifle with women or snooze in the green grass. After all, if I must pursue a mirage I prefer the highest. . . . Let me die like a dog rather than produce a sentence before it is ripe. . . .

Frédéric, giddily launched into Vanity Fair, ignores such uncompromising pride. He wants women, boots, social suc-

cess, the pleasures of art, and literary fame into the bargain —
in other words he wants nothing seriously and that is what he
will have to pay for. Not indeed with his life — he is not cut
out for tragedy and Flaubert would not dream of killing him
off — but through the gradual erosion of the existence his
petty ambitions have precluded him from putting to good use.
Condemned to live, or rather to vegetate in the inferno his
frustrated ambition deserves, he is only required to serve the
humiliating sentence of being a bourgeois — a harsh enough
sentence, it is true, amounting for its author to the greatest of
intellectual degradations.

Though Flaubert was never quite sure of having shed his
middle-class characteristics ('I am a bourgeois living in the
country and dabbling in literature' he occasionally declared),
on the other hand he never doubted that literature — Art, as he
called it (which has been inaccurately interpreted as: Art for
Art's sake) — was the only means by which his better pride
could overcome the lesser. For one who realised from his
earliest efforts that 'to write, oh to write is to possess the
universe', the art of making up stories and telling them to
others meant supreme power, a kingship compared to which
all temporal powers, including the worldly fame of a successful writer, are nothing but vulgar baubles. Already as a child
Flaubert knew that pen and ink gave him a right to infinity 'an
infinity greater, perhaps, than God's'. Armed with his pen he
can be lord and master of all the characters his fancy conjures
up, whom he sees 'performing before his eyes like a god
contemplating the spectacle of his creations'. Armed with this
wand whose magic power bestows on phantoms a material
body, he can 'frighten the world with a frown' and play now
the Divine Creator, now the Devil intent on destruction. He
has 'ready-made tragedies in his head full of frantic scenes and
untold anguish'. Style flows from his pen like the blood in his
veins and, overcome by visions that annihilate his identity, he
possesses instant knowledge of past and present events, 'from
the babe in its cradle to the corpse in its coffin, humanity
resounded within me in all its echoings; at times gigantic ideas
flashed through my mind like those great flares of silent
summer lightning that light up a whole city, exposing each
building and cross-road in detail'. And in such moments of
illumination which compensate a hundred-fold for his innate

insignificance, he combines words and images and traps life itself on the page, thus experiencing the unequalled satisfaction of 'putting live beings into the frying-pan of style and making them bounce like hot chestnuts'. Live beings — not just the eventual reader. For the great writer he wants to be does not aspire to actual fame with its powers restricted to delighting and moving a given public — he wants to put all humanity into the frying-pan of his style, just as God would do if he condescended to being a novelist.

The writer in full possession of his talent never disowned such childish and adolescent notions of art. Indeed they form the basis for his famous theory of impersonality, and for the categorical imperatives to which he was to submit all his life in order to be worthy of the deified artist's prerogatives. As God the writer is no longer a private individual, at any rate he must remain invisible: 'An artist must exist in his writing like God in his creation, invisible and omnipotent.' 'I belive moreover that a novelist *has not the right to express his opinions* on anything whatsoever. Has God ever given his opinion? . . .'.[25] The creator's narcissism is thus exalted to the point where it becomes humility: 'Anybody is more interesting than Mr G. Flaubert', and Mr G. Flaubert has nothing to say about himself (he has every reason to exclude himself from his books), he is entirely dissolved into the artist who derives invisible omnipotence and total neutrality from his mission.

Thus the creator's narcissistic ecstasy, source of delights that surpass all those derived from personal relationships or from the exercise of temporal powers, is counterbalanced by the strictest possible discipline — discipline the writer only evades at the risk of being evicted from paradise. If the art of writing is of divine essence and the artist is God's equal — or the priest's social equivalent, Flaubert is never very explicit on this point, perhaps to underplay his megalomania — then writing can achieve its purpose only when it is life's supreme asset, the law to which all others are subordinate and which even controls the modulation of thought: 'Finally I try to think right *in order to* write well. But to write well is my aim, I readily admit . . .'.[26] Thus for the 'saints' of literature form takes precedence over content, or rather the content is only a means of creating a perfect form where art's sublimity is reflected in each word.

Moreover the Foundling has a further reason for trying to subject the contents of his dreams to the perfection of writing — for the stories he invents are very far from innocent. They all derive from seriously criminal intentions and the main virtue of their formal perfection consists in its ability to distract attention from these while simultaneously making amends for them. He who murders his mother to go off and live in the wilderness of art and who, moreover, wants to make humanity bounce in the frying-pan of his style, can only be restored to grace in his own eyes if he puts all he is and all he has into the quest for unparalleled beauty. Alone against all and guilty towards all, his only means of justifying himself consists in paying for the savagery of his aggressive instincts in aesthetic currency — even if he thus simultaneously aggravates his misanthropy. However such justification, in fact, is endless, like the guilt it would abolish — conscious of being the murderer by intent of the mother who taught him his first words, he has no other means of justifying himself in his own eyes than through the expiatory sacrifice to his mother tongue of his own life, dedicated entirely to his writing or, as it were, converted into writing, positively consumed by pen and ink (he might indeed have dedicated his oeuvre to 'Madam, my Mother Tongue' more aptly than the old German writer, or than any other writer captivated by perfection, who succeeded him).

Flaubert's prose is purged, by its faultless beauty, of the infantile crime whose intention surfaces in each image. But it is in the nature of such beauty, acquired through 'anguish' at the price of renouncing all the ordinary pleasures of the world, never to be quite equal to its overwhelming task: imperfect, it offends the sublimity of art and is nothing but inflated vanity, a caricature and thus a further imposture; overperfect, it is a dangerous incentive to the artist's delirious megalomania and, insofar as it is self-sufficient, intensifies the destructive urge from which his passion stems. Do as he may such beauty, bearing the indelible stigma of the child-demon who sees himself as God in spite of the whole world, inevitably fails to break free from the vicious circle of his guilt. Thus, ever questionable and ever to be renounced,[27] it will only lead to a Quixotic pursuit of the impossible where the author cannot, or will not find a single instant of respite.

The Foundling who hopes to allay his guilt by writing faultless prose, is naturally drawn to strange and bewildering subjects. He likes highly colourful stories, oriental splendour, the exotic quaintness of past ages, barbaric tinsel and all manner of excess and monstrosity. He delights in describing fantastic costumes, bloodthirsty crowds, human sacrifices not solely to satisfy his hatred for the novel but, on his own assertion, by 'distaste for taste'. Yet all these typical ingredients of his mythology are not there entirely for their own sake — they are mixed, measured and assessed in view of stylistic perfection and of a technique which will enable him to achieve or at least approximate to such perfection. For the sentence with its balance, its rhythm, its shape and the cadence which keeps it alive in the reader's memory; the sentence with its inventories of rare objects and litanies of ideas; the sentence, spacious or brief, bawling, musical, gaping, down-to-earth or lyrical, is the very soul of the text for Flaubert, the source of beauty and of the only kind of truth he wants to express. An adverb in the right place can make all the difference. To change a word can have fatal consequences (when the editor of the *Journal de Rouen* asked him to change the name of the paper to which Homais contributes to *Progressif de Rouen* Flaubert was terribly upset: 'It will break the rhythm of my poor sentences!'), an adjective too many is a slur, assonances and rhymes must be eliminated, alliterations controlled, clichés tracked down, prepositions properly spaced out. Furthermore it is a major crime to write a sentence before it is ripe and, if Flaubert had dared to be entirely consistent he would have written nothing but stories without plots and only been preoccupied with fitting sequences of faultless sentences together in the best way possible. Style is art and art is pure form like the wall of the Acropolis he describes for the benefit of George Sand:

I remember having heart-tremors, experiencing violent joy when contemplating one of the walls of the Acropolis, a bare wall (the one to the left when you go up to the Propyleis). Well! I wonder if a book, *quite apart from what it says* [28] cannot produce the same effect. In the precision with which it is put together, the exceptional quality of its elements, the polish and harmony of the whole, is there not a specific quality, almost a divine power, something as timeless as a fundamental truth?

Flaubert, perhaps fearing to be taken for a madman by his old friend, suggests rather timidly here this notion of a book's value being independent of what it says (indeed it was the first time such a radical notion had ever been considered by a novelist and George Sand was surely the last person to appreciate its significance), yet he was nonetheless entirely convinced of its validity — at least for the writer he was when he wrote anti-novels in order to achieve 'something timeless'.

Although when nowadays we try to find impressive antecedents for discontinuous writing we tend to think otherwise, Flaubert *never wrote* the novel without a plot, based entirely on the perfection of stylistic constructions which he undoubtedly visualised as the model of liberated prose. He never wrote it because he was obsessed by another ideal which constrained him no less peremptorily to serve traditional Romantic literature, overflowing with subject matter and able to express the slightest tremor of life as though it were real. Art is more than the mysterious divinity which bestows eternity on its worshippers in exchange for their humanity: it is also the opposite, a pre-eminently human phenomenon, 'realistic' as Flaubert says in the same letter to George Sand, and its value, in fact, far from being independent of what it says, consists in its ability to recreate the flesh and blood of living creatures, even their smell:

What a feeble creation is Figaro, for instance, compared to Sancho Panza! How the latter comes to life, astride his ass, eating raw onions and spurring on his steed while conversing with his master. How clearly we see those Spanish roads which are never described. . . .

Together with the art of the wilderness thanks to which, according to Saint Anthony's prayer, 'lost, obscured, the world below would soundlessly disappear', Flaubert loved 'books that smell of sweat, those whose muscles ripple beneath the binding and that go barefoot. . . .' Together with the stylistic 'howl' that buries the world in oblivion, he loved realism, getting to grips with the world, capturing its noises, stinks, all the pungent emanations of its pleasures and toil. Together with a Beauty devoid of sense, he loved the sense of novels laden with experience and observation and which take life as it comes, refuse and all. And nothing to bridge the gap,

no possibility of a compound, unless the urge for impossible
perfection finally reconciled artist and novelist — at the cost of
untold suffering, doubt and torment.

It might seem that in this perpetual conflict between these
two conceptions of art — themselves stemming from the two
conflicting tendencies which divide the 'faiseur de roman' —
the Foundling is the advocate of pure style, its beauty unrelated to what it says, like the bare wall of an ancient, ruined
temple; while the Bastard, that realistic observer, witness of
the world as it is and participating in its animation strives to
feed his narrative on concrete plots and, if need be, to include
'tanglible' objects as an antidote to insanity. Although such a
concept is both too abstract and too simple to account for the
subtle process of creativity, it may nonetheless be seen as
accurate were it only because it conforms so exactly to the
dynamics of those 'two ideals' between which Flaubert was
torn. With his profound distaste for reality and, on the other
hand, his urge to indulge in a form of writing totally devoid of
plot — the kind he was overtly referring to when he advised a
friend to read 'utopian and unadulterated dreamers' — he
cannot confine himself to telling tales of adultery, boots,
women and down-to-earth adventures such as are assumed to
be part of his trade. For in addition he has to base his descriptions on a carefully controlled material which includes everything experience, direct observation and scholarship can teach
him. Anthony may ramble, but his hallucinations are none
other than those which one of his cultural traditions might
provide. He does not invent a single monster, heresy or vision
that was not conceived and duly testified by some reputable
writer of the past. Flaubert had no difficulty in justifying, with
references to the various works from which they were drawn,
the improbabilities in *Salammbô* that Sainte-Beuve had noted
with such unmotivated pedantry. For he who was so upset at
breaking the rhythm of his 'poor sentences', knew that in this
respect he was way above the attacks of his critics. He researched on the spot all the details of the Comices in *Madame
Bovary*, obtained the necessary information to describe someone afflicted with a club foot, and sought the advice of a man
of law when writing about Lheureux's shady dealings which
would cause Emma's downfall. As soon as he had decided to
resume *l'Education* he undertook Frédéric's trip to Montereau,

later visiting a china factory, then a pottery in Creil, so as to describe that owned by Arnoux. He studied the works of social reformers, researched all the ideological trends contemporary to the novel's action, and visited the Hospital of Sainte Eugénie to observe at first hand children suffering from croup, because Madam Arnoux's child was taken ill with it. As to *Bouvard et Péchuchet*, the incredible amount of research he undertook so as to situate his two heroes gradually became disturbingly similar to their own ridiculous pilgrimage through the labyrinths of learning. The files he kept to fill in their enquiries could have been compiled by them. Indeed this pointless task — whose absurdity could well have come from the pen of Cervantes — destroyed him long before it was completed. For literature has never known a more scrupulous observer nor a more accurate witness than this 'unadulterated dreamer' who was forced, whether he liked it or not, to dream 'true'.

However the common sense and meticulousness with which the Bastard was always modifying his opponent's utopias did more than influence the contents of his fiction. They were equally instrumental in consolidating the aesthetic imperatives of what Flaubert referred to cumulatively as 'style'. Doubtless the Bastard's main function was to provide the narrative with carefully controlled information — he goes so far as to stipulate that one should 'know everything in order to write', 'everything' referring here to a patiently acquired aggregate and not to the unmediated 'all' Anthony dreamt of possessing. But as soon as information is understood to be a condition of writing it naturally has repercussions on the style itself, since it then dictates the choice of material, the relative length of each section, in short the creation of a complex organism possessing the appearance and coherence of existence. If the Foundling indisputably governs *style*, the Bastard on the other hand is responsible for the overall shape. To him devolves the task of discovering 'by what degrees the infinite descends into reality' and how poetry can become prose without disintegrating. Thus the need to know everything thoroughly — and not superficially like the Balzacian dilettante who thinks he is above expert knowledge — enormously increases the demands for that formal perfection already posited by the magic of the 'howl'. And Flaubert, compelled to satisfy the requirements of the plot while preserving the freedom of his style, does not write a single page without first making a rough copy and not a single line in which the act of writing is not confronted with the impossibility of writing. Obliged to work like a whole gang of drudges whose number increases at every word, yet condemned by his method to produce very little, he becomes a martyr to his trade without even the benefit of fame which is always relative to the abundance and freedom of the output. The Foundling's insane narcissism and the Bastard's stern super-ego having finally concluded a truce against him which places him before the absurd alternative of having either to live without writing or to write without living, from which stems his doctrine of exclusive art, Flaubert is relegated to the wilderness he had formerly conceived as his own choice — he will be the Hermit of Croisset beset by the regrets, self-doubt and incurable melancholy which solitude involves. But if he was deprived of all human satisfactions at least he was able to raise the novel to that perfection of French prose which, as he said, nobody had yet dreamt of, and thus to become the founder of a literature for which the very significance of the word 'literature' would be transformed.

★

And now where is the novel going? What balance has it achieved between the two basic fictional tendencies Flaubert managed, in his consistently uncompromising literary output, to play off against each other? What has happened to the earthly carriage drawn by unearthly horses which carried Kafka's country doctor on his endless journey? From a superficial viewpoint it seems that the Bastard's great venture into Western fiction is a thing of the past, or is at least coming to an end. Doubtless the Oedipal novel still thrives in the lofty regions of the avant-garde — Joyce's *Ulysses*, that parody of a soul's odyssey in quest of a father, overtly translates it into the epic form which, simultaneously imposing and absurd, is the most fitting for its waning condition, while *A la Recherche du temps perdu*, obsessed as it is with titles and genealogies, probes the snobbish Bastard's secrets, not indeed to expose them but to fragment them and conceal the pieces in a syntactical maze. As to Kafka, who undertakes both to oppose and to defend the world, he instals the Bastard as tutor and judge over the untamable Don Quixote whose rejections — metaphysical rejection of life's limitations and social rejection of hierarchies — lead the hero inevitably to a vacuum. Thus we have Joseph K.'s Trial and the pointless quest of the Castle in which the Land Surveyor wears himself out to no purpose because, rather than acknowledge and follow his true Oedipal assistants he expects salvation from a non-existent spiritual messenger. So in the outposts of literature the Family Romance still pursues (as it has always done in popular literature) the task which answers our irresistible urge to rise above our station. But, apart from Kafka who, as Flaubert's true disciple, writes his Quixotic tales in the frigid style of an official report conceived by a legal Bastard, the great writers of the avant-garde usually allow the Foundling to *unravel* his narrative of rebellion in a skilfully disorganised form and, by so doing, to question the stereotyped expressions and ideas of a threadbare cultural heritage. In Joyce as in Proust the Bastard is already less predominant. He does little more than provide the raw material which the Foundling manipulates according to his fancy, often turning it into something unrecognisable or dissolving it completely into the very substance of language. Henceforth stories do not have to represent 'slices of life' in a time and place resembling as much as possible those with which we are familiar. But neither are they required to try and make us believe in some kind of Utopia. Their principal preoccupation is with the formal mechanism which enables them to express themselves in unpredictable ways. This is the time when Don Quixote, tired of brandishing his paper sword and beginning to doubt his chances of converting life into literature, disowns the 'maker' of stories he has been for so long to become a 'maker' of sentences solely intent on creating new figures of speech and startling juxtapositions. It is no longer a question of fighting the windmills of reality or of representing real battles in the form of dream battles, but of grasping the world at one go without the help of suggestive romanticism, simply by exploiting the magic of the printed word. The Bastard who, since he has more or less lost the ability to pass off his love of success stories as World History,

appears at best as a touching memory, at worst as the representative of an odious convention, is naturally excluded from
the lofty spheres where his adventures are considered ever less
worthy of being recorded (which does not stop him from
recording them copiously and enjoying excellent sales). Thus
for the first time since it was launched by Don Quixote and
Robinson Crusoe on the roads of adventure, the novel can
dispense with the conflicts of interest, desire and emotion
which had made it throughout the ages one of the most
important modes of communication between one man's
dream and the profound reality of every man. It is free to be a
sequence of sentences without history or story, free to express
nothing but the narcissistic giddiness of its own writing, and
even free to claim that this is the only respectable aspect of its
vocation. Free, certainly, but what then? Then, we can only
wonder — while avoiding the ridicule of prophecy, for in this
strictly incalculable field a single book might still constitute the
whole of literature — we can only wonder if the unfettered
novel's style will ever have the subversive power and the
perfection of Flaubert's frying-pan where the reader was so
willing to be fried, and if, once free of the immemorial myth
from which till now it derived its true significance, the novel
will still be able to justify its name.

Notes

1   Cf. *Correspondance*, third series 1852-1854, letter to Louise Colet, 27
     December 1852.
2   J.-P. Sartre, *l'Idiot de la famille*, Vol. II, Paris 1970, pp. 1098-9. (Vol. III
     has in fact since been published).
3   The letter to Louise Colet ingeniously combines the dream work —
     based on condensation, displacement and symbolisation of uncon-
     scious elements — with the work of mourning, or a kind of mental
     cannibalism whereby the survivor embodies, or as the psychoanalysts
     say 'introjects' the lost beloved, so as to overcome the sorrow of
     irreversible loss. Usually the 'introjected' object is idealised and the
     survivor acquires additional inner power from it; when it is, on the
     contrary, debased, mourning becomes pathological and deteriorates
     into melancholia. Thus Flaubert's idealisation of Alfred has nothing to
     do with 'play-acting'. It is merely a sign that mourning has proceeded
     normally. Cf. Sigmund Freud, *The Interpretation of Dreams*, Ch. IV,
     'The Dream-Work'; also 'Mourning and Melancholia' (1917), in
     Collected Papers Vol. III, and the famous dream *Non vixit* where Freud
     plays the part of survivor opposite his departed friend.

4 Which would account for Flaubert's refraining from mentioning it in his letter, while giving Louise another of his juvenilia shortly after. This was the short story called *Novembre* which deals with similar experiences.

5 The seven or eight fathers recall the six or seven wolves Freud's most famous patient dreamt about at the age of eighteen months. Cf. S. Freud, 'From the History of an Infantile Neurosis' (1918) in *Collected Papers Vol. III.*, and in particular the dream analysis. Of course associative materials are not available to us, that might enable us to make a serious analysis of Flaubert's childhood dream. Yet we can nonetheless discern the main themes — desire to be penetrated by the father and castration phobia — which constitute the traditional latent themes of a small boy's Primal Scene. As in the childhood dreams reported in 'The Wolf Man', *motionless* people *stare* at Gustave, which, when translated according to the grammatical inversion proper to dreams, reverses the circumstances so that in fact *it is he who stares* at violently *active* people. As to the number seven *or* eight, such precision qualified by vagueness and thus leaving a certain amount of freedom to the over-definite image, probably expresses a desire to potentialise the father's phallic power, and furthermore, since the young victim has identified with his aggressor, to annihilate the threat of castration terrifyingly symbolised by the steel blades.

6 In his analysis of the Wolf-Man the witnessing of the Primal Scene which leaves an indelible psychic mark is assumed by Freud to take place in the very first months of a child's life, although at the time he obviously cannot grasp its significance. The act witnessed may be the copulation of parents or domestic animals; the child, for whom an animal is still largely an equal, has no difficulty in making the transposition. In any case the Primal Scene is always interpreted after the event according to the child's greater or lesser sexual sophistication. We cannot tell how old Flaubert was when he witnessed the scene responsible for his nightmare, nor how old he was when he dreamt it. At fifteen he is obviously sufficiently sophisticated for the emotional tone of the dream to be substantially transformed (at nineteen, in *Novembre*, he stresses his 'voyeurism' by making Marie, the young prostitute with whom he ostensibly identifies say: 'I watched out for my mother's and father's embraces and at night for the sounds from their bed.') But we may presume that the traumatism played a decisive part in his constitution, from the peculiarities of his love life and notably from the convulsive fits — epilepsy or histero-epilepsy — from which he suffered intermittently and which were largely responsible for his 'secluded' existence. Moreover there are a number of passages in his works which express just such infantile 'voyeurism'. In this respect the famous hansom cab scene in *Madame Bovary* might well have scandalised the judges had they sensed its true purport. For in fact what takes place in that hermetically sealed black box, shaken with ridiculous jolts and bumped along the deserted streets of Rouen in full daylight, is no other than the forbidden scene, except that ridicule and exaggeration have dispelled its dread.

7   The seven or eight men whose verility is so prominent could also be
     seen as the countless lovers the Bastard is always ready to impute to his
     mother.

8   Flaubert's refusal to father children is evidence that the traumatism
     connected with the Primal Scene had profound repercussions. He
     wrote in *Novembre* at the age of nineteen: 'He earnestly believed that it
     was less harmful to kill a man than to conceive a child.' And at
     twenty-five in a letter to his friend Vasse: 'Stay as you are, always,
     don't marry, don't have children. . .'. For him the child one conceives
     is death ('I have never seen a child without thinking that he will
     become an old man, nor a cradle without thinking of the grave.')
     Similarly the Primal Scene finds its epilogue in the cemetery where the
     dead still try to copulate: 'If the dead think at all in their graves it is of
     burrowing underground till the next grave so as to raise the dead
     woman's shroud and merge with her slumber.' (*Novembre*)

9   Whether his disease is diagnosed as epilepsy, histero-epilepsy or,
     according to Sartre, as simple hysteria, Flaubert was more predis-
     posed by his psychic constitution to violent, impulsive paroxysms
     than the ordinary neurotic (the destructive tendencies of his nightmare
     are very different from the apparent innocence and purity of similar
     visions in an obsessive neurotic such as the Wolf-Man). In this respect
     Flaubert could be compared to Dostoevsky who was also obsessed by
     the Primal Scene.

10   Instead of admiring the lucidity and frankness of the youth who shows
     such exceptional perceptiveness where so many poets tend to avoid
     the truth, Sartre (op. cit.) quotes this passage as proof that Flaubert
     never really loved Elisa Schlesinger. Had he loved her, Sartre sug-
     gests, he could not have degraded her in this way. Such is the voice of
     common sense — but it cannot help us in this case. Indeed from a
     psychoanalytic point of view the loved one is degraded precisely in
     proportion to the passion's authenticity. It is a reversal of the mother
     figure's former idealisation, which has been seriously jeopardised
     during the Oedipal phase, at puberty when the conflict is revived. The
     mother falls from grace as soon as it becomes clear that she betrays the
     child by giving herself to a man: if she gives herself to one why not to
     any number? This tendentious assumption constitutes, as we have
     seen, the basis of the Family Romance's second version, where
     everything derives from this conflation of the two conventionally
     most contradictory images of woman. By identifying the loved one
     with a prostitute, man protects himself against his own incestuous
     impulses (this is not my mother but, as it were, her opposite). On the
     other hand he obtains both consolation and revenge from the ima-
     gined or true prostitute who, at least, gives herself to him where the
     mother withholds her favours.

11   Were it not for the co-presence of these two aspects of Marie — which
     was eminently significant for his emotional life and for the creation of
     his most accomplished masterpieces — the final words of *l'Education
     sentimentale* ('Yes, perhaps you're right. That was the happiest time we
     ever had') would be truly incomprehensible. The brothel Frédéric

Moreau and Deslauriers frequented with so much pleasurable apprehension in their youth, is a debased mirror-image of the equally enclosed home whose integrity is maintained by the mother. Frédéric had never possessed Madame Arnoux; twenty years after their relationship had begun she comes to see him one day and he suddenly understands the significance of his aborted sentimental education: 'Frédéric suspected Madame Arnoux of having come to offer herself to him' (that is, to realise his degrading fantasies) 'and he was seized once again with desire, a desire more violent and frenzied than ever before. Yet he experienced an incomprehensible sensation, revulsion and dread similar to those provoked at the thought of incest. . .'. And it is indeed the horror of incest that permeates the whole of this simultaneously perverse and chaste relationship. And incest is precisely what the novel tries both to express and to conceal in all its epic recapitulations and its vicissitudes. In such a context Frédéric's visits to the brothel are indeed the happiest time he has had, for there he possessed his mother but 'without degrading his ideal' and incurring guilt. By and large a rewarding study could be made of the role of the brothel and of prostitution in the sentimental education of nineteenth and twentieth century middle-class young men. It would probably reveal that without such institutions — reversed and profaned images of the family — the great Romantic novels would have gone in a very different direction. One thinks of the theme's significance for Balzac (the death of Coralie, who sacrifices herself to Lucien's social advancement), for Dostoevsky, whose Sonia, among other prostitutes, is the criminal hero's redeeming mother substitute; and even for Kafka in *The Castle*, for instance, where admittedly in a skilfully ironic disguise, the 'Gentlemen's inscrutable omnipotence encompasses even a common brothel.

12   As a child Flaubert was subject to fits of obtuseness or inattention and was, besides, somewhat slow in learning to read, which according to Sartre caused his father to see him as an 'idiot' and lose interest in him. At fifteen he was able, thanks to the medical connections he then had, to glean a rudimentary knowledge of heredity which induced him to lay the blame for his shortcomings on a family taint or, in other words on his father (I am an idiot because that is what you made me with your profligate's corrupt seed and unhealthy blood). But even if such accusations — stemming from an offended narcissism — are based on old wives' tales, it is a fact that the high rate of infant mortality in the Flaubert family (surprisingly high even for the period) together with Gustave's nervous fits which denote a marked congenital predisposition, would favour his diagnosis (without necessarily proving that Achille Flaubert was a drunken profligate).

13   Sartre (op. cit.) sees here a further proof of Gustave's bad faith. He writes: 'There is little evidence of Flaubert's parents indulging in such orgies.' Maybe, but that is not really the question. The revolting, shocking event to which the child belives he owes his existence is only a transposition of the Primal Scene he has witnessed — with the addition of a few realistic details he is now able to provide.

14   By no means the first. Flaubert, the 'idiot' who could not learn to read
      the alphabet, was writing at the age of nine, and the list of his juvenilia
      is impressive. After *Mémoires* the most important is *Smarh*, written at
      seventeen and already foreshadowing *la Tentation de Saint Antoine*.

15   Flaubert's pronounced bisexuality — and the latent homosexuality
      which was to influence his relationship with his friends — corresponds
      to a need to deny sexual distinction in order to see himself not as a half,
      requiring completion, but as an indivisible whole (during his fits of
      depression he referred to himself as a 'hysterical old woman'). The
      Foundling, in this respect, is always obsessed with the Platonic myth.

16   He wrote to Louise Colet: 'That is another of my ambitions! To write
      a fairy tale!' And again: 'You know that one of my dreams has always
      been to write a romance of chivalry . . .'. He doubtless knew *Don
      Quixote* by heart and Cervantes was always one of his most venerated
      masters. But fairy tales *and* Madame d'Aulney? As the author of
      Madame Bovary he would certainly have no truck with them, yet
      insofar as he is a Foundling inextricably entangled in his dreams he
      could not resist them. In fact the over-Quixotic are invariably at-
      tracted to fairy tales and romances of chivalry. Thus Kafka expresses a
      similar ambition in almost identical terms: 'I would love to write
      Märchen! . . .' True he felt for the author of *l'Education* (a book he
      thought of as his literary bible during his whole life) such profound
      and exceptional affinities that, despite his pathological humility, he
      claimed to be his spiritual heir. Kafka criticism, misled by historical,
      linguistic and social contrasts between the two writers, has not
      generally considered this kinship although Flaubert is far more signi-
      ficant for Kafka's art than all the existentialist writers with whom he is
      always associated.

17   Flaubert's relentless attitude to the mother figure, explicitly indicated
      as such, is one of the more striking features in his writings and
      probably stems from his inability to accept the Oedipal fate, or more
      precisely from a pronounced emotional regression. Though the
      Oedipal Bastard could obviously claim to have adored his mother,
      since he had broken off with Louise Colet because of her, cherished
      and avoided her reflection in Elisa Schlesinger and had never been able
      to leave her, the Foundling who created his Saint undoubtedly desired
      the death of the white-haired woman who keeps recurring in his
      hallucinations — or at least thought about it more overtly than it is
      customary to do consciously. During a certain period the phrase:
      'Should my mother die my plans are made . . .' became almost a
      leitmotif in his correspondence.

18   Sartre (op. cit.) censures him for this: 'To make an impact on society?
      No ambition could be sillier . . .'. Silly or not this is what gives the
      Bastard's novel its strongest motivation. It is the original source of all
      popular and highbrow fictional literature and the model for all the
      fictional situations on which novels of every description thrive.

19   Sartre notes this feature, apparently so inconsistent with the call of the
      wilderness: 'Is Gustave distressed at not being *well born*? . . . He may
      indeed have dreamt of it at times: middle-class youths tended to do so

in his day — Hugo for instance, and Baudelaire, even Mallarmé, alas. . . .' Why alas? And why only middle-class youths contemporary with Flaubert? Indeed, for such a basically dissatisfied creature as the innovator tends to be in whatever intellectual climate he may find himself, *snobbishness is the most powerful incentive to creativity* (as instances we have only to name Balzac, James, Proust and even the humblest, purest and most ascetic of writers, Kafka, who raised the *pariah's snobbishness* to practically mythical heights.

20   Copious psychoanalytical observations stress the remarkable role played by Red Indians in North American and especially Canadian Family Romances where they presumably replace the historically non-existent aristocrat. The characteristics traditionally associated with them would favour such a substitution: the Red Indian is proud, noble, indomitable, generous and the rightful owner of the land. Compared to those who exterminate them the Indians can easily be seen as superior beings and thus replace Kings and Noble Fathers who occupy the most exalted position in the European Romance. The fact that Flaubert should have discovered a hypothetical 'savage' ancestress is noteworthy in that it provides him with a more singular nobility and a more vigorous blood than those of the Parisian aristocrat. Moreover this Natchez or Iroquoi lady must have appealed to his taste for 'barbaric' societies.

21   Goethe's influence is obvious here too: if *la Tentation* mirrors *Faust*, *l'Education* is Flaubert's *Wilhelm Meister*, the 'Bildungsroman' which was the model of all educative novels.

22   Flaubert was aware of the fact that Frédéric was a passive undistinguished replica of Balzac's hero. Thus he puts into the mouth of Frédéric's Sancho, his inseparable friend Deslauriers, the words: 'Remember Rastignac in *la Comédie humaine*! You will succeed, I am certain!'

23   Mirrors have the same fascination for him as for the hero of *Novembre* who would have liked to have been a woman so as to admire his reflection in streams — and as for Gustave himself who confesses: 'People would laugh at me if they knew how much I admire myself . . . .'

24   Flaubert was not unaware of the cowardice his choice of the 'wilderness' denoted: 'I was a coward in my youth, *I was afraid of life!* Everything must be paid for. . . .'

25   Flaubert's italics.

26   Flaubert's italics.

27   Cf. Michel de M'Uzan, 'Aperçus psychanalytiques sur le processus de la création littéraire', in *Tel Quel*, No. 19, August 1964, where the author makes a penetrating analysis of the desire for perfection and of its relation to deep-rooted guilt.

28   My italics.